D1585894

Text, Context, Pretext

Language in Society

GENERAL EDITOR
Peter Trudgill, Chair of English
Linguistics, University of Fribourg

ADVISORY EDITORS
J. K. Chambers, Professor of Linguistics,
University of Toronto

Ralph Fasold, Professor of Linguistics,
Georgetown University

William Labov, Professor of Linguistics,
University of Pennsylvania

Lesley Milroy, Professor of Linguistics,
University of Michigan, Ann Arbor

1 Language and Social Psychology,
*edited by Howard Giles and
Robert N. St Clair*

2 Language and Social Networks
(2nd edn.), *Lesley Milroy*

3 The Ethnography of Communication
(3rd edn.), *Muriel Saville-Troike*

4 Discourse Analysis, *Michael Stubbs*

5 The Sociolinguistics of Society:
Introduction to Sociolinguistics,
Vol. I, *Ralph Fasold*

6 The Sociolinguistics of Language:
Introduction to Sociolinguistics,
Vol. II, *Ralph Fasold*

7 The Language of Children and
Adolescents: *Suzanne Romaine*

8 Language, the Sexes and Society,
Philip M. Smith

9 The Language of Advertising,
Torben Vestergaard and Kim Schrøder

10 Dialects in Contact, *Peter Trudgill*

11 Pidgin and Creole Linguistics,
Peter Mühlhäusler

12 Observing and Analysing Natural
Language: A Critical Account of
Sociolinguistic Method, *Lesley Milroy*

13 Bilingualism (2nd edn.),
Suzanne Romaine

14 Sociolinguistics and Second Language
Acquisition, *Dennis R. Preston*

15 Pronouns and People, *Peter Mühlhäusler
and Rom Harré*

16 Politically Speaking, *John Wilson*

17 The Language of the News Media,
Allan Bell

18 Language, Society and the Elderly,
*Nikolas Coupland, Justine Coupland, and
Howard Giles*

19 Linguistic Variation and Change,
James Milroy

20 Principles of Linguistic Change, Vol. I:
Internal Factors, *William Labov*

21 Intercultural Communication (2nd edn.),
Ron Scollon and Suzanne Wong Scollon

22 Sociolinguistic Theory (2nd edn.),
J. K. Chambers

23 Text and Corpus Analysis,
Michael Stubbs

24 Anthropological Linguistics,
William Foley

25 American English: Dialects and Variation,
Walt Wolfram and Natalie Schilling-Estes

26 African American Vernacular English,
John R. Rickford

27 Linguistic Variation as Social Practice,
Penelope Eckert

28 The English History of African American
English, *edited by Shana Poplack*

29 Principles of Linguistic Change,
Vol. II: Social Factors, *William Labov*

30 African American English in the
Diaspora, *Shana Poplack and
Sali Tagliamonte*

31 The Development of African American
English, *Walt Wolfram and
Erik R. Thomas*

32 Forensic Linguistics, *John Gibbons*

33 An Introduction to Contact Linguistics,
Donald Winford

34 Sociolinguistics: Method and
Interpretation, *Lesley Milroy and
Matthew Gordon*

35 Text, Context, Pretext: Critical Issues in
Discourse Analysis, *H. G. Widdowson*

Text, Context, Pretext

Critical Issues in Discourse Analysis

H. G. Widdowson

Blackwell
Publishing

© 2004 by H. G. Widdowson

BLACKWELL PUBLISHING
350 Main Street, Malden, MA 02148-5020, USA
108 Cowley Road, Oxford OX4 1JF, UK
550 Swanston Street, Carlton, Victoria 3053, Australia

First published 2004 by Blackwell Publishing Ltd

Library of Congress Cataloging-in-Publication Data

Widdowson, H. G.
    Text, Context, and pretext : critical issues in discourse analysis / H. G. Widdowson.
        p.   cm. — (language in society)
    Includes bibliographical references and index.
    ISBN 0–631–23451–9 (hardback : alk. paper) — ISBN 0–631–23452–7 (pbk. : alk. paper)
  1. Discourse analysis.   I. Title.   II. Series: Language in society (Oxford, England).
    P302.W533 2004
    401'.41—dc22   2004016920

A catalogue record for this title is available from the British Library.

Set in 10.5/12.5pt Ehrhardt
by Graphicraft Ltd., Hong Kong
Printed and bound in the United Kingdom
by MPG Books Ltd, Bodmin, Cornwall

For further information on
Blackwell Publishing, visit our website:
www.blackwellpublishing.com

Contents

for barbara

Preface

This book is, in a sense, a reconceptualized and extended version of one that was unwritten and unpublished thirty years ago. This itself would have been a revised version of my PhD thesis, entitled 'An applied linguistic approach to discourse analysis', submitted in 1973, in the early stages of my academic career.

Immodest though it might seem, I would like to acknowledge the work of this author, my former self, for it was here that many of the issues in discourse analysis (then a newly burgeoning growth in the field of linguistics) were first addressed and tentatively explored. To my later regret, I declined the offer to publish a write-up of my thesis, preferring to draw on it in the writing of a number of papers in applied linguistics and language education. Not surprisingly, when discourse analysis subsequently became fashionable within mainstream linguistics, my own early efforts in the applied linguistics backwaters went unnoticed, much, I must confess, to my chagrin. It was irritating to find ideas that (as I saw it) I had anticipated in my own writing, and expounded with such brilliance, re-emerging with all the appearance of novelty in the work of other people without so much as a nod of recognition or acknowledgement. But this is, of course, a familiar academic experience and as the years go by the frustrations fade, resentment is revealed as petty and misplaced, and a new and wiser realization dawns that ideas, like a kind of benign intellectual infection, spread in different minds in all sorts of ways and cannot be readily or reliably traced to particular sources.

Times have moved on since 1973. I have changed, and so has the field. Both, I like to think, for the better. Although many of the issues discussed in this book were first broached in the earlier unpublished one, they have also been taken up independently, conjured with, reformulated in a variety of ways by scholars of different disciplinary persuasions under the names of discourse analysis, conversation analysis, speech act analysis, pragmatics and so on. The concepts of discourse, text and context, which figure prominently in the work of my prentice period, have all been subjected by others to extensive and impressive enquiry over the intervening years, and many a textbook is available to bring enlightenment on these matters to the novice student. Even so, it seems to me that the relationship between them remains problematic, and it is this that justifies the reconsideration I give to them in the early chapters of this present book. The third term that appears in my title, pretext, calls for more detailed comment, and I will come to that presently.

My interest in these theoretical matters remained a steady current in my mind over twenty years, but was galvanized by the rapid rise to fashionable prominence of Critical Discourse Analysis (CDA). Here was a development in linguistics which claimed to be applicable to the immediate and pressing concerns of the non-scholarly world. Here was, it seemed, work which came under the very rubric of my thesis all those years ago: an applied linguistic approach to discourse analysis; but with an important difference. Whereas I had thought of language teaching as the main area of practical concern which discourse analysis could be relevant to, CDA had a much more ambitious and much more significant agenda. Its concern was to educate people more broadly in the abuse of power by linguistic means, to reveal how language is used for deception and distortion and the fostering of prejudice. Here was an approach to discourse analysis whose significance could hardly be exaggerated.

For there has surely never been a time when the need for such an investigation is so urgent, when public uses of language have been so monopolized to further political and capitalist interests to the detriment of public well-being and in denial of human rights and social justice. Over recent years, the cynical abuse of language to deceive by doublethink that characterizes the fictional dystopia of Orwell's *1984* has become a reality of everyday life. Ecological devastation goes under the verbal guise of economic development, and millions of people are kept subject to poverty, reduced to desperation, deprived of liberty and life in the name of democratic values and a globalized market economy that is said to be free. So much of the language we come across in print and on screen seems to be designed to deceive, used as a front, a cover-up of ulterior motives. This is an aspect of discourse, the effect that a particular use of language is designed to bring about, that I refer to as pretext.

And it was just this aspect that CDA focused attention on, particularly as it related to the insinuation of ideological influence and the covert control of opinion. It had, in principle, an initial appeal for me on two counts: it promised not only to extend the scope of discourse analysis as such, but to do so with the express applied linguistic purpose of engaging with real world issues of immediate and pressing importance.

Regrettably, my further acquaintance with CDA had an adverse effect on this initial appeal, for reasons which I discuss in detail in the second half of this book. Whether these reasons are valid or not I must leave the reader to decide, but what I want to stress here is that it is not the cause of CDA that I call into question, for it is one that, as will be evident from my earlier comments, I wholeheartedly endorse. Where I take issue with CDA is in the mode of analysis and interpretation it adopts by way of promoting this cause. The need to demonstrate how discourse analysis can contribute to a critical awareness of the ways in which language is used, and abused, to exercise control and practise deception remains as pressing as ever. CDA, to its great credit, has alerted us to this need, and although, as will be apparent in this book, I have serious reservations about the way it does its work, I recognize too that it has the effect of giving point and purpose to discourse analysis by giving prominence to crucial questions about its socio-political significance which might otherwise have been marginalized.

This book is confrontational and uncompromising in its criticism, and I am aware that it will not endear me to some of my colleagues working in the field of discourse analysis, critical or otherwise. But my quarrel is with arguments, analyses, and the claims that are made for them, and not with people. We are all concerned with issues which have a significance compared with which individual sensitivities are trivial, and it should be possible to engage in adversarial argument about them without causing any serious hurt. But this, of course, is easier said than done, for people, and I am myself certainly no exception, quite naturally invest their emotional selves in their thinking, and the animation and animosity of intellectual exchange are always difficult to keep apart. All I can say is that no offence is intended, and I hope to be forgiven if any is taken. And in mitigation, I acknowledge, in all sincerity, the achievement and distinction of those people whose work has inspired my criticism: Norman Fairclough, Michael Halliday, Michael Stubbs, Ruth Wodak in particular. My disagreement with them does not diminish my indebtedness: they have all made crucial and indeed indispensable contributions to this book.

I also owe thanks to the counsel and support of those colleagues whose views are more congruent with mine, and in particular to two people, Kieran O'Halloran and Peter Trudgill, who have read and commented with impressive insight on an earlier draft of this book. My thanks, too, to Katharina Breyer for all her dedicated work on the index. Most thanks of all go to the person to whom the book itself is dedicated, Barbara Seidlhofer,

who gives me counsel and support, intellectual and emotional, in everything
I do.

H. G. W.
Vienna, February 2004

Sources

Certain chapters of this book are developed from papers published in various places
over the past ten years.

*Discourse analysis: a critical view. *Language and Literature* 4.3, 157–72, 1995
(chapters 1 and 6).

Review of Fairclough: *Language and Social Change. Applied Linguistics* 16.4, 510–16,
1995 (chapter 6).

*Discourse and interpretation: Conjectures and refutations. Reply to Fairclough.
Language and Literature, 5.1, 57–69, 1996 (chapters 8 and 10).

The use of grammar and the grammar of use. *Functions of Language* 4.2, 145–68,
1997 (chapter 2).

The theory and practice of critical discourse analysis: A review article. *Applied
Linguistics* 19.1, 136–51, 1998 (chapters 6 and 8).

The conditions of contextual meaning. In K. Malmkjaer and J. Williams (eds),
Context in Language Learning and Language Understanding. Cambridge: Cambridge
University Press, pp. 6–23, 1998 (chapter 3).

Critical practices: On representation and the interpretation of text. In S. Sarangi
and M. Coulthard (eds), *Discourse and Social Life*. London: Longman, pp. 155–
69, 2000. (chapter 8)

On the limitations of linguistics applied. *Applied Linguistics* 21.1, 3–25, 2000
(chapter 7).

Interpretations and correlations: A reply to Stubbs. *Applied Linguistics* 22.4, 531–8,
2001 (chapter 7).

Verbal art and social practice: A reply to Weber. *Language and Literature* 11.2, 161–
7, 2002 (chapter 8).

*These, along with a reply by Fairclough, also appear in B. Seidlhofer (ed.),
Controversies in Applied Linguistics. Oxford: Oxford University Press, 2003.

1

Text and discourse

Although discourse analysis has been a busy field of activity for many years, there is a good deal of uncertainty about what it actually is. The generally accepted view is that it has something to do with looking at language 'above' or 'beyond' the sentence, but this is hardly an exact formulation. Even when the term *discourse analysis* is used as a book title, as it is in a key work by Michael Stubbs, it is not always clear just what the term is intended to signify: 'Roughly speaking, it refers to attempts to study the organization of language above the sentence, or above the clause, and therefore to study larger linguistic units, such as conversational exchanges or written texts' (Stubbs 1983:1).

Even roughly speaking, this is an unsatisfactory description on a number of counts. To begin with, it is not clear whether Stubbs is using the terms *clause* and *sentence* to mean the same thing or not. This is not a terminological quibble. It makes a good deal of difference whether the linguistic organization to be analysed is above a clause or above a sentence. If it is above the clause, analysis would presumably take into account complex and compound units which would be conventionally defined as syntactic constituents and so below the sentence. Rules for co-ordination and embedding, which figure prominently, for example, in transformational grammar, would in this case be considered examples of discourse analysis.

This would actually be consistent with what Zellig Harris had in mind when he first used the term fifty years ago. He too was looking at how language is organized as 'connected discourse', by which he meant how patterns of formal equivalence might be discerned across sentences in stretches of what he calls morpheme sequences in actually occurring text. Equivalence, as Harris is at pains to point out, has nothing to do with what semantic meaning these stretches have but with the textual environments in which they appear. He illustrates the notion by asking us to suppose that in a particular text the following sentences occur:

The trees turn here about **the middle of autumn**; The trees turn here about **the end of October**; *The first frost comes* after the middle of autumn; *We start heating* after the end of October.

The expressions I have put in bold here would be equivalent in that they share the same environment, and being equivalent they provide the same environment for the italicized expressions in the second pair of sentences, so that they too are equivalent with each other. If the text were to continue:

<u>We always have a lot of trouble</u> when we start heating **<u>but you've got to be prepared</u>** when the first frost comes.

By the same process, the underlined expressions here are assigned equivalent status on the basis of their environment, which has already been established as the same by the preceding analysis. And we proceed in a kind of chain reaction mode, with one set of equivalences providing the environmental conditions for another (Harris 1952:6–7).

So far, the analysis simply involves identifying recurrent morpheme sequences which are actually present in the text, but Harris then goes on to assign equivalence on the basis of underlying structural similarity established by means of transformations. So, for example, we can say that a sentence that occurs in the text, like **We start heating after the end of October**, is equivalent to its transform **After the end of October, we start heating**, which does not. By the same criteria any sentence like **Casals plays the cello** is equivalent to one that takes the form **The cello is played by Casals** (these are Harris's examples). This procedure of establishing equivalence in absentia, so to speak, is, says Harris,

> the same basic operation, that of comparing different sentences. And it will serve the same end: to show that two otherwise different sentences contain the same combination of equivalence classes even though they may contain different combinations of morphemes. What is new is only that we base our equivalence not on a comparison of two sentences in the text, but on a comparison of a sentence in the text with sentences outside the text. (Harris 1952:19)

The transformations that Harris uses to identify structural equivalences underlying different morphemic manifestations on the surface are essentially devices of the same order as those subsequently adopted by Chomsky in the design of generative grammar. They are in both cases formal operations on sentence constituents. What Harris was doing would appear on the face of it to be discourse analysis as Stubbs defines it, for he was studying how language is organized above the sentence by analysing 'larger linguistic units'. Discourse analysis in this conception is simply a matter of extending the scope of grammar. Though this is itself not, of course, a simple matter, there is, as Stubbs would agree, rather more to it than that.

Harris himself acknowledges as much by pointing out the limitation of his enterprise: identifying the underlying structural patterns that make connections across sentences tells us nothing about what they might mean. As he puts it:

> All this, however, is still distinct from an *interpretation* of the findings, which must take the meaning of morphemes into consideration and ask what the author was about when he produced the text. Such interpretation is obviously quite separate from the formal findings, although it may follow closely in the directions which the formal findings indicate. (Harris 1952:29)

For Harris, clearly, discourse analysis is a set of procedures for establishing underlying formal equivalences within a text. Although his work is motivated by the belief that 'Language does not occur in stray words or sentences, but in connected discourse' (Harris 1952:3), it is the connectedness itself that is focused on rather than on its discourse implication. He looks beyond the bounds of the sentence, it is true, but his vision is essentially that of the sentence grammarian.

Discourse analysis can be said to date back to Harris. But his celebrated article is of more than just historical interest. Even this very brief discussion of it raises a number of questions which have remained stubbornly problematic to this day. I mark them down here as issues to be taken up in this book.

- If discourse analysis is defined as the study of language patterns above the sentence, this would seem to imply that discourse is sentence writ large: quantitatively different but qualitatively the same phenomenon. It would follow, too, of course, that you cannot have discourse *below* the sentence.
- If the difference between sentence and discourse is not a matter of kind but only of degree, then they are presumably assumed to signal the same kind of meaning. If sentence meaning is intrinsically encoded, that is to say, a semantic property of the language itself, then so is discourse meaning.

- In the quotation cited above, however, Harris talks about interpretation as involving two factors: 'the meanings of the morphemes', which presumably refers to semantics and 'what the author was about when he produced the text', which brings in pragmatic considerations like intention. So interpretation cannot just be read off from the text as if it were an elongated sentence. But then if semantic and pragmatic meanings are different, *how* are they different, and by what principles can they be related?

- Harris says that interpretation 'may follow closely in the directions which the formal findings indicate'. How then do such findings direct interpretation?

- In the quotation, Harris talks of interpretation as if this were a matter of finding out 'what the author was about', thereby equating it with the discovery of intention. But what a first-person author means by a text is not the same as what the text might mean to a second-person reader (or listener), or indeed to a third-person analyst. How then are these different perspectives to be reconciled?

- Harris uses the term *discourse* in the title of his paper, and occasionally within it; the term that figures most prominently in the account of his analysis is *text*. It would seem that for him the terms are synonymous. Is there a case for making a conceptual distinction between them?

These issues are closely interrelated, of course, and, as we shall see, the discussion of any one of them will necessarily bring others in by implication. Let us begin with the synonymous use of the terms *text* and *discourse*. We have already noted that Harris appears to conflate them, using both to refer to the language that an author produces. Stubbs does not distinguish them either: both terms refer to 'language above the sentence, or above the clause', that is to say 'larger linguistic units, such as conversational exchanges or written texts'. I pointed out earlier that there is a crucial difference between language above the sentence and language above the clause. A consideration of the latter will include syntactic relations among sentence constituents and will come within the scope of grammar. If one looks for patterns of language above the sentence, however, then one goes beyond the bounds of conventional grammar and one needs to look for other principles of ordering.

What further confuses the issue is the reference that Stubbs makes to 'written texts'. For here we find sentences of an orthographic kind, the written utterances of actually performed language of a different order from sentences as abstract grammatical constructs. And these written utterances will often take the form of linguistic units consisting of many grammatical sentences, or (as we shall see) of no sentence, or clause, at all, and the form they take is determined by just the kind of pragmatic intention that Harris excludes from consideration.

Since *discourse* analysis is said to apply to written *texts*, Stubbs, it would seem, makes no clear distinction between the terms. And this is borne out by remarks he makes a little later in the same (introductory) chapter to his book. The terms, he tells us, are 'often ambiguous and confusing', but seeing no need to disambiguate or clarify them, he simply comments: 'One often talks of "written text" versus "spoken discourse" . . . "discourse" implies length whereas a "text" may be very short' (Stubbs 1983:9). Presumably a text cannot be all that short since, by Stubbs's own definition, it would have to be a larger linguistic unit than a sentence to qualify for discourse analysis at all. But for Stubbs the fact that the terms *text* and *discourse* are 'confusing and ambiguous', does not really matter, since for him nothing essential hangs on the distinction: his 1983 book is called *Discourse Analysis*, his later book has *text analysis* in its title. Clearly he finds no place for the distinction in his own work, and seems sceptical of its significance in the work of others. He comments:

> One brief point about terminology. There is considerable variation in how terms such as *text* and *discourse* are used in linguistics. Sometimes this terminological variation signals important conceptual distinctions, but often it does not, and terminological debates are usually of little interest. These distinctions in terminology and concept will only occasionally be relevant for my argument, and when they are, I draw attention to them (e.g. in section 7.2). (Stubbs 1996:4)

No indication is given as to when the distinction is conceptually significant and when it is not. One may concede that debates about terminological distinctions as such are of little interest, but they clearly cannot be so summarily dismissed when they have conceptual substance, as they apparently do, occasionally, in Stubbs's own work, though just where and how is actually never made evident. Section 7.2, to which he draws the reader's attention, does not actually address the issue at all.[1]

Stubbs is not alone in the indiscriminate use of the terms *text* and *discourse* to refer to language above the sentence. It is indeed so orthodox a view that it seems perverse, not to say foolhardy, to question it.[2] Here it is again as expressed without equivocation by Wallace Chafe in no less authoritative a work than the *Oxford International Encyclopedia of Linguistics*:

> The term 'discourse' is used in somewhat different ways by different scholars, but underlying the differences is a common concern for language beyond the boundaries of isolated sentences. The term TEXT is used in similar ways. Both terms may refer to a unit of language larger than the sentence: one may speak of a 'discourse' or a 'text'. (Chafe 1992:356, 2003:439–40)[3]

One may indeed so speak, and scholars do. But is it helpful so to speak? Hoey, noting how some scholars are indifferent to the distinction, and other inconsistent in their use of it, makes the observation: 'And yet the distinction continues to be made. It is as if some basic differentiation is felt to exist that people cannot quite agree on but cannot leave alone' (Hoey 1991:197). Let us then consider how far this feeling might be substantiated and the differentiation justified.[4]

We can begin with the question of how we deal with uses of language which are indeed very short texts, taking as they do the form of isolated sentences. The most obvious instances of such texts are public notices like

TRESPASSERS WILL BE PROSECUTED
STICK NO BILLS
HANDLE WITH CARE

and so on. These, on the Chafe criterion, are not texts at all since they have no other sentences to keep them company. And yet they are intuitively textual in that they are not fragments or components of any larger linguistic whole but are complete communicative units, separate speech events as Hymes might call them (Hymes 1968).

In view of this, we might concede that in certain circumstances single, isolated sentences can serve as texts. But then the question inevitably arises as to what these circumstances might be. And this in turn might lead us to suspect that perhaps it is these circumstances and not the size of the linguistic unit which determines textuality, and that whether a piece of language is larger than a sentence has little if anything to with it. This suspicion is strengthened by the obvious fact that there are instances of language which have all the appearance of complete texts, but which do not even consist of separate sentences but of isolated phrases and words. Public notices again:

NO ENTRY
      CHILDREN CROSSING
            HARD HAT AREA
TRAINS   TOILETS   GENTLEMEN   LADIES   SILENCE   PRIVATE
OPEN   CLOSED   IN   OUT

and so on. Here there is no sentence in sight, but only noun phrases, nouns, adjectives, adverbs, parts of speech in grammatical limbo, constituents that have somehow declared independence from syntax and are on their own.

But it is not only that parts of sentences seem to take on textual independence. Parts of words do as well, even those parts, like the graphological letter, which have no encoded meaning whatever. Thus the single letter **W** signals to me where I am to register for a conference. The single letter **P** tells me where to park my car. These are notices which apparently function in just the same way as others less sparing with language. Do we say that they are non-texts on the grounds that they are smaller than a sentence? This does not seem to be a very satisfactory way of proceeding.[5]

It might be objected that I am giving unwarranted attention to relatively trivial uses of language. These are texts, if you like, but minimal texts. But the interesting question surely is how they can be texts when they *are* so minimal. One answer might be that they are a sort of shorthand: they stand for larger texts, rather like acronyms. Just as **PTO** at the bottom of a letter stands for the sentence *Please turn over*, so **P** stands for *Parking*. But this is still a one-word text. Well then, *Parking* in turn stands for *Parking is permitted here* or *Here is a place for parking your car*, or something along these lines: shorthand.

These still do not meet the Chafe criterion, of course, since we have still not gone 'beyond the boundaries of isolated sentences'. But quite apart from that, how do those who write such shorthand know that I will interpret it as intended? How do they know how minimal they can be? The letters BBC can indeed be said to stand for the *British Broadcasting Corporation*, BC for *Before Christ* (or *British Columbia*), NYPD for *New York Police Department*, and so on. These are established encodings with fixed denotations, symbolically secure. But **P** does not have the same fixity of meaning. If I see it as a notice at the side of a country road I interpret it as referring to a small space at the side of the road, a so-called lay-by, where I can pull in for a brief stay. If I see the letter **P** as a notice in a street in the middle of the city, I know that it refers to something entirely different: to a covered concrete place, a multi-storey edifice, where I pay to leave my car. In other words, how I interpret the text **P** depends on where I see it and what I know about the lay-by and the multi-storey car park. It depends, in other words, on relating the text to something outside itself, that is to say to the *con*text: to where it is located on the one hand, and to how, on the other hand, it keys in with my knowledge of reality as shaped and sanctioned by the society I live in – that is to say, my social knowledge. **P** is a linguistic symbol, a letter of the alphabet, an element of English graphology. But that is not how I *interpret* it when it figures as a text. I read it not as a conventional element of the code but as an index whose function is to point away from itself to the context, and so indicate where meaning is to be found elsewhere.

The same point can be made about the other texts we have been considering. When I see the one word TRAINS, for example, written on the wall of Russell Square underground station in London, I know that it refers to the trains of the Piccadilly Line proceeding westbound towards Hammersmith. And I also know that it not only has reference to a particular direction – westwards, but it has the force of a direction in a quite different illocutionary sense as well – come this way to the trains. But the same word can serve as a totally different text and invoke a quite different interpretation, where reference is to other trains with the force of a warning. Similarly, when I see the notice TRESPASSERS WILL BE PROSECUTED, its location and my familiarity with such notices will lead me to infer that it is meant to have the force of prohibition in reference to individuals who might be tempted to stray onto this particular piece of private land. I know that it is not meant to refer generically to all who trespass or to have the force of a general assertion about their fate; like SINNERS WILL BE DAMNED or THE MEEK WILL INHERIT THE EARTH.

How do I know all these things? Obviously because I have been socialized into a particular reality and know how to use language to engage indexically with it. I recognize a piece of language as a text not because of its linguistic size, but because I assume it is intended to key into this reality. Texts can come in all shapes and sizes: they can correspond in extent with any linguistic unit: letter, sound, word, sentence, combination of sentences. To put the matter more briskly, I identify a text not by its linguistic extent but by its social intent.

But identifying something as a text is not the same as interpreting it. You may recognize intentionality but not know the intention. This is where discourse comes in, and why it needs to be distinguished from text. As I have tried to show, we achieve meaning by indexical realization, that is to say by using language to engage our extralinguistic reality. Unless it is activated by this contextual connection, the text is inert. It is this activation, this acting of context on code, this indexical conversion of the symbol that I refer to as discourse. Discourse in this view is the pragmatic process of meaning negotiation. Text is its product.[6]

The main concern of this book is to explore the relationship between text and discourse, between the language people produce and which provides objective data for linguistic analysis, and the way this is processed by the parties themselves, which is a matter of interpretation. We can begin by noting obvious differences between spoken and written text as discourse realizations.

The spoken text of conversational interaction is the direct reflex of the discourse enacted between two, or among several, parties. The discourse may be prepared, pre-scripted in different degrees. Interviews, for example, may be structured in advance, though the actual wording of the participants cannot be entirely predicted. Casual conversation is, of course, much less structured, but even here the participants have some expectation as to how the discourse is likely to proceed, the relative informality of the engagement, the kind of topics which would count as normal, and so on. As Firth put it, conversation is a 'roughly prescribed social ritual' (Firth 1957:31). But whatever the degree of prescription, the text, the actual language which realizes the interaction, is immediate to it, and is directly processed on line. As such it provides only a fugitive and partial record of the discourse. It is fugitive because its sound simply disappears into thin air unless it is artificially recorded. And when it is recorded, it necessarily changes in character, for it no longer represents the actual experience of the participants themselves. What is recorded, and subsequently analysed, therefore, is a second-hand derived version of the original: not the reflex of interaction but the result of intervention. It is a partial version too because it records only the linguistic text, and not other features of interactive behaviour of a para-linguistic kind other than what is vocally realized. Transcription can of course be refined to take some of this into account, but no means all. Even a visual record on film is bound to miss some interactive features, like eye contact and direction of gaze which may be highly significant for the participants themselves. And most accounts of spoken text are anyway based on written transcriptions. It has long been recognized that speech and writing are quite different modes of interaction, and the differences have been extensively documented (see Halliday 1989, Stubbs 1983). Nevertheless, in practice what is studied as speech is a derived version of it, stabilized and objectified by transcription as a kind of written text.

Now if one compares a text which is originally written as such with one which is the partial transcription of speech, the differences between them become obvious. What is most immediately striking about the transcribed record of unscripted conversation is its non-linearity. Though the interacting parties in the conversation may make satisfactory sense of what is going on, and feel that they are co-constructing their discourse in a reasonably orderly fashion, the transcription of their actual text usually records it as being fragmentary and discontinuous. And of course the greater the precision the transcription strives for by the use of elaborate notation to signal these features, the more fragmentary and discontinuous the discourse appears to be, and the further removed the transcribed text becomes from that which served to realize the discourse in the first place. People are usually surprised to discover how incoherent recorded conversation is, even their own. The transcribed written version of conversation is even more remote from the reality of immediate interaction.

In short, the textual record of speech is a poor representation of the discourse which gave rise to it, and the more precise the analytic account, the further removed it is from the actual experience of the speakers. Making sense of a spoken interaction from the insider point of view of the participants is very different from making sense of it as an outsider third person transcribing it. We have here an observer's paradox, but not that which Labov points out, and resolves, whereby a non-participant third-person presence impinges on the participation process itself (Labov 1972). This is the more intractable paradox that the very observation of an interaction necessarily misrepresents it, and the more precise the observed record, the greater the misrepresentation. The text of spoken interaction can only have an immediate discourse effect and is of its nature fugitive and partial. When transcribed, these features necessarily disappear. This we might call the paradox of irreducible subjectivity.

Recognition of this paradox does not, of course, imply that there is no point in transcribing speech, but only that it sets limits on its claims to representation. Transcriptions can reveal a great deal about the textual reflex of spoken discourse by focusing attention on specific linguistic features. They can record the occurrence of certain speech sounds, lexical items, grammatical structures and so on, and these are clearly relevant to the analysis of text as such, and indeed it may be possible to infer from them something of the significance they might have had for the discourse process which gave rise to them. The point I would wish to make is that the transcribed record of spoken text cannot capture the experience of its original use. This is recognized well enough in the analysis of speech at the phonetic level: what is acoustically recorded is not the same as the auditory apprehension of sounds. Nor of course can such analysis capture the paralinguistic features of spoken utterance, let alone the significance attached to them by interlocutors (see Cook 1995). I would simply extend the same principle to the textual level. Analysis does not match interpretation. But this raises an interesting question: why is this experience so elusive of analysis? Why is there a disparity between what is recorded as text and what that text means to its speakers? Discourse participants seem to be able to make coherent sense of what on the face of it, on the evidence of the textual record, is a fragmented patchwork of utterance. The key question that needs to be addressed here is how they manage to do this. I shall return to this question later in the book (particularly in chapter 5).

Given these difficulties with spoken text, it is with some relief that we turn to written text. This, surely, is more straightforward. No transcription problems are involved: it comes in only one version. You do not have to depend on some third-person intervention to record it; it is participant-produced, self-authored as a direct record of the discourse intentions of a first-person party. The text is there at first hand, stable, continuous, well ordered, fixed on a page, or on a screen. But these very features of the textual record can mislead us into thinking that its relationship with the discourse that gave rise to it is relatively unproblematic, and we are drawn into the delusion that meaning is inscribed in the text itself, and that what the writer intended to mean can be discovered, inferred, directly from textual evidence. There is no sign here of the disorderly fragmentation that is obvious in the text of spoken discourse. But appearances are deceptive. The orderliness and apparent completeness of written text disguises the fact that it too is only a partial record of intended meaning. Garfinkel, in outlining his approach to conversation analysis, says that 'what the parties said [i.e. the spoken text] would be treated as a sketchy, partial, incomplete, masked, elliptical, concealed, ambiguous, or misleading version of what the parties talked about [i.e. their discourse]' (Garfinkel 1972:317). The same applies, I would argue, to written text.

Indeed, written text, as distinct from the written transcription of spoken text, poses even greater problems of interpretation. For whereas transcription records, however imperfectly, the discourse of both parties to the interaction, written text records only that of the first party, who can only account for second-person reaction by proxy. The writer enacts a discourse with a projected reader who may be very different from the actual readers who derive their own discourse from the text. Consequently the piecing out of the imperfections of the text on the page (its sketchiness, partiality, incompletion and so on) does not yield the writer's version of the originating discourse, but the reader's version of it. And unlike spoken conversation, there can be no on-line negotiation to enable the two parties to converge on a common understanding. In this respect, the stability of the text conceals an intrinsic instability of meaning.

When discourse takes the form of spoken interaction, the text is simultaneous and transitory and leaves no trace unless recorded. Since there is continual textual reflex of the discourse, it is easy to suppose that they are the same thing, although a glance at a transcription makes it immediately obvious how little of the discourse is actually made textually manifest. Written text is different. Here we have a record made by one of the discourse participants, the writer, who enacts the discourse on behalf of both first- and second-person parties, but who, usually, only records the contribution of the first. The textual record is always necessarily one-sided.

The actual second-person reader, as distinct from the projected one, then has to interpret this text, that is to say, to realize a discourse from it. The discourse which the writer intends the text to record as output is, in these circumstances, always likely to be different from the discourse which the reader derives from it. In other words, what a writer means *by* a text is not the same as what a text means *to* a reader.

So in reference to what Zellig Harris has to say, interpretation is not simply a matter of what the author was about when he produced the text. It is also what the reader is about when processing it. There may often, of course, be a close correspondence. This seems fairly clearly to be the case with public notices. There are, to be sure, anecdotal counterexamples. There is the man who misunderstood the force of the notice DOGS MUST BE CARRIED and declined to take the escalator because he had no dog. There is Jonathan Miller in the revue *Beyond the Fringe* reflecting on the notice in the toilet in a train GENTLEMEN LIFT THE SEAT. This, he suggests, might not actually be an injunction, but a statement of general truth about gentlemen and their habitual behaviour, or even a loyal toast ('Gentlemen, lift the seat!').

But these are comical anecdotes: comical precisely because such incongruous instances of mistaken reference and force are rare. And indeed in most of our daily transactional uses of language we are so contracted into the conventions of belief and behaviour that define them that we can fairly confidently count on an unproblematic convergence of intention and interpretation. It is hard to see how social life would be possible otherwise.

In other cases, however, convergence is less straightforward. This is particularly so when our individual identity is implicated, when the values, attitudes and beliefs which provide us with our security are brought into play. I have talked about (locutionary) reference and (illocutionary) force as aspects of pragmatic meaning achieved in discourse. When we talk of such values, attitudes, beliefs and individual identity, we introduce a third, and much more problematic aspect: that of (perlocutionary) *effect*.

A simple example, and a traditional one. I can make reference to the same person in a variety of ways: the Duke of Wellington, the Iron Duke, the victor of Waterloo; or, to be a little less dated, the Prime Minister, Mr Blair, our Tony, Bush's poodle, and so on. The difference between these phrases lies in the attitude they appear to express, in how I seem to position myself in respect to the person referred to. So I might be deemed to indicate deference, admiration, disrespect. And of course, since communication is a matter of convergence, my choice of referring expression can be seen as an attempt to persuade my intended interlocutor into the same position. So it is that expressions can be said to be indexically the same in reference but different in effect. The same point can be made about force. I can report an event with the intention to alarm or amuse or impress, to incite your sympathy or your contempt, and you may recognize the intention and so ratify the effect intended.

But equally, of course, you may not. And there's the rub. For, like reference and force, effect is not a feature of the text but a function of the discourse, either as intentionally written into the text or interpretatively read into it. You may *deem* me to have said or written something disrespectful, or rude, or ironic, or racially biased, but to do so you have to make assumptions about my intentions, which, in accordance with normal pragmatic practice, can only be partially signalled in the text. These assumptions are naturally and inevitably made on the basis of *your* conception of the world, *your* social and individual reality, *your* values, beliefs, prejudices. This is the necessary consequence of discourse conceived as social action. It is your discourse you read into my text. You can only interpret it by relating it to your reality. Where your reality corresponds to mine, or where you are prepared to co-operate in seeing things my way, then there can be convergence between intention and interpretation. Otherwise, there will be a disparity. You will be taking me out of context – out of the context of my reality. What for me is a statement of fact may for you be an assertion to be challenged.

When we are engaged in face-to-face interaction, this challenge can, of course, be made directly and will be immediately textualized as a constituent part of the ongoing discourse. Thus the second person jointly constructs the spoken text, so long as this is the reflex of reciprocal interaction, as in conversation. But with other kinds of spoken language, there is no such possibility of intervention, and it is the first person who is in complete control of text production. And this, as we have already noted, is also the case with written text. In some kinds of discourse, most obviously in writing, the participants are kept apart, and there can be no possibility of reconciling their positions by overt negotiation. Intention and interpretation cannot mutually modify each other: they inform different discourses, and only the first is textualized.

In this chapter I have argued the case for making a conceptual distinction between text and discourse, and this has involved rejecting as unsatisfactory, and misleading, the definition of either of them in terms of language 'above the sentence'. The sentence is an abstract unit of syntax which can be adduced to account for linguistic competence, what people know of the encoding possibilities of their language. Whatever reality it has as knowledge, made explicit by linguistic analysis, it is not actually realized as performance in normal language behaviour. It can be *manifested* if people (like language learners) are asked to display their knowledge by giving examples of well-formed sentences, but that is a very different thing, a matter of mention, of usage rather than use (Widdowson 1978). Normally people do not manifest their knowledge as sentences, but realize it as utterances. This is readily recognized in the case of spoken language use, which is frequently so textually fragmented that forms corresponding to sentences are hard to find. But since such forms normally do appear in writing, it is easy to suppose that here the text *does* consist of sentences. And we do indeed commonly refer to sentences, rather than utterances, when talking about written text.

But these are sentences in a different sense. For here they are units of actual written performance bounded by a capital letter and a full stop, which may (though, as we have seen need not) correspond with any number of units which can be analysed into sentences in the syntactic sense. Sentence in this case is the word we use for written utterance.

Since the production of text, written as well as spoken, is performance it cannot be accounted for as such by invoking the competence category of the syntactic sentence. It is not, as I have argued earlier, an encoded arrangement of language above, or below, the sentence but a different phenomenon altogether: the overt linguistic trace of a process of negotiating the passage of intended meaning, the pragmatic process of discourse realization, whereby the resources of the language code are used to engage with the context of beliefs, values, assumptions that constitute the user's social and individual reality. In this sense, text is an epiphenomenon. It exists as a symptom of pragmatic intent. Of course, you can ignore this symptomatic function, disregard any discourse significance a text might have, and treat it simply as the manifestation of linguistic data. But since text always carries the implication of discourse, to do this is to analyse the textual product in dissociation from the pragmatic process which realizes it, and without which it would have no point.

Notes

1 What we do find in 7.2 in fact is a reaffirmation that there is no conceptual distinction between the two. Where a distinction is made, however, is between two senses of the term *discourse*: 'In previous chapters, I have used text and discourse to mean naturally occurring instances of language in use. However, discourse is also used to in a very different sense to mean recurrent phrases and conventional ways of talking, which circulate in the social world, and which form a constellation of repeated meanings.' Such 'discourse patterns' are said to 'embody particular social values and views of the world' (Stubbs 1996:158). This, we are told, is the sense of discourse that is developed in Foucault 1972 and Fairclough 1992. What makes this sense 'very different' is not explained. The difference is certainly not apparent in Stubbs's own work: the immediately preceding chapter of his book actually deals with discourse in this second sense, being a detailed analysis of 'how language mediates and represents the world from different points of view' (Stubbs 1996:128). I consider this analysis in chapter 7.

2 Just how orthodox it has become is indicated by the following entry in a recently published glossary of sociolinguistics: 'Discourse analysis. A branch of linguistics which deals with linguistic units at levels above the sentence, that is texts and conversations. Those branches of discourse analysis which come under the heading of sociolinguistics presuppose that language is being used in social interaction and thus deal with conversation. Other non-sociolinguistic branches of discourse analysis are often known as text linguistics' (Trudgill 2003).

3 A new edition of the encyclopedia was published in 2003. Chafe's entry, however, is unchanged.

4 It is perhaps of interest to note that the distinction between text and discourse, drawn very much along the lines proposed in this chapter, figures explicitly and prominently in the first edition of Coulthard's *Introduction to Discourse Analysis* (Coulthard 1977), but unaccountably disappears in the revised edition (Coulthard 1985).

5 In his later work, Stubbs concedes that the definition of text (or discourse) as language above the sentence needs to be revised to account for the textual status of such notices: 'It is therefore more accurate to say that text and discourse analysis studies language in context: how words and phrases fit into both longer texts, and also social contexts of use' (Stubbs 2001a:5).

6 Note that the distinction between text and discourse in terms of product and process is clearly drawn in Brown and Yule 1983: 'In summary, the discourse analyst treats his data as the record (text) of a dynamic process in which language was used as an instrument of communication in a context by a speaker/ writer to express meanings and achieve intentions (discourse)' (Brown and Yule 1983.26). For arguments along similar lines to those in this chapter against defining discourse as structural units 'above the sentence or clause' see Schiffrin

1994, chapter 2. Schiffrin contrasts this with 'discourse as language use'. Interestingly, this distinction parallels one that I proposed myself in earlier days. Discourse, I suggested then, might be defined as 'the use of sentences in combination' but added: 'This is a vague definition which conveniently straddles two different, if complementary, ways of looking at language beyond the sentence. We might say that one way is to focus attention on the second part of my definition: *sentences in combination*, and the other to focus on the first: *the use of sentences*' (Widdowson 1979:90). I later recognized (as does Schiffrin) that discourse as use has to do not with sentences but with utterances, and for me it followed that a distinction needed to be made between text and discourse. Schiffrin does not come to that conclusion: for her, as for Stubbs, the difference between these latter terms has no conceptual significance, and she uses the two in free variation. She prefers to assign different kinds of significance to the term *discourse*. As we see, however, she does not do this along the same lines as Stubbs: there is no recognition in her account of the distinction he makes.

2

Text and grammar

As was pointed out in the preceding chapter, Zellig Harris conceived of discourse analysis as the discovery of patterns of formal equivalences across the sentences in a text, and therefore, essentially, as an extension of the scope of grammar. His device for establishing such textual constituents was the transformation, by means of which he sought to identify regularities underlying different surface appearances. This device was then adopted by Chomsky not to extend the scope of grammatical analysis but to focus it more exclusively on the constituent relations within the sentence itself. The generative grammar that Chomsky developed does not account for textual relations of the kind Harris was concerned with, and makes no claim to do so.

There is, however, an approach to grammar that does. I refer to systemic-functional grammar, as developed by Michael Halliday. This presents itself in opposition to a generative grammar of the Chomskyan stamp in that it accounts not only for the formal properties of sentence constituents as such, but for how they function in texts. This functional perspective is entirely consistent with Halliday's conception of language as 'social semiotic' and his concern for language in use, and the fact is, as Harris himself noted, language use takes the form of texts, not isolated sentences. The question is how far grammar can be designed to take account of this fact.

Systemic-functional grammar (henceforth S/F grammar) has the express purpose of analysing language into systems of options which constitute the 'meaning potential' for the creation of text. As Halliday puts it: 'The aim has been to construct a grammar for the purposes of text analysis: one that would make it possible to say sensible and useful things about any texts, spoken or written, in modern English' (Halliday 1994:xv). Although English is specifically mentioned here, the same would presumably apply to any language. Perhaps the first thing to be clear about is that the aim of the grammar so formulated is to account for text as a linguistic unit in its own right, to explain it as such and not simply to use it to exemplify the occurrence of other structural units, like clauses or phrases. The purpose, it would appear, is not therefore to show how different grammatical features simply show up in stretches of language, but how they operate to form larger units of meaning. As Halliday says: 'The grammar, then, is at once both a grammar of the system and a grammar of the text' (Halliday 1994:xxii).

One might reasonably infer from this statement that text analysis is taken as a straightforward matter of applying the categories of the grammar. But only, it would appear, up to a point. Halliday explains that analysis works on two levels:

> One is a contribution to the *understanding* of the text: the linguistic analysis enables one to show how, and why, the text means what it does. In the process, there are likely to be revealed multiple meanings, alternatives, ambiguities, metaphors and so on. This is the lower of the two levels; it is one that should always be attainable provided the analysis is such as to relate the text to general features of the language – provided it is based on the grammar in other words.

At this level, then, application of grammatical categories reveals the properties of the text, not only, we should notice, how it is constructed, but what it means. That is to say, the meaning is internally in the text, and understanding derives directly from analysis. Analysis, it would seem, does not just *contribute* to, but actually *constitutes* understanding. Certainly there is no mention here of where any other contribution might come from. But this is the lower level of analysis. There is a higher one:

> The higher level of achievement is a contribution to the *evaluation* of the text: the linguistic analysis may enable one to say why the text is, or is not, an effective text for its own purposes – in what respects it succeeds and in what respects it fails, or is less successful. This goal is much harder to attain. It requires an interpretation not only of the text itself but also of its context (context of situation, context of culture), and of the systematic relationship between context and text. (Halliday 1994:xv)

At this level, the text is interpreted externally in relation to context. We are concerned here not with what texts mean but what users mean by texts in the realization of their communicative purposes. At this level, presumably, the multiple meanings, ambiguities and so on which emerge from the first level get resolved by reference to contextual factors.

Halliday, then, like Harris, talks about the processing of text at two levels. But whereas for Harris the first level is concerned only with the *identification* of textual features, for Halliday it is concerned also with an understanding of their meaning, and therefore some degree of *interpretation* as well. So it would appear that for Halliday the meaning of a text is compounded of the meanings of its constituent sentences, so that understanding it is a cumulative matter. A text, it seems, is taken to be simply a sum of its sentential parts, so understanding it is straightforwardly a function of a grammatical analysis which reveals the multiple meanings, alternatives, ambiguities, metaphors encoded in the separate sentences it is composed of.

Halliday's first level of analysis looks to be more comprehensive than that of Harris in that it takes meaning into account. It is less comprehensive, however, in that it seems not to address the question of how sentences are related to form larger linguistic units, and so long as it does not do that, it is hard to see how the grammar that is applied is actually a grammar of text as such as distinct from the sentences in a text. Furthermore, the meaning that is taken into account at this level of 'understanding' is not of the kind that Harris has in mind: it has to do not with the pragmatic matter of 'what the author was about when he produced the text', but with what is semantically encoded in the sentences of the text itself. The pragmatic meaning of a text only comes into consideration at the second level of 'evaluation' when attention is shifted from the text itself to its relationship with context.[1]

The model that we are presented with here is based on the assumption that there is meaning contained within a text, an understanding of which will result directly from a linguistic analysis of its constituent sentences. Thus text is isolated as a linguistic object for analysis (and understanding), but in consequence, of course, it is dissociated from the contextual conditions which make it a text in the first place. For, as I have argued, text only exists in conjunction with context, as the reflex of discourse, and understanding in the usual sense would normally imply not the identification and subsequent elimination of alternatives, ambiguities and so on, but a more direct homing in on relevant meaning. The two levels of analysis that Halliday proposes would not appear to correspond with the normal process of assigning meaning to texts. In normal circumstances of use, people do not process utterances (spoken or written) as separate sentences, one by one, and then consider how the text so analysed might relate externally to contextual factors. We do not first come to an understanding of the semantics of a text, and then evaluate what its possible pragmatic import might be. We do not read possible meanings *off* from a text; we read plausible meanings *into* a text, prompted by the purpose and conditioned by the context. In other words (in my words) you derive a discourse from it and it is that which realizes the text as text. What is happening in Halliday's formulation,

I suggest, is that analysis is confused with interpretation. This confusion, as we shall see in later chapters (chapters 6 and 7) has far-reaching consequences.

The confusion might be remedied (in some degree at least) if we relate analysis and interpretation to the text/discourse distinction I proposed in the preceding chapter and take analysis to be a process of identifying what semantic features are manifested in a text and interpretation as one that involves recognizing how a text functions as discourse by discriminating which, and how, these features are pragmatically activated. From this perspective, it is only at the evaluation level, in Halliday's terms, that we are dealing with a text at all. At what he calls the understanding level, we are dealing only with textual data and using it as evidence for how semantic meaning is encoded in sentences. With regard to the analysis of text, S/F grammar is, in this view, systemic, but not functional. Now of course this is not to deny that S/F grammar is *based* on text in the sense that its systems reveal all manner of detail about the semantic resource that is textually deployed in the making of meaning. This is where its unique achievement lies. But a text-based grammar is not at all the same as a grammar of text.

Systemic-functional grammar is an account of the meaning potential that is encoded in formal systems. These systems are functional in the sense that their development reflects the essential social functions that language has to serve. But how this semantically encoded potential, this social semiotic resource, gets actually, and pragmatically, realized in particular occasions of use is quite a different matter. Here we are concerned with function in a different sense, not with how use is abstracted as code but how code is actualized as use. It is easy to see how the two senses might be confused, and so to suppose that in dealing with the functional features of sentences one is at the same time dealing with how they are functioning in the text. Consider the following remarks in another introduction to S/F grammar:

> For Halliday, the only approach to the construction of grammars that is likely to be successful will be one that recognizes meaning and use as central features of language and tackles the grammar from this point of view. It follows from this that Halliday's grammar is *semantic* (concerned with meaning) and *functional* (concerned with how language is used). (Bloor and Bloor 1995:2)

Here the grammar is represented as having two central features: meaning, which is semantic, and use, which is functional. There is, however, no such distinction in S/F grammar: the two are conflated in that the systemic/semantic systems which encode meaning potential are functionally informed. Furthermore, the grammar itself cannot be concerned with how language is used, how the potential these systems encode gets pragmatically realized in use. S/F is functional not because it deals with how language is used, here and now, in actual acts of communication, but because it reflects how language *has been used*, and how these uses have over time been abstracted and semantically encoded. Language is as it is, as a system, because of the social functions it has evolved to serve. This is a diachronic statement. From this starting point, you can explain the functional provenance of form, show it to be socially motivated and not just inexplicably random, and so provide an immensely rich account of how meanings get to be encoded in the language. This is the great achievement of S/F grammar. But it cannot be an account of how language is used. These authors, however, appear to think that it can: 'Since a speaker's or writer's choice of words is constrained by the situation of utterance, and since words and groups of words take on special significance in particular contexts, the grammar must be able to account for the way in which the language is used in social situations' (Bloor and Bloor 1995:4).

Presumably it is the 'functional' feature of the grammar which is supposed to account for the way language is used in social situations. The difficulty is that there is no such separate feature in systemic-functional grammar: it is incorporated into the semantic. But, as we have noted, how language is used in social situations is a matter of contextual conditioning and belongs to what Halliday calls the higher level of text evaluation. It is decidedly not a function of linguistic analysis, or what he calls understanding, which is entirely derived from text and does not depend on context at all. So Bloor and Bloor seem to be calling on the grammar to do something which is in principle beyond its scope. But we can see how the confusion arises. If a grammar claims to be a grammar of text, then it surely follows that it should account for the 'special significance' that language takes on when it used *as* text, that is to say in context. Halliday talks about evaluation, the higher level of analysis, as requiring an interpretation of the 'systematic relationship' between text and context. In what respects the relationship between text and context is systematic is a key issue in discourse analysis, but systematic or not, it is hard to see how it can be *systemic* in an S/F grammar sense.

We might agree with Bloor and Bloor that *significance* is the meaning a text takes on when it is used in association with context. It is a function of what Halliday calls evaluation, and it is necessarily a pragmatic matter. But this cannot be equated with the *signification* of the formal components which constitute the text as linguistic object, and which can be exemplified without reference to any context at all. As a simple illustration, take the following:

They are arriving tomorrow.

The signification of the auxiliary is that it simultaneously encodes present tense, third person plural subject and (in combination with the present participle) continuous aspect. But since all of these are signalled elsewhere in the clause, the auxiliary in fact has no auxiliary significance whatever. So we can dispense with it in actual use, and if we have access to contextual information, we can dispense with the subject too. So it is that we have no difficulty interpreting the reduced clause as a text in the form of a telegram:

ARRIVING TOMORROW

So it is too that communication can often be achieved by minimal linguistic effort so long as an effective contextual contact is thereby achieved:

Me Tarzan. You Jane.
Mistah Kurtz – he dead.[2]

Of course, one can accept that signification is a function of significance in that it is historically derived from it: contextual uses of language find formal expression in the code. But the relationship is not reflexive: significance is not a function of signification. You cannot read it off from linguistic features. Text does not signal its own meaning, so, to refer back to Halliday's first level, linguistic analysis, no matter how detailed, cannot result in an understanding of 'how and why a text means what it does', for this must also take into account, among other things, what Harris refers to as 'what the author was about when he produced the text'.

Indeed, one might argue that the more detailed the linguistic analysis, the further one is likely to get from the significance of the text. And this follows because only some of the semantic meaning encoded in linguistic form is activated as contextually appropriate on a particular occasion. What is distinctive about S/F grammar is that it shows how the language code is informed by the range of contextual functions it is called upon to discharge in the social process. These external contextual functions become encoded as internal semantic relations. Every clause represents a convergence of options from the different semantic networks, and can be analysed as message, exchange, representation, at different constituent ranks and at different levels of delicacy. Analysis can, in principle, take anything that has been encoded into account, and the decision to select certain features to attend to is essentially arbitrary, a matter of descriptive convenience.

But it is a pragmatic commonplace, of course, that when this system is actually exploited in use only a part of its potential is realized, quite simply because if the actual context provides sufficient information for your communicative needs, you do not have to pay much attention to how this contextual information has been encoded in the language. In exploiting the meaning potential of the system you also exploit its redundancy. You regulate your attention and select what is significant: you activate whatever in the text seems to be contextually relevant and disregard the rest. Otherwise, language use would be an intolerably cumbersome process. So significance, the contextual functioning of language, depends on paying selective heed to the contextually derived signification inscribed in the code.

Texts, indeed, are very commonly designed to make the most economical connection with context precisely to *avoid* unnecessary linguistic processing, so that understanding them is not a function of analysis at all. Understanding the text CLOSED on a shop window does not require me to recover a clause like **This shop is closed**, and then analyse it for its meaning. I relate it directly to context and make an immediate pragmatic inference. It would appear then that in this case, Halliday's first level can be dispensed with altogether, and the text is evaluated without being understood. Of course, one might argue that if one cannot apply the first level of grammatical analysis to instances of use, such as public notices, then they are not texts at all. But then, as we saw in chapter 1, this takes us back to a definition of text in terms of its formal properties rather than its pragmatic use. Such a formalist definition is not one which is likely to find much favour in functionalist circles.

It seems clear that the linguistic analysis of text is not necessary for understanding. Indeed, it would appear that, if anything, it deflects attention from an inference of meaning and interferes with interpretation, so that the first level of analysis in Halliday's scheme has a way of obstructing the processing at the second level. Consider the case of multiple meanings and ambiguities. These occur in texts with a fair degree of frequency. But in many cases, though they can be revealed by semantic analysis, they are not pragmatically activated because the signification is overridden by contextual factors. So it is that we might conceive of the man in the London underground (referred to in the preceding chapter) setting about understanding the text DOGS MUST BE CARRIED by semantic analysis and being confused by two possible meanings:

(1) *It is necessary to carry dogs* (by analogy with TICKETS MUST BE SHOWN)
(2) *If you have a dog, it is necessary to carry it.*

It seems more likely, however, that the man, like thousands of other passengers, would simply identify the text as a notice, relate it to context and notice nothing ambiguous about the language at all. The same applies to the following utterance that occurred some time ago in a the text of a news broadcast about stormy weather on the British coast:

Five people were lost in a rowing boat.

This too is semantically ambiguous:

(1) *Five people in a rowing boat were lost.*
(2) *Five (very small) people were lost in(side) a rowing boat.*

Normal listeners, concerned with interpretation, do not notice ambiguities of this kind. Linguists do. This is because their attention is attuned to semantic analysis, and in the process they abstract sentence from utterance and thereby detextualize the text.

Ironically enough, the level of text understanding in Halliday's scheme would seem to involve the same kind of fixation on isolated sentences that is associated with the formalist linguistics that a functional approach to analysis sets out to oppose. Consider the celebrated, not to say notorious, example of:

Visiting aunts can be boring.

Ambiguity here can be explained in the formal terms of generative grammar as resulting from the convergence in one surface form of two distinct underlying syntactic structures:

(1) *Aunts who visit can be boring.*
(2) *To visit aunts can be boring.*

By the same process of analysis one can reveal ambiguity in the following expressions as well:

Visiting lecturers can be boring.
Visiting foreigners can benefit the economy.
Closing doors can be hazardous.
Melting wax is messy.
Melting ice is dangerous.
Following motor-bikes could get you into trouble.

And so on.

In all of these, and in innumerable other cases, grammatical analysis will yield the same kind of semantic ambiguity, but even as utterances in isolation we relate them to the context of our knowledge of the world and one interpretation gets preferred by pragmatic default. This default interpretation could, of course, be changed under more particular contextual conditions:

Doors should be kept open in case you need to get out quickly.
Closing doors can be hazardous.
If you melt the ice on the path with hot water, it will be dangerous when it
    freezes again.
Melting ice can be dangerous, etc.

But the point is that it is generally only one semantic alternative that is pragmatically activated and the other left as a potential unrealized. So if we take these expressions as *textual*, that is to say as used in a communicative context of some kind, and not as exemplifying the semantic resources of the system, the ambiguity will, likely as not, pass unnoticed. Noticing it, indeed, is likely to interfere with communicative efficiency. So making ambiguity noticeable by analysing semantic features out of text would actually be *dys*functional as far as interpreting the text is concerned.

One might, of course, argue that though we may not be consciously aware of ambiguities, or other alternative meanings, they are nevertheless activated at some subliminal level of text processing, where they are all sifted through and selected as pragmatically required. One might even suggest that this process leaves a trace, and that alternative meanings remain as a shadowy presence in the mind which have an effect on the interpretation even though it appears to have eliminated them. If this is so, then it can be argued not only that interpretation presupposes analysis, but that analysis actually represents meaning which is taken in subliminally, and so makes explicit how the text acts upon the mind of interpreters subversively in ways they are unaware of. I shall return to this argument in chapter 6 when I consider the principles and practices of critical discourse analysis. Meanwhile, there is another issue about S/F grammar that we need to address.

I have been arguing that when language is put to use, the resulting text acts upon context, and in this pragmatic process the encoded semantic potential is only partially realized. This is why evaluation cannot be a function of understanding in Halliday's sense. But there is a further difficulty: the semantic analysis is bound to be partial on its own terms as well. This is because the potential that the grammar seeks to capture is misrepresented by the very process of accounting for it. The grammar, in other words, can never be an account of what people can mean. A model, of its very nature, classifies and categorizes, makes divisions and distinctions which separate aspects of language out from each other. But these aspects co-occur in texts in complex relationships which cannot be grammatically accounted for.

An S/F grammar analyses language as networks of options which constitute distinct systems associated with three metafunctions. The analysis requires disjunctive categorization. Some allowance can no doubt be made for tactical cross-classification, but this must of its nature be limited. Essentially linguistic analysis is disjunctive. Language experience, on the other hand, is not: in language use, we commonly find a complex functional *con*junction of features across categories.

As we have already noted, it is taken as axiomatic in S/F linguistics that a model of description should reflect the essential social nature of language. Human language did not just take the form it did by random mutation, but evolved in the process of adaptation to human need, and a linguistic model should reflect this fact. So it is that S/F grammar is functionally iconic in that its design is meant to represent the essential human purposes which language has evolved to serve. Thus we arrive at the tripartite structure of the model. This is how the general design principle is expressed:

> All languages are organized around two main kinds of meaning, the 'ideational' or reflective, and the 'interpersonal' or active. These components, called 'metafunctions' in the terminology of the current theory, are the manifestations in the linguistic system of the two very general purposes which underlie all uses of language: (i) to understand the environment (ideational), and (ii) to act on the others in it (interpersonal). Combined with these is a third metafunctional component, the 'textual', which breathes relevance into the other two. (Halliday 1994:xiii)

We might formulate the ideational and interpersonal functions in terms of the relationship between the trinity of positions which are linguistically encoded in the personal pronoun system. Thus the ideational function can be understood as the relationship between ego, first-person self, to third-person reality out there, and the interpersonal function as the relationship between first-person self and second-person other. Diagrammatically:

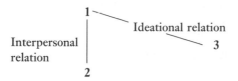

Figure 2.1

Since this trinity does indeed seem fundamental to human perception, we can acknowledge that there is good reason for basing the design of a model of language on the two functions which express their essential relationship.

There is, however, a difficulty about the third of the metafunctions which Halliday identifies. It is different in kind from the others in that it is not related to any external social or communicative need. It simply serves an enabling purpose: it is a kind of functional catalyst which combines with the other functions only in order to 'breathe relevance into them'. This implies that these other functions are inert and are only made relevant (presumably to the communicative process) when acted upon by the textual. But how this comes about is far from clear. If the textual function is to combine with the others and make them relevant, then one would expect that the grammar would reveal how the various options associated with the other functions are realized through the options associated with the textual. We would expect to find some clear indication of functional interrelations and interdependencies. But what the grammar does is to show how the three metafunctions are encoded in three separate systemic components: theme, mood and transitivity. They are categorized as three distinct kinds of meaning, and options from each constitute separate strands, three lines of meaning which come together in the clause. There they coexist but they do not act upon each other. So each clause can be characterized as message or exchange or representation in respect to the theme, mood and transitivity systems respectively. Consider the following clauses (Halliday's own examples):

The duke gave my aunt this teapot.
This teapot, the duke gave my aunt.

These do not differ as exchange or representation: *the duke* is subject (in respect to mood) and actor (in respect to transitivity) in both cases. But in the second clause it is *this teapot* which is the theme, and so the clause is different as message. What though if we put *my aunt* in theme position by means of the passive?

My aunt was given this teapot by the duke.

In this case we are involved not in an option from the theme systems but from the mood systems, since *my aunt* now becomes the subject. The participant roles in the process remain the same, however (*the duke* is still the actor, *my aunt* the goal), so on this account there is no change in the clause as representation. But since it is the function of the passive to provide an alternative thematization, we really need this option in the theme systems as well, alongside, for example, thematic variants like:

What the duke gave my aunt was this teapot.
This teapot is what the duke gave my aunt.

Furthermore, if we want to argue that the use of the passive (and of these thematic variants too for that matter) not only reorganizes information to alter the clause as message, but actually represents a different ideational perspective on the event, then we need to account for it in the transitivity systems as well. In short, what we have is a complex set of implicational relations across the different divisions of the grammar and what we need is some explanation of the interpersonal and ideational consequences of alternative thematizations, of just *how* the textual function combines with the others to breathe life into them. The clause is, after all, only a message to the extent that it is also both exchange and representation, and it would seem that the meaning of a clause is a function of the dynamic interplay of the mood and transitivity systems as realized by the textual.

As I indicated earlier, all models of description are based on idealization, and S/F grammar is no exception. It is convenient, and indeed necessary, to assign different linguistic phenomena to different components of the grammar. But this is a function not of the language but of its analysis.

In the grammar, the systems are kept apart. In actual use, however, they are not. When the semantic resources are actualized pragmatically as text, they act upon each other in various ways. Consider theme and rheme, for example, as constituents of the clause as message. In actual use they do indeed combine with other meanings: indeed their *only* function is to realize other functions. The organization of information in the clause is motivated by some ideational or interpersonal purpose. Thus, theme and rheme may be associated with topic and comment, in which case the first person adopts a position in relation to the third-person world, interprets reality, if you will, in reference to self. In this sense, assignment of topic and comment is an ideational matter. Alternatively, theme and rheme may be associated with given and new. In this case the information is being organized to key in with what is assumed to be known by the second person, so the thematic arrangement now discharges an interpersonal function. We can show this diagrammatically as follows:

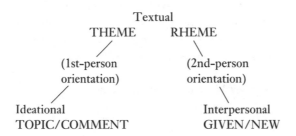

Figure 2.2

What this diagram represents, in a modest way, is one case of interrelationship across the systems of the grammar. It may be that there are other and more specific inter-systemic dependencies that could be identified and made explicit in the grammar. It might be possible, for example, to establish that particular theme options co-occurred regularly with particular options in the transitivity and mood systems so that they are bound implicationally together. The more such inter-systemic dependencies could be accounted for, the closer the grammar of the system would approximate to the grammar of text in that it would obviously increase semantic constraints on pragmatic meaning, and narrow down interpretative possibilities. But the quest for such relational dependencies seems to be precluded by the divisions built into the design of a S/F grammar whereby each of the three system types is singled out for separate treatment: the emphasis is on intra-systemic distinctions rather than inter-systemic connections. But even if S/F grammar were to become a more integrated model along these lines, it would still not account for all possible textual realizations. It could not determine which combination of theme, transitivity and mood features was operative on a particular textual occasion.

So whether a particular thematic arrangement is to be understood as having ideational or interpersonal significance is a matter of interpretation beyond analysis. The textual function in the grammar does not, in fact, reveal how the text functions. Consider the case of the passive as a thematic device for message organization. When it occurs pragmatically in text it is bound to take on ideational or interpersonal significance. It is indeed frequently cited by critical discourse analysts as an example of specific representation, of how a particular first-person perspective is projected on reality. I shall be looking more closely at this kind of analysis in chapter 6, but it will perhaps clarify the present argument to cite one simple example.

In Lee (1992) we are presented with an analysis of two texts, extracts from two newspapers which deal with same event. The texts differ in their organization of the clause as message, that is to say in the way the information is thematically organized. One of them uses the active, and the other the passive. The *Guardian* newspaper has the headline:

Police (*theme*) shoot 11 dead in Salisbury riot

The text then continues:

Riot police (*theme*) shot and killed 11 African demonstrators . . .

The *Times* text has the headline:

Rioting blacks (*theme*) shot dead by police as ANC leaders meet

followed by:

Eleven Africans (*theme*) were shot dead . . .

Lee comments: 'It is noticeable that *The Guardian* uses active structures in both the headline and in the text . . . whereas *The Times* uses passives. The effect of the passive is to further attenuate the agentivity of the police, particularly in the case of the truncated passive with agent deletion' (Lee 1992:100).

It is a matter of fact that these texts manifest active and passive structures. The question is: what meanings do they realize? Lee asserts that the selection of the passive necessarily implies a first-person position on the event, presents the topic in a certain light. This may be the effect of the passive on him, but it has no warrant in the grammar. For he takes the passive here not as a message-forming option from theme systems, but as if it were an option from the transitivity systems of the grammar: he reads the passive, as opposed to the active, as signalling a different representation of the event. But the specific ideational meaning which Lee assigns to the passive is actually a function of his interpretation of this structure as it occurs in this particular text, an interpretation which is itself related, of course, to a context of socio-political beliefs and values. If the passive is textualized differently, it becomes more difficult to assign such a meaning to it. Suppose, for example, we were to give the event described in these newspaper texts the following wording:

Police opened fire on African demonstrators in Salisbury today as ANC leaders were meeting. Eleven Africans were shot dead.

It would surely be somewhat perverse in this case to interpret the passive ideationally as representing the event as happening without agentivity, since the agentivity is explicitly described in the preceding clause. It would seem more reasonable to suggest that this is not a case of reference evasion, but reference avoidance, motivated by communicative economy. The agent is deleted because it is redundant. The writer, we might suggest, is cooperatively taking account of what the reader already knows and fashions the message accordingly on given/new considerations. The passive with deleted agent in this case can be understood not ideationally as representing the event in a certain way, but as having the interpersonal function of facilitating the exchange.

Lee talks as if the passive structure always signifies a particular kind of representation, a signification that is carried over from grammar into text. But as we have seen, the significance of the structure depends on how it relates to others in a text. Even if one could show systematically (and systemically) that agentivity is a function of the convergence of theme and transitivity options in the grammar, it does not follow that this semantic feature is focused on in a particular instance of text, or even pragmatically activated at all.

It would seem then that active/passive message forms can, as parts of *text*, function in different ideational and interpersonal ways. But these cannot be captured by the grammar. Here the functions are kept apart. This is made quite clear in another introduction to S/F grammar. Lock (1996) illustrates the relationship between textual and ideational (what he calls experiential) systems of the grammar by referring to the following two clauses:

Michelangelo finished the statue of David in 1504.
The statue of David was finished (by Michelangelo) in 1504.

He then comments as follows:

> In the active voice clause the noun group functioning as Actor (Michelangelo) also functions as Subject and as Theme. However, in the passive voice clause, the Actor is either not expressed at all or occurs in the Rheme as the Object of the preposition *by*. The Theme and the Subject of the passive version is the Goal, which in the active voice version is mapped on to the Direct Object. In other words, the two clauses have the same experiential meanings, but differ in their textual meanings, having two different points of departure. (Lock 1996:233)

The meanings referred to here are semantic, intrinsic to the linguistic forms themselves. But the difficulty is that the term *textual* is ambiguous. It can either (as here) refer to the thematic component of the grammar, or to the way forms function pragmatically in text. Thus, as we have seen, for Lee textual differences of the grammatical kind that Lock is talking about carry ideational implications when used in text, and so do *not* have the same experiential meaning. The point, again, is that such *significance* is a function of the pragmatic interplay of different semantic features and cannot be referred to the *signification* of these features as specified in the grammar itself.

Halliday himself seems to provide corroboration of this. Consider, for example, his comments on the two material process clauses:

> The lion caught the tourist. (*Actor Process Goal*)
> The tourist was caught by the lion. (*Goal Process Actor*)

> Material processes are processes of 'doing'. They express the notion that some entity 'does' something – which may be done 'to' some other entity. So we can ask about such processes or 'probe' them, in this way: What did the lion do? What did the lion do to the tourist? Looked at from the tourist's point of view, on the other hand, the process is not one of doing but one of 'happening'; we can also say: What happened to the tourist? Consequently if there is a Goal of the process, as well as an Actor, the representation may come in either of two forms: either active, *the lion caught the tourist*, or passive, *the tourist was caught by the lion*. (Halliday 1994:110)

The representation comes in two possible forms, active and passive, but the representation itself is the same, unaltered by the different shaping of the clause as message. They are variants of what Halliday refers to elsewhere as effective clauses. These contrast in respect to representation with what he calls middle clauses which are ergative and not transitive in character. So the middle clause

The glass broke.

contrasts with the two effective clauses:

The cat broke the glass. (*effective active*)
The glass was broken by the cat. (*effective passive*)

He comments:

> Strictly speaking an effective clause has the feature 'agency' rather than the structural function Agent, because this may be left implicit, as in *the glass was broken*. The presence of an 'agency' feature is in fact the difference between a pair of clauses such as *the glass broke* and *the glass was* (or *got*) *broken*: the latter embodies the feature of agency, so that one can ask the question 'who by?', while the former allows for one participant only. (Halliday 1994:169)

Although, rather misleadingly, active and passive figure here as options in the ideational component, there seems to be no distinction between them in respect to agency: the roles of actor and goal in relation to the process remain unaffected by the alternative thematic formulations. The cat is the agent in both cases (as is the lion in the earlier example) and the glass is the goal in both cases (as is the tourist). As Halliday says, the same representation comes in two different (message) forms. So it would appear that, *in the grammar*, the distinction between middle and effective is ideational, but that between passive and active effective is thematic. The choice between them in actual text use, however, as between any thematic option, is likely to have ideational or interpersonal implications, which, as I have suggested, are impossible to confine within the disjunctive systems of the grammar.

In text analysis, however, it is just these implications that we are concerned with, and it is of course very tempting to ascribe such implications as a direct function of semantic signification in the grammar itself, thereby conflating the levels of 'understanding' and 'evaluation (in Halliday's terms), and making the task of interpretation a relatively simple matter of semantic projection

In this chapter I have been exploring the relationship between text and grammar by questioning the S/F claim that it can account both for the systems of the code and for their textual use within the same model of description. I have argued that this claim is sustained by a confusion in the concept of function. S/F grammar is functional in the sense that the systems of semantic encodings that it identifies are derived diachronically from how language has developed as social semiotic as a formal reflex of the functions it is required to serve. It does not follow at all, however, that the functioning of language pragmatically as discourse is simply a function of these systems. The fact that S/F grammar is modelled *on* use does not make it a model *of* use. So I think it is misleading to claim that it is 'at once both a grammar of the system and a grammar of the text'. It cannot be an account of text as the pragmatic use of language, the product of a discourse process.

What it can, and does, provide is an extremely detailed set of descriptive devices which can be used in specifying the linguistic features of texts, and it may be that this description of semantic signification might serve as a pointer to where pragmatic significance is to be found. It might indeed be that, in Harris's words, the interpretation of text 'may follow closely in the directions which the formal findings indicate'. But just what these directions are, and how closely interpretation follows them, are precisely the kinds of question that discourse analysis needs to grapple with. There must obviously be a crucial relationship between semantic and pragmatic meaning, between the potential and its realization, between abstract systems that are informed by function and the functions that are actualized in their use. But we cannot look for relationships between phenomena without first making a distinction between them.

And this point applies, most crucially of all perhaps, to the notions of text and discourse that I discussed in chapter 1. Like Chafe, Schiffrin and Stubbs, Halliday makes no distinction between them, as is evident from the following: 'A text is meaningful because it is an actualization of the potential that constitutes the linguistic system; it is for this reason that the study of discourse ("text linguistics") cannot properly be separated from the study of grammar that lies behind it' (Halliday 1994:366).

If by actualization is meant the *realization* of potential (as distinct from the manifestation of the system that encodes it), then a text can only be meaningful as a text when we recognize it as a product of the discourse process, and as such has no self-contained meaning of its own to be understood by grammatical analysis. In this respect what lies behind the text is discourse, not grammar. The study of discourse, in this sense, crucially involves relating text with context, so it *has* to be separated from the study of grammar. This is not, of course, to say that such study can be conducted *separately* from grammar, for this, as Halliday says, provides the essential semantic resource to be drawn on, the potential to be realized. The point I would make is that the notions of grammar, text and discourse need to be clearly distinguished so that we can enquire more explicitly into the ways in which they are related.

Discourse analysis, as I see it, has to do not with what texts mean, but with what might be meant by them, and what they are taken to mean. In this view there is no 'understanding' of texts as a semantic process, separate from, and prior to, a pragmatic 'evaluation' which brings context into play. Text implies context right from the start, so textual interpretation necessarily involves a consideration of contextual factors. Just what such contextual factors might be, and how they come into play, are matters to be taken up in the next chapter.

Notes

1 Halliday does not talk about his two levels of text interpretation in terms of semantics and pragmatics. There is every indication that, as with the terms *text* and *discourse*, they are taken as terminological variants which have no conceptual significance in his scheme of things. The term *pragmatics*, indeed, rarely, if ever, occurs in his writing: it makes no appearance, for example, in the index of Halliday (1994). *Semantics*, on the other hand, does, and this term is used to cover all aspects of meaning. Thus he refers to 'the semantic system of the language', 'the semantic interpretation of a text' (xx) and 'discourse semantics' (15). There is no recognition of the distinction I drew in chapter 1 between (semantic) meaning that is encoded in the language and (pragmatic) meaning that is realized in language use. Halliday talks about realization, but in a very different sense: 'The relation between the semantics and the grammar is one of realization: the wording "realizes", or encodes, the meaning' (Halliday 1994:xx). For Halliday, encoded and realized meanings are, it would appear, the same (semantic) thing.

2 'Mistah Kurtz – he dead.' This comes from Joseph Conrad's novel *Heart of Darkness*, and the context in which the utterance occurs gives it a significance well beyond what the words signify. It also occurs in a totally different context as a quotation preceding T. S. Eliot's poem *The Hollow Men*, where it takes on additional intertextual meaning which, again, cannot possibly, of course, be derived from the words alone.

3

Context

I suggested in chapter 2 that we *identify* a stretch of language as text when we recognize that it is intended to be related to a context. How we *interpret* a text is a matter of realizing that relationship. Thus we can identify a text, but be at a loss to know how it might be interpreted because we cannot make an effective contextual connection. Since the text is a linguistic object, we can also, of course, decode it semantically as such, but we thereby dissociate it from context and disregard its textual nature, for interpretation is a matter of assigning pragmatic significance to such encodings. In this view, the realization of text as discourse is a matter of establishing some appropriate relationship between code and context. In the preceding chapter we considered how the code figures in this relationship. The focus of the present chapter is on the context.

The term *context* is of very common occurrence in the literature on discourse and text analysis and, like the term *discourse* itself, is elusive of definition. Just as we began our exploration of the meaning of the latter term by tracing it back to Harris, so we can proceed in like fashion with the term *context* by tracing it back to Malinowski. Both scholars sought to broaden the scope of linguistic description, but in very different ways. For Harris, we might say, it was a matter of bringing aspects of use under formal control, whereas for Malinowksi it was a matter of showing how the code functions in contexts of use. In this respect, one might say that of the two it was Malinowski who was actually engaged with discourse, as it has been defined in this book, not Harris, whose attention was, as we have seen, confined to the features of its textual trace.

Malinowski invoked the notion of context to account for the way language was used among the Trobriand islanders in the Western Pacific. In such non-literate communities, he observed, language functioned as 'a mode of action'. But it could only do that if what was said was made meaningful by being keyed into a particular 'context of situation' familiar to the participants concerned. Malinowski associates this context-dependent functional use of language with spoken interaction in 'primitive' communities, such as the Trobriand islanders: 'in a primitive language', he says, 'the meaning of any single word is to a very high degree dependent on its context' (Malinowski 1923:306). He then goes on to suggest that this also applies to 'a modern civilized language', but we are prevented from seeing it because of the priority accorded to writing. So he takes his observations about a particular 'primitive tongue' to warrant a conclusion about spoken language use in general:

> it should be clear at once that the conception of meaning as contained in an utterance is false and futile. A statement, spoken in real life, is never detached from the situation in which it has been uttered. For each verbal statement by a human being has the aim and function of expressing some thought or feeling actual at the moment and in that situation, and necessary for some reason or other to be made known to another person or persons – in order either to serve the purposes of common action, or to establish ties of purely social communion, or else to deliver the speaker of violent feelings or passions. Without some imperative stimulus of the moment, there can be no spoken statement. In each case, therefore, utterance and situation are bound up inextricably with each other and the context of situation is indispensable for the understanding of the words. Exactly as in the reality of spoken or written languages, a word without *linguistic context* is a mere figment and stands for nothing by itself, so in the reality of a spoken living tongue, the utterance has no meaning except in the *context of situation*. (Malinowski 1923:307)

The meaning of an utterance (as distinct, I would add, from a sentence) is contextually dependent. Words in use can only be understood in terms of what we do with them. Statements are actions. There is a remarkably close correspondence between what Malinowski has to say here and what Labov describes, nearly fifty years later, as the domain of discourse analysis:

> Commands and refusals are actions, declaratives, interrogatives, imperatives are linguistic categories – things that are said, rather than things that are done. The rules we need will show how things are done with words and how one interprets these utterances as actions: in other words, relating what is done to what is said and what is said to what is done. This area of linguistics can be called 'discourse analysis'; but it is not well known or developed. Linguistic theory is not yet rich enough to write such rules, for one must take into account such sociological non-linguistic categories as roles, rights and obligations. (Labov 1969:54–5)

Although Malinowski provides abundant ethnographic illustration of how 'utterance and situation are bound up inextricably with each other' in the language use of the Trobriand islanders, he proposes no specific rules to account for this binding. Furthermore, in his view, the relationship between the two is not, it appears, one of bilateral interdependency: it is the situation which is in unilateral control. 'The utterance', he tells us, 'has no meaning except in the context of situation'. This would seem to imply that meaning is not only context-dependent but context-*determined*, that pragmatic significance can be created on line out of nothing. There is no recognition here that there is an encoded semantic resource available for the users to draw on. Malinowski here overstates his case. But at the same time he actually contradicts the immediately preceding statement that he makes. For if a word can be meaningful in a linguistic context, then it cannot be simply a figment or stand for nothing unless it occurs in a context of situation.

If we are to understand how what is said relates to what is done, and vice versa, let alone propose rules, we need to recognize that code and context act upon each other bilaterally. As Hymes puts it: 'The use of a linguistic form identifies a range of meanings. A context can support a range of meanings. When a form is used in a context, it eliminates the meanings possible to that context other than those the form can signal: the context eliminates from consideration the meanings possible to the form other than those the context can support' (Hymes 1968:105). What was discussed in the preceding chapter was the tendency, in Halliday's S/F model, to overextend the semantic reach of grammar and so to undervalue the eliminating function of context. What we see in Malinowski is the reverse: an extension of the pragmatic reach of context so as to undervalue the eliminating function of linguistic forms.

I suggested earlier that Malinowski's work can be seen as an excursion into discourse analysis (in a way that Harris's work is not). But we can agree with Labov that it is not well developed. Malinowski's ethnographic observations, suggestive as they are, are not so systematized as to constitute a linguistic theory. It is not entirely clear indeed just how the key concepts context, situation and context of situation are to be distinguished. The terms are often used interchangeably. Nor is it clear how far what he says about the spoken language of 'primitive' orate communities has a more general application to written language use, or even to the spoken use of 'civilized' literate people.

Labov says that 'linguistic theory is not yet rich enough' to account for the relationships that he and Malinowski were concerned with. That was in

1969. But there was a linguist who had been busy in the development of such a theory almost twenty years earlier, namely J. R. Firth.

Firth takes up the notion of context of situation and turns it into a key concept in his linguistic theory by giving it a more abstract character, and, more significantly, by incorporating language within it. This is how he formulates it:

> My view was, and still is, that 'context of situation' is best used as a suitable schematic construct to apply to language events, and that it is a group of related categories at a different level from grammatical categories but rather of the same abstract nature. A context of situation for linguistic work brings into relation the following categories:
>
> A. The relevant features of participants: persons, personalities.
>   (i) The verbal action of the participants.
>   (ii) The non-verbal action of the participants.
> B. The relevant objects.
> C. The effect of the verbal action.
>
> Contexts of situation and types of language function can then be grouped and classified. (Firth 1957:182)

Just how this schematic construct works as a means of analysis is not made clear. There is no demonstration of how it operates on actually occurring language, and all that Firth provides by way of exemplification is a single invented utterance.[1] But even as a theoretical construct it is elusive, and Firth's own explanation is obscure, so much so as to prompt John Lyons to comment: 'there are those who would deny that Firth ever developed anything systematic enough to be described as a theory' (Lyons 1966:607). There are, however, two points about it that have a particular bearing on the present discussion in that they bring the problem of accounting for the code–context relationship into sharp relief.

The first concerns the issue raised in the last chapter about the difference between the way language in use is analysed and the way it is experienced. Firth's construct is very definitely a device for analysis. He talks about it as forming 'the basis for a hierarchy of techniques for the statement of meanings . . . a sort of hierarchy of techniques by means of which the meaning of linguistic events may be, as it were, dispersed into a spectrum of specialized statements' (Firth 1957:183). So each technique analyses the linguistic event at a different level – phonological, syntactic and so on. The obvious problem with this is that having dispersed the event in this way into its component parts there is no indication as to how they are to be reconstituted so as to reveal the nature of the event itself. We are told that the phonological analysis is 'linked to the processes and features of the utterance' and that the sentence analysed at the syntactic level 'must also have its relations with the processes of the context of situation' but there is no indication how one might proceed to identify these links and relations, nor indeed what these processes and features are. Firth, we should note, makes no distinction of the kind I proposed in chapter 1, between sentence and utterance,[2] and so he assumes that in accounting for the sentence by means of specialized statements about linguistic form one necessarily makes statements of meanings at the same time. As we have seen, in the earlier quotation he talks about applying his schematic construct to *language events*. Here he refers to *linguistic events*. Whether a distinction is intended here is impossible to say, but what is clear is that the language event, the mode of social action as conceived by Malinowski, is, in Firth's scheme of things, converted into convenient data for linguistic analysis.

'A context of situation', Firth tells us, 'brings into relation' the categories of his schematic construct. But he does not demonstrate, nor even discuss, how this relation comes about. In fact, all he does is talk about the linguistic analysis of one of these categories, namely what he calls 'the verbal action of the participants', and though he says it is related to the others, he then proceeds to deal with it in unrelated isolation. So, in taking over Malinowski's notion and making it into an abstract schematic structure, Firth actually misrepresents and reduces it. The separate categories he proposes, and his techniques for analytic dispersion, do not deal with the interplay of code and context factors in discourse at all. What Firth is proposing is, in effect, an approach to text analysis. We are still left with the question of how to account for discourse as a pragmatic process of bilateral modification, for the mutual elimination of meanings that Hymes talks about.

I said earlier that the notions of context and situation are not clearly distinguished in Malinowski. Nor are they in Firth. In his schematic construct he talks about 'the relevant features of participants' and 'the relevant objects' but without indicating how relevance might be determined. Clearly there will be many features of the situation in which a language event occurs which are not relevant at all, but are simply contingent circumstances with no bearing on the nature of that event. And it is not, of course, only features of the immediate spatio-temporal setting that we are talking about, but conceptual realities internalized in the minds of the participants as well. In view of this, it is not surprising that Firth just invokes relevance as a condition and leaves it at that. But unless this condition can be applied so that context can be identified as a subset of situational features (those which, in Hymes's terms, have an eliminating function) then, of course, it is indeed synonymous with situation, and it is hard to see how one might give any definition to such an inclusive and amorphous notion. This is how Mey puts it:

> Many linguists assert that that it is the 'context' that we must invoke to determine what an ambiguous sentence means. This sounds OK, perhaps, if by 'context' we understand a rather undefined mass of factors that play a role in the production and consumption of utterances. But 'context' is a notoriously hard concept to deal with (I shall have more to say on this later; see sections 3.3 and 9.1); often it is considered by linguists to be the sum and result of what has been said up to now, the 'prehistory' of a particular utterance, so to speak, including the prehistory of the people who utter sentences. (Mey 1993:8)

Here Mey seems reluctant to credit context with being a concept at all, and puts the term in scare quotes to signal a certain reservation about taking it seriously. We might then turn to section 3.3 of his book to see if the concept is dealt with more precisely there.

> context is a dynamic, not a static concept: it is to be understood as the surroundings, in the widest sense, that enable the participants in the communication process to interact, and that make the linguistic expressions of their interaction intelligible.
>
> The difference between a 'grammatical' and 'user-oriented' point of view is precisely in the context: on the former view, we consider linguistic elements in isolation, as syntactic structures or parts of a grammatical paradigm, such as case, tense, etc., whereas on the latter, we pose ourselves the all-important question, how are these linguistic elements used in a concrete setting, i.e. a context? (Mey 1993:38)

The scare quotes have disappeared, but the concept remains indeterminate. Context is 'the surroundings in the widest sense', an undefined mass indeed. It does then seem as if Mey, like Malinowski before him, thinks of context *in rebus*: a concrete situational setting, and so not, by definition, abstract at all. What *is* abstract is the grammar: the categories of tense and case and so on, the formal properties of sentences in isolation from context. And so we have an opposition between language, which is entirely abstract, and context, which is entirely concrete.

The question then arises as to whether context can be defined in more stringent abstract terms to mean something more significant than just the undifferentiated contingent circumstances of utterance. Mey talks about context as a concrete setting. It is of interest to note that Hymes, in quest of what he calls (significantly enough) 'some schema of the components of speech acts' also makes reference to setting. He describes it as follows: 'Setting refers to the time and place of a speech act and, in general, to the physical circumstances.' However, he acknowledges that these physical circumstances are only part of the story. There is also an abstract and internal location for communication as well as a concrete external one, and this he refers to as the scene: 'Scene, which is distinct from setting, designates the "psychological setting," or the cultural definition of an occasion as a certain type of scene. . . . In daily life the same persons in the same setting may redefine their interaction as a changed type of scene, say, from formal to informal, serious to festive, or the like' (Hymes 1974:55). In reference to this distinction, we can say that setting refers to the situation and scene to the context of utterance, the latter having to do with how the parties concerned abstract what is relevant from the material circumstances. Hymes is talking more particularly here about the *location* of utterance, but his psychological interpretation can be extended to all other factors as well, to the concept of context in general.

The definition of context as a psychological construct is to be found too in Sperber and Wilson's theory of relevance. They express their position as follows:

> The set of premises used in interpreting an utterance (apart from the premise that the utterance in question has been produced) constitutes what is generally known as the *context*. A context is a psychological construct, a subset of the hearer's assumptions about the world. It is these assumptions, of course, rather than the actual state of the world, that affect the interpretation of an utterance. A context in this sense is not limited to information about the immediate physical environment or the immediately preceding utterances: expectations about the future, scientific hypotheses or religious beliefs, anecdotal memories, general cultural assumptions, beliefs about the mental state of the speaker, may all play a role in interpretation. (Sperber and Wilson 1995:15–16)

So let us suppose then that context is abstract and in the mind rather than concrete and in the world. This clearly distinguishes it from situation understood as the material circumstances of utterance. But on the face of it, it still remains an undefined mass of factors: the fact that they are abstract entities in the mind rather than actual entities in the world does not make them any more manageable. On the contrary, it makes them more difficult to discern.

In reference to Firth's scheme, what the Sperber and Wilson proposal amounts to is an incorporation of 'the relevant objects' into 'the relevant features of participants': it is how such objects are cognitively abstracted that counts as context. But we are still left with the problem of how to recognize which features are relevant and which are not.

We should note, however, that Hymes defines 'scene' not only as a psychological construct, but as a *socio*-psychological one: it is something that is *identified* by the parties concerned as a culturally familiar type of occasion, that is to say, an abstraction from the situation of what is deemed to be schematically relevant. This suggests that one way of finding a way through the 'undefined mass of factors' that Mey refers to is to invoke the idea of the schema.

The schema can be defined as a cognitive construct, a configuration of knowledge, which we project on to events so as to bring them into alignment with familiar patterns of experience and belief (see Freedle 1977, de Beaugrande 1980, Widdowson 1983).[3] While it may be true that ultimately what is inside the individual's head is an idiosyncratic medley of contextual assumptions of all kinds born of personal experience which cannot be pinned down, it is also the case that there are a wide range of assumptions that are culturally shared as schematic knowledge, which define an individual as the member of a community. It was indeed reference to such schemata ('the native customs and psychology' as he put it) that enabled Malinowski to make sense of the behaviour, verbal and otherwise, of the Trobriand islanders.

Since these schemata are social constructs, it is not surprising to find that they correspond to the two basic components of an S/F grammar. They are the contextual counterparts of the encoded social semiotic. Thus, some of these schemata are of an ideational kind in that they have to do with the way third-person reality is constituted by custom or shared experience. These are frames of reference which provide us with bearings on propositional meaning. Thus, by relating what the fishermen said to what he knew to be their customary practices, Malinowski was able to infer what they were talking *about* beyond what was made verbally explicit. Their words keyed into their culturally specific schematic world. Similarly, though engaged in a very different kind of communication, I make assumptions, as I write this book, that readers will understand what I say by relating it to a frame of reference, part of which is in place beforehand, part of which I have been at some pains to construct. Reference is only achieved when words are referred to such a frame.

Other schemata are of an interpersonal kind and have to do with how people in a particular community interact with each other, the conventions of customary communication. Among such conventions are the speech act conditions which define different illocutionary acts. The *locus classicus* usually cited for the specification of such conditions is Searle 1969 (itself a development from Austin 1962), but it should be noted that, quite independently, Labov, in his own quest for discourse rules which relate what is said to what is done, has proposed contextual conditions of a comparable kind, based on the analysis of actually occurring data (Labov 1972:252–8). What is of primary interest for Labov, however, is not the abstract specification of ideal illocutionary conditions, but how discourse is enacted through their actual realization. His enquiry is thus related to other interpersonal schematic conventions of turn taking and interaction management that conversation analysis has been concerned with.[4]

If we define contextual features in this schematic way, then they would seem to constitute the kind of abstract categories at a social level of analysis that Firth was speculating about. They are also consistent with Mey's point that 'context is a dynamic, not a static concept'. For these schematic assumptions are simply guidelines which allow room for manoeuvre, and of course they are modified in the communicative process. In this respect they are no different from the categories of language itself, which are also subject to change. They are enabling constructs. One can think of them as contextual parameters which are given particular settings in actual use, or, to use a more traditional formulation, variables which take on different values as occasion requires.

The question we must now address is how the different settings or values are achieved. Firth talks about his own schematic construct as a basis of techniques for the statement of meanings, but, as we have seen, gives no clear idea about how they might actually operate. This is not to be wondered at since he provides no guidance as to how the crucial condition of relevance might be established. Sperber and Wilson (1995), though making no mention of Firth, in effect sets out to repair the omission. In their relevance theory, the authors refer to contextual assumptions as a 'set of premises used for interpreting an utterance'. How then are these abstract assumptions used to actualize meaning? What techniques or procedures are put into operation to realize features of knowledge as relevant to particular instances of communicative behaviour?

As I have said, Sperber and Wilson do not mention Firth. But there is hardly any discussion either of the schematic constructs of social knowledge which I have been referring to as necessary conditions on contextual meaning. Only cursory mention is made of schema theory; speech acts are treated to what Sperber and Wilson acknowledge is a 'very sketchy discussion' at the end of their book. What they are interested in is the process of logical inference whereby meaning is actualized, the procedural work that has to be done to work out communicative intentions on the basis of contextual assumptions. What they are *not* interested in is what these procedures work on, where the contextual assumptions come from.

How do these inferential procedures work, then? Let us consider an example.

> Imagine the following scenario. I am a keen club tennis player, and you know that I have recently begun playing with a new doubles partner. When we meet, you ask me what my new doubles partner is like, and I reply:
>
> **He has much in common with John McEnroe**
>
> At least for readers of the English tabloid press, the intended interpretation of this utterance will be immediately obvious. You are intended to use the contextual assumption that John McEnroe is extremely bad-tempered on court, and draw the conclusion that my new doubles partner is also bad-tempered on court. The question is why is this so? (Wilson 1994:42)

The answer, it seems, is provided by relevance theory (henceforth RT). This holds, essentially, that we home in on an interpretation which is relevant to the occasion when we conjoin what is actually said in the text with existing assumptions in the context and draw a meaning from the conjunction, a contextual effect, which could not be inferred from either text or context on their own. Notice that this is indeed a matter of conjunction and not simply addition. You do not just put two and two together: the information from text does not co-exist with but interacts with that of context. So in the case of this utterance about John McEnroe, the second-person recipient relates the proposition expressed to what he or she knows about this particular tennis player, and thereby infers the required, and relevant, contextual effect.

This seems reasonable enough. Indeed, it can be seen as an alternative formulation of the basic (and obvious) point made in the preceding chapter that meaning is a function of the interaction of code and context so that the significance of what people say transcends the signification of the words they use to say it. I will return to this presently. But meanwhile there is another obvious point to be made. It is quite simply that the scenario provided constitutes just the schematic knowledge that must be presupposed for the whole inferential process to get off the ground. Shared knowledge is established (*I am a keen tennis player . . . you know I have a new partner*, etc.), a particular discourse community is specified (*readers of the*

English tabloid press). In these respects, the utterance is already provided with a likely frame of reference, and it is only within this that relevance can be inferred.

Of course, it may turn out that the supposition of shared contextual assumption on the part of the first person is unwarranted. In the present case, for example, the second person may home in on McEnroe's tennis skill rather than his temperament, and one might imagine the following exchange:

A. How is your new tennis partner?
B. He has much in common with John McEnroe.
A. Good server?
B. Bad temper.

It is clear, even from this small invented example, that procedures for homing in on intended contextual assumptions, and so establishing relevance, are not confined to covert inference based on pre-existing knowledge, as Sperber and Wilson sometimes seem to suggest. They are also externalized as interaction whereby the relevant contextual assumptions are overtly negotiated, not just identified but created in the interactive process itself. This relates to what I said earlier about the malleability of schematic knowledge in agreement with Mey's point that context is not a static but a dynamic concept. These schemata, or shared contextual assumptions, are of their nature unstable, subject to continual modification. They cannot just be taken as given, the secure premises for covert inference. They are also negotiable in the process of overt interaction. You do not always infer relevance in the privacy of your own head; you may interact your way towards it in public.

In a way, RT seems altogether too cerebral to account for how meanings are contextually achieved. The subtitle of the Sperber and Wilson book is *Communication and Cognition*. The conjunction would seem almost to indicate equivalence. But communication cannot be *only* cognitive, and I think that the neglect of other factors, and particularly those of interaction, leads to curious conclusions. Let me explain, and exemplify.

Sperber and Wilson acknowledge the work of Grice and say that their theory builds on the basis he provided with his co-operative principle. What they do is to reduce his multiple maxims to one. But in so doing they also radically reduce the scope of the original proposal. For, philosopher though he may be, Grice is concerned not with thought but with action, not with cognition but co-operation. His maxims are essentially ground rules for the interactive management of intentions, and they are couched accordingly in the idiom of injunction: *make your contribution as informative as is required, do not say what you believe to be false, avoid obscurity, be brief,* and so on (Grice 1975). These are all injunctions directed at the first person about what to do in order to effectively interact, not how to think as a second person in order to effectively interpret.[5]

RT, on the other hand, is concerned with how to think in order to reach a relevant interpretation, and is essentially a model of cognition rather than co-operation. In reference to Malinowski, it conceives of language not so much as a 'mode of action' as a mode of thought. Interpretation is said to be conditional not only on the contextual effects which we discussed earlier, but also on processing effort. Processing effort may be contextually required, if a plausible context for an utterance proves elusive; or textually required, if the utterance is encoded in complex language. The effect factor and the effort factor act upon each other and are represented as in complementary opposition; so that relevance is accounted for by the following formula: 'The greater the contextual effects, the greater the relevance; but the greater the processing effort needed to obtain these effects, the *lower* the relevance' (Wilson 1994:46).

Let us see how this works. Wilson herself takes us through an example in the following text:

> Greater complexity implies greater processing effort; gratuitous complexity detracts from relevance. Thus, compare (9a) with (9b):
>
> (9) a. It's raining in Paris.
>   b. It's raining in Paris and fish swim in the sea.
>
> In circumstances where the hearer needs no reminding that fish swim in the sea, the extralinguistic complexity of (9b) will not be offset by any extra contextual effects, and will detract from the overall relevance of (9a) as compared with (9b). (Wilson 1994:46)

Leaving aside (for the moment at least) the question whether (9b) can be said to be more linguistically complex, rather than simply containing more information, let us concede that it takes more effort to process it. But why should that detract from its relevance? If the hearer has no need of information about fish, then why does the speaker mention fish in the first place? The co-operative principle does not allow for the neutral utterance of gratuitous information. There can, of course, be an inadvertent miscalculation in the regulation of information required, when you say more than your hearer needs, but that is not gratuitous. And if someone were to utter (9b) (a fairly remote contingency, one has to say) it is unlikely to be inadvertent in this sense. It is more likely to be deliberately designed for effect. If the circumstances of this utterance are such that the hearer needs no reminding that fish swim in the sea, this is indeed gratuitous as information, but, for this very reason, it is significant by implication. The quantity maxim is thereby violated and in consequence an implicature is created. So there are contextual effects, arising from the very redundancy which, as defined by Sperber and Wilson, needs to be disregarded for relevance to be achieved. If one accepts the co-operative principle (as relevance theory does), then deliberate redundancy of this kind creates implicatures, and so cannot be edited out by invoking the notion of processing effort.

The difficulty seems to be that Wilson is taking this utterance out of the context of interaction and is in effect treating it in isolation as a sentence. Its processing, therefore, is a matter of decoding its semantic content in detachment. This, ironically enough, calls to mind the experiments which were inspired by the derivational theory of complexity which was based on the same idea – that there is a direct correspondence between processing effort and linguistic encoding.[6]

The fact is that the least-effort principle is not just applied to information processing in the abstract, but is implicated in interaction and is part of the co-operative principle. That is why it is pragmatically significant. If it is violated, and the violation taken as deliberate rather than accidental, it *necessarily* creates implicatures. It is simply not the case that 'the greater the processing effort needed to obtain contextual effects, the lower the relevance.' As we have seen, the very reverse may be case. It all depends on what kind of contextual effects one has in mind. In the case of (9b), for example, the utterance could easily be taken as an expression of the effect that Wilson calls attitude:

It's raining in Paris and fish swim in the sea.

That is to say:

It's raining in Paris, as usual.
It's raining in Paris, and how about that as a banal statement of the obvious.

One limitation of RT, then, as an account of the conditions of contextual meaning, is that it dissociates inference itself from interaction, and therefore from the on-line context which is interactionally constructed in the actual activity of interpretation. The contextual effects they discuss are inferred as a function of the language itself, and no systematic account is taken of how extralinguistic factors might impinge upon them. I will take up this matter in more detail a little later. Meanwhile, there is a second reservation to be made, and this has to do with how code and context factors figure in the process of inference itself. Consider these remarks:

> Inferential and decoding processes are quite different. An *inferential process* starts from a set of premises and results in a set of conclusions which follow logically from, or are at least warranted by, the premises. A *decoding process* starts from a signal and results in the recovery of a message which is associated to the signal by an underlying code. (Sperber and Wilson 1995:12–13)

According to Sperber and Wilson it is the inferential process, rather than the decoding process which yields the pragmatic meaning of utterances. Now one can readily agree that, as was argued at some length in the preceding chapter, what people mean by their utterances pragmatically cannot be equated with what the corresponding sentences mean semantically as exemplars of the language code. If this were not the case, we would not be bothering our heads about the conditions of contextual meaning at all. But this is not to say that semantic meaning is not implicated in the process. Indeed Wilson concedes as much:

> The intended interpretation of an utterance is not decoded but inferred, by a non-demonstrative inference process – a process of hypothesis formation and evaluation – in which linguistic decoding and contextual assumptions determine the class of *possible* hypotheses, and these are evaluated in the light of certain general principles of communication which speakers are expected to obey. (Wilson 1994:43–4)

There seems to be some ambivalence here about where decoding comes in. We are told in no uncertain terms that it is quite distinct from inference. At the same time, it figures in the inferring process. It is apart from inference, but a part of it at the same time. How is this to be explained?

This question takes us back to Halliday's model of interpretation discussed in the preceding chapter. Interpretation here, it will be remembered, was represented as a two-level process: the first involving the understanding of a text by linguistic analysis and the second its evaluation in relation to contextual factors. It was suggested that the difficulty with this two-level process is that it implies that a text can be understood in dissociation from context as a linguistic object and indeed *has* to be understood first as such before it can be evaluated as discourse. In other words (in Wilson's words, in fact) interpretation is first decoded and then inferred. For Wilson, interpretation is inferred and not decoded, which would rule out Halliday's first level as a separate process altogether. But decoding nevertheless does have a role to play, but only in relation to contextual assumptions. Here, as in Halliday, it is this relationship that is evaluated in interpretation. The difference between them is that with Halliday decoding is given a prominent, even prior, role in interpretation, whereas with Wilson it makes a much less significant contribution to the interpretation process. But just what this contribution amounts to is difficult to tell.

Part of the difficulty at least has to do with what is intended by the term 'decoding'. If we take it in its usual sense to mean the recovery of semantic meaning as linguistically manifested (to use the term proposed in chapter 2), then we stay confined within the text as linguistic object and closed off from the context. In consequence, no pragmatic meaning can be inferred. Decoding in this sense is explicitly ruled out in RT: 'the inferential and decoding processes', we are told, 'are quite different.' So in what sense *is* decoding involved in pragmatic inference?

The answer would appear to be that decoding in RT is a matter of recovering the underlying propositional content of utterances rather than of assigning meaning to the surface forms of the actual wording. This can be illustrated by reference to the examples we considered earlier. First the one about the new tennis partner:

He has much in common with John McEnroe.

Given the appropriate frame of reference (a crucial proviso, as we have seen), this utterance can be interpreted as implying that the new tennis partner is bad-tempered or has tantrums on court. The crucial condition concerns what the language refers to, the propositional content of the utterance. But what about the manner in which it is expressed? No allowance seems to be made for the possible relevance of this. Indeed, the least-effort principle would seem to preclude it, particularly if we take it as applying pragmatically, for efficient processing commonly involves what I have referred to elsewhere (Widdowson 1990) as taking an indexical beeline, and disregarding the details of linguistic form. But it will not do in the present case to derive contextual effects only from the proposition expressed without regard to the manner of the expression. For there is surely something in the turn of phrase itself which signals an attitude on the part of the speaker: a certain formality, suggestive of irony, which would alert the hearer to the intended implication. The same effects are not as likely to be activated by the proposition expressed in different terms:

He is a bit like John McEnroe.
He is similar to John McEnroe.

Furthermore, if the proposition is negated it seems more likely that, even though the person referred to remains the same, it is indeed tennis ability rather than temperament which is called to mind:

He does not have much in common with John McEnroe.

What all this suggests to me is that the language not only serves up propositions as premises for the inferencing process to work on but can itself, as a form of words, project its own contextual implications, which are then checked out (or evaluated) against extralinguistic contextual factors. Realizing the ironic effect of the utterance 'He has much in common with John McEnroe' is not only a matter of analysing its propositional content, but also, and perhaps more crucially, of taking note of its actual wording. In both cases, this textual processing has to be referred to (and in consequence perhaps even overridden by) the contextual factors concerning the participants' knowledge about John McEnroe.

A similar point can be made in reference to the other example. In the unlikely event of anybody actually producing the utterance

It's raining in Paris and fish swim in the sea.

then this would require the recipient to rummage around among contextual assumptions to find out what possible relevance the second proposition has to the first. But consider:

It's raining in Paris and I'm a Dutchman.

No rummaging is called for here. All you need to know is what the second expression means as a formulaic phrase in the language.

Although RT takes a rather different line on linguistic decoding from S/F grammar, it too represents pragmatic interpretation as a matter of relating decoding with extralinguistic contextual assumptions. The focus of attention, however, is on the decoding. The assumptions seem generally to be taken as given, and there is little indication of how they might act upon the decoding process. As with Malinowski and Firth, the importance of context is acknowledged, but exactly what it is, and how it is implicated in the achievement of pragmatic meaning, remain unclear. As was pointed out earlier, Firth talks about 'techniques for the statement of meaning' but gives no demonstration of how they might operate. With Sperber and Wilson there is abundant demonstration of the working of the techniques they propose for their statements of meaning. But these statements do not really account for the contextual factors that Firth, and Malinowski before him, were centrally concerned with. RT deals with the contextual effects that are brought about by inference, but not with the effects of context on the inferential process itself.

The basic assumption of RT is that people interpret language in use by the application of the inferential processes of propositional logic. It rejects linguistic analysis, but only to replace it by logical analysis. Like S/F grammar it is fixated on what the language means, on the text itself (which in the RT case take the form of invented isolated utterances) rather than on the processes whereby discourse is derived from it. In the quotation cited earlier, Wilson talks of the inferential process as yielding a 'class of possible hypotheses', rather as decoding might, in Halliday's terms, yield the meaning potential of the language used. But the crucial question is how possible or potential meanings are actually realized. They 'are evaluated', we are told, 'in the light of certain general principles of communication which speakers are expected to obey.' But it is the nature of this evaluation that is central to any pragmatic enquiry into how discourse is realized. So what are these general principles, and what does it mean to say that this evaluation is made 'in the light of' them?

One set of such general principles has, of course, been proposed by Grice, as was mentioned earlier in this chapter. Here we have maxims for conversational engagement which participants are expected to obey, and they are indeed very general. What is more to the point, however, for our present discussion is that they are contextually constrained. The co-operative principle is formulated, as we noted earlier, as an injunction. It runs as follows: 'Make your conversational contribution such as is required, at the stage at which it occurs, by the accepted purpose or direction of the talk exchange in which you are engaged' (Grice 1975:46).

As was indicated earlier, for Grice, the pragmatic process of making out what is meant by what is said is one of bilateral interaction rather than unilateral inference, with the focus on co-operation rather than cognition. Participants make contributions, but they do so *as required by the accepted purpose or direction of the talk*. So what they say is designed to fit into some agreed pattern of interaction which is accepted as appropriate for the occasion; they recognize what kind of exchange they are engaged in and act accordingly. Co-operation then involves conformity to certain conventions defining kinds of communication, that is to say to what was referred to earlier as interpersonal schemata. The maxims can only be recognized as being disregarded or flouted in relation to the accepted schematic conventions, and this would be true not only of conversation but of all kinds of discourse, spoken and written. There is no way in which maxims can be violated in schematic isolation. If you say that an instance of speech or writing is obscure, or over-elaborate, or irrelevant as such, without regard to what is required by its accepted purpose, then you are making a statement about text in dissociation from the discourse it is designed to realize. So the manner maxim, for example, which enjoins the language user to be perspicuous is not violated by the use of prolix and obscure expressions in a legal document if such expressions are conventionally accepted as appropriate to their purpose. Implicatures would arise if the expressions were *not* appropriately prolix and obscure. Similarly, in an obituary, or other kinds of ritual encomium, the quality or quantity maxims are not violated by being economical with the truth.

The same argument applies to ideational schemata. The activation of the Gricean maxims is similarly regulated by assumptions about how the world is ordered and conceived by cultural convention. Reference is effective by default: information which is schematically recoverable is left unverbalized. You do not avoid the truth by not mentioning it if you have reason to believe it is known already. The maxims do indeed work on the least-effort principle that RT talks about, but only in alliance with schematic requirement. Least effort does not mean little effort. It may mean a good deal. It all depends on how much verbal effort is needed to be indexically effective in making a schematic connection.

To summarize: if we are to account for discourse, as I defined it in chapter 1 of this book, we need to be clear about the nature of context, for it is only when the linguistic features of the text are related to contextual factors that discourse is realized. In this present chapter, I have been examining various ways in which context has been represented, starting with Malinowski. The difficulty with his notion of the context of situation, I suggested, is that it is indeterminate, and that it remains so even when Firth takes it up as the basis for his contextual theory of meaning, essentially because the theory depends on the concept of relevance, which is left undefined, and there is little in the way of explanation or illustration of how the theory would be empirically applied in description. Where we do find the concept explained, with impressive precision, is in Relevance Theory. Here, however, it gets detached from the socio-cultural context of situation as Malinowski and Firth conceived of it and becomes the function of an inferential process whereby contextual effects are derived from given contextual assumptions without any account of where such assumptions come from, or how far contextual factors in general might influence, or even override, the inferential process itself. The problem here, I suggested, is that communication is represented as too exclusively a cognitive process, dissociated from the socio-cultural conditions in which it normally takes place. A consideration of such conditions then led me to propose that one way of being specific about context (and distinguishing it from situation) is to define it as a schematic construct. In so doing, we return to Malinowski's original socio-cultural notion of context of situation but give it a more precise formulation. And we also return to Firth and *his* schematic construct, but taken now not as a device for linguistic analysis, for the grouping and classifying of 'types of language function' after the event, but as a discourse process engaged in by the participants themselves in the online achievement of pragmatic meaning.

Contexts as schematic constructs are not fixed. They are socio-cultural conventions from which the online pragmatic processing of language takes its bearings, but they do not determine what course it takes. For the processing of the language of a text involves contextual projection too, which modifies these constructs. Context and text, as I have said, interact with each other. To the extent that RT represents meaning not as a semantic aggregate but as a relational function, it is consistent with the view of interpretation proposed in the last chapter. I have expressed reservations about it, however, because it seems to me that it focuses attention too exclusively on contextual effects that are generated intra-linguistically by inference and does not take adequate account of extralinguistic contextual factors. But this is not to deny that contextual effects *are* generated from linguistic processing. It could hardly be otherwise if we accept the idea of language as meaning potential, as the semantic encoding of previous conventions of pragmatic use. What RT demonstrates is how different parts of a text are interpreted as acting upon each other so as to give rise to contextual projection. One question that arises from this, as I have said, is how such projection relates to extralinguistic contextual factors of a pre-existing schematic kind. A second question concerns the nature of the intra-textual relationships that are activated between different parts of a text. We consider this question more closely in the next chapter. It will take us back to the distinction made in chapter 1 between text and discourse, and to matters concerning the grammatical analysis of text discussed in chapter 2.

Notes

1 Firth presents his example as follows:

> If I give you one brief sentence with the information that it represents a typical Cockney event, you may even be able to provide a typical context of situation in which it would be the verbal action of one of the participants. The sentence is:
>
> **'Ahng gunna gi' wun fer Ber'.'**
> **(I'm going to get one for Bert)**
>
> What is the minimum number of participants? Three? Four? Where might it happen? In a pub? Where is Bert? Outside? Or playing darts? What are the relevant objects? What is the effect of the sentence? 'Obvious!' you say. So is the convenience of the schematic construct called 'context of situation'. It makes sure of the sociological component. (Firth 1957:182)

Although it may be obvious that the schematic construct will prompt such questions, it it not at all obvious how it can be applied to resolve them. How far does the effect of Bert's verbal action depend on how many other people are present, or where he is, or his non-verbal action of playing darts, or innumerable other features of the context of situation that one might think of? Some might be relevant, others not. If the schematic construct is to be convenient for analysis, and 'make sure of the sociological component', it will need to give some guidance as to how such relevance is to be determined, and in what respects, therefore, this event can be taken as typical.

2 Firth makes no distinction, either, between semantics and pragmatics. Like Halliday, he uses the former term to cover all aspects of meaning.

3 The origin of the term is usually credited to Bartlett. He used it to account for the results of an elicitation experiment whereby he asked readers to recall and record a North American story, 'The War of the Ghosts'. His subjects, he found, organized the new information in memory by reformulating the unfamiliar detail of the story to fit their own cultural structures of reality, or schemata (Bartlett 1932). I have occasion to refer to Bartlett's experiment again in chapter 10.

4 Both Searle and Labov specify conditions on the act of request or command, and it is interesting to compare their formulations. This is Searle:

Propositional content:	Future act A of H
Preparatory:	1. H is able to do A. S believes H is able to do A.
	2. It is not obvious to both S and H that H will do A in the normal course of events of his own accord.
Sincerity:	S wants H to do A
Essential:	Counts as an attempt to get H to do A

Comment: Order and command have the additional preparatory rule that S must be in a position of authority over H. (Searle 1969:66)

Labov's formulation, as he points out, is focused on rights and obligations 'which are plainly social constructs':

If A requests B to perform an action X at a time T, A's utterance will be heard as a valid command only if the following pre-conditions hold : B believes that A believes (= it is an AB event) that

1. X should be done for a purpose Y
2. B has the ability to do X
3. B has the obligation to do X
4. A has the right to tell B to do

(Labov 1972:255)

Speech act theory (SA) deals with conventions of use at a level of philosophical abstraction and focuses on the conditions that have to met for utterances to count as particular acts of communication. Conversation analysis (CA), sociological rather than philosophical in orientation, is different in two respects: it focuses attention on the conventions that affect how interactions are managed and it deals with actually occurring conversational data. The two approaches are generally seen as quite distinct, and discussed separately in the literature (see, for example, Levinson 1983, Schiffrin 1994). There would seem to be a good case, however, for considering how they might be related, how, for example, the abstract illocutionary conditions proposed by SA get discoursally realized through interactive negotiation.

5 Since the maxims are taken to be co-operative conventions, however, they constitute shared knowledge. The first person depends on the second person knowing what the maxims are, and assumes they will be taken into account in interpretation. Adherence to them would not otherwise be recognized, of course, and no implicatures would arise by flouting them.

6 The derivational theory of complexity (DTC) hypothesized a correspondence between the syntactic complexity of sentences, as measured by their transformational history, and their intelligibility, as measured by the time taken by subjects

to assign them meaning. It turned out that there was no necessary correspondence, even when subjects were presented, unprompted, with sentences in isolation. This in itself does not invalidate DTC, for it is possible that other measures of complexity, based on different models of linguistic description, might indeed match up with processing difficulty.

There is, however, one point to be made of particular relevance to the arguments I am putting forward in this book. DTC is concerned with the decoding of sentences, and how subjects go about this experimental task tells us nothing about how people go about interpreting utterances experienced as language use in context. The problem with DTC, then, is that it confuses sentence decoding, which is a semantic matter, and utterance interpretation, which is a pragmatic matter. As I have suggested in the preceding chapter, this is also the problem with Halliday's model of text interpretation. And it is a problem that will recur as a continuing theme in the chapters that follow. For a discussion of DTC, see Aitchison 1998, Garnham 1985.

4

Context and co-text

At one point in a paper commending corpus descriptions to language teachers, Sinclair proposes a number of pedagogic precepts. I have expressed my reservations about these elsewhere (Widdowson 2003) and it is not my purpose to discuss them here. However, one precept is relevant to the present discussion, namely:

Inspect contexts.

Sinclair then goes on to correct himself with a disclaimer: 'Strictly speaking, I should write "inspect co-texts", because "context" often has a wider meaning than the surrounding text . . . I would advocate a much closer inspection of the verbal environment of a word or phrase than is usual in language teaching. A great deal is to be learned from this exercise' (Sinclair 1997:34). We have already seen in the preceding chapter that the term 'context' has indeed been used to refer to much more than the verbal environment. The inspection of co-texts involves a consideration of the textual product as such without regard to the discourse that gave rise to it. The exercise of co-textual inspection that Sinclair refers to is now conducted by means of computer analysis and a great deal has indeed been learned from it. But what has been learned concerns the internal patterns of text, not the way they are activated as discourse, for the kinds of extralinguistic contextual factors we have been considering in the last chapter are left out of account. This is readily acknowledged by the authors of the *Longman Grammar of Spoken and Written English*, the result of a massive exercise in the kind of co-textual inspection that Sinclair refers to:[1] 'Under natural circumstances, texts occur and are understood in their discourse settings, which comprise all of the linguistic, situational, social, psychological, and pragmatic factors that influence the interpretation of any instance of language use' (Biber et al. 1999:4). Since co-textual and contextual relations are very different, the one concerned with text and the other with discourse, we need to be clear which we are setting out to inspect, so strict speaking would seem to be in order. Let us then look more closely at what it is that can be learned from co-textual inspection.

We can begin by considering the following statement about the nature of co-text:

> In our discussion so far we have concentrated particularly on the physical context in which single utterances are embedded and we have paid little attention to the *previous discourse* co-ordinate. Lewis introduced this co-ordinate to take account of sentences which include specific reference to what has been mentioned before as in phrases like *the aforementioned*. It is, however, the case that any sentence other than the first in a fragment of discourse, will have the whole of its interpretation forcibly constrained by the preceding text, not just those phrases which obviously and specifically refer to the preceding text, like *the aforementioned*. Just as . . . the token [p] in [greɪpbrɪtn] (is) determined by the context in which (it) appears, so the words which occur in discourse are constrained by what, following Halliday, we shall call their *co-text*. (Brown and Yule 1983:46)

There are a number of points here that touch on matters that have already been discussed. We might note, for example, that in the light of our discussion in the preceding chapter, Brown and Yule's notion of context as 'physical' is somewhat limited.We might note too that the terms 'discourse' and 'text' are used synonymously here, as are the terms 'utterance' and 'sentence'. What is of particular significance for our present concerns, however, is that as a result there is an apparent confusion here between two quite different ways of conceiving of co-textual constraint. On the one hand we are told that what is co-textually constrained is the *interpretation* of linguistic features, as in the case of reference to previous mention, but we are also told that it is the *occurrence* of linguistic features that is co-textually constrained, as in the case of phonetic modification ([p] in [greɪpbrɪtn]). This is not a pedantic quibble. The two phenomena are (strictly speaking) crucially different.

With co-textual constraints on occurrence we are back with Zellig Harris and his quest for linguistic patterns, which, as he pointed out, are quite separate from interpretation (see chapter 1). True, Harris's patterns were somewhat restricted and rudimentary when compared with what concordances can now reveal in such detail. Nevertheless, his point about interpretation still applies. What corpus analysis can do is to process vast amounts of observed language behaviour and abstract from it patterns of lexical and lexicogrammatical co-occurrence, collocational and colligational regularities, not immediately accessible to introspection or elicitation. But by the same token, these regularities are not a matter of deliberate intention either. What we learn from this is that actual language behaviour is much more formulaic than its users might suppose, and that to a considerable degree they conform unwittingly to idiomatic custom. Furthermore, we can infer from a concordance display more general dependencies that hold between cooccurring linguistic features. Thus, for example, on the evidence of their customary collocates, particular words can be shown to have a typical positive or negative prosody, and it can be plausibly suggested that facts of co-textual co-occurrence should be recognized as part of the semantic signification of such words.[2] But this, of course, does not tell us about what pragmatic significance might be assigned to such a co-occurrence in a particular text. The point about these co-textual findings is that they are a function of analysis, with texts necessarily reduced to concordance lines. One might trace a particular line back to its text of origin, but then if it is to be interpreted, it has to be related not to other lines in the display but to the other features of the original text.

We come to co-textual constraints on interpretation. Here we need the distinction between sentence and utterance that Brown and Yule disregard. As Sperber and Wilson put it:

> The semantic representation of a sentence deals with a sort of common core of meaning shared by every utterance of it. However, different utterances of the same sentence may differ in their interpretation; and indeed they usually do. The study of the semantic representation of sentences belongs to grammar; the study of the interpretation of utterances belongs to what is now known as 'pragmatics'. (Sperber and Wilson 1995:9–10)

We may accept that it is reasonable for typical co-textual occurrence as revealed by corpus analysis to be incorporated into the semantic representation of sentences, but what of the particular co-textual effects of the corresponding utterances? Is it the case, as Brown and Yule claim, that the interpretation of an utterance 'will have the whole of its interpretation forcibly constrained by the preceding text'? Let us consider an example they themselves provide from Darwin's *Journal during the Voyage of HMS Beagle around the World*:

> When we came within hail, one of the four natives who were present advanced to receive us and began to shout most vehemently, wishing to direct us where to land. When we were on shore the *party* looked rather alarmed. (Brown and Yule 1983:47)

The point that Brown and Yule make in their comments on this text is, as they say, the obvious one, that the different semantic possibilities encoded in this italicized lexical form, as specified by a dictionary, are narrowed down by co-textual association. Thus we can in this particular case eliminate the meaning of *party* as a group bound together by political conviction, as in the *communist party*, or a group assembled to socialize as in *cocktail party*. There seems to be nothing contentious about that. But we should note that the co-text only partially constrains interpretation, for the phrase *the party* is ambiguous here. The lexical item semantically encodes 'a group of people who are involved in an activity together' (as the *Cambridge International Dictionary of English* defines it), and the definite article signals that the identity of such a group has been previously established. But two groups have been mentioned previously in the text: 'we' and 'four natives'. The expression *the party* could therefore refer to either of them: either to Darwin and his group coming on shore, or the group of four natives on shore already. Or even both groups, if it comes to that. Which party looked alarmed? No matter how closely we inspect the co-text, it gives us no definitive answer. We can, of course, make a guess, and so arrive at the more plausible interpretation, but to do that is to go *beyond* the text, to impressions and assumptions that arise in relation to what is schematically familiar.

And when we consider the matter it is obvious that this is very generally the case. As was noted in chapter 2, there are innumerable instances of textual imprecision and ambiguity in actual language use which simply pass unnoticed because we of course quite naturally complement what we read with what we know. It is true of all texts that, to adopt a phrase of Shakespeare's, we 'piece out their imperfections with our thoughts'. Of course we can make an anaphoric connection across textual points by noting that a particular lexical item copies certain semantic features from previously occurring items, thereby establishing a pattern of co-occurrence, and narrowing down the referential possibilities. But the identification of this textual pattern does not, of itself, yield an interpretation, as we have seen. What interpretation involves is the relating of the language in the text to the schematic constructs of knowledge, belief and so on outside the text. In this way, discourse is achieved. Co-textual connections are semantic in character, and are only relevant to the pragmatic process to the extent that they can be contextually realized.

Brown and Yule equate co-textual lexical relations with those which obtain between phonological elements such that a particular phonetic environment constrains the occurrence of a particular sound: for example [p] in [greɪpbrɪtn]. But these are constraints not on interpretation but on the co-occurrence of encoded forms. They exemplify what Labov refers to as a variable rule, which expresses the conditions that affect the probability of co-occurrence of particular linguistic features. Thus Labov shows how the deletion of stop consonants across a wide range of usage is variably affected by both the phonological and morphological environments in which they occur. As he puts it: 'a stop is variably deleted after a consonantal segment at the end of a word, often if it is not a separate inflectional morpheme, and more often if it is not followed by a vowel.' This rule, he adds, 'will now apply generally to a wide variety of dialects. Wherever variability exists, these constraints are binding on all speakers of English' (Labov 1972:220). Just *how* the rule applies will itself vary and particular dialects may be characterized by the different ordering and weighting of these two variables, and such different settings of probability can therefore serve as what Labov calls *indicators*. These 'show a regular distribution over socioeconomic, ethnic or age groups, but are used by each individual in more or less the same way in any context' (Labov 1972:237). So co-textual indicators of this kind serve to identify varieties of encoded usage that typify particular communities.

Labov also talks about variables of another sort, sociolinguistic *markers* which 'not only show social distribution, but also stylistic variation'. These have to do not just with features which indicate a user's dialect but with how these are adapted in certain conditions of its use. Here, then, we are concerned not just with internal co-textual constraints but with shifts in style induced by external contextual factors. Labov in fact deals with only one factor, the amount of attention paid to speech, but it is easy to see how this can be refined to focus on others like topic, setting, kinds of participant relationship and so on. Sociolinguistic markers relate to the external context, but it is still the occurrence of linguistic features that Labov is concerned with rather than their interpretation. In his discussion of indicators and markers his central interest lies in the correlation of code elements with contextual factors and not with the way the two are pragmatically engaged in the communicative process. So the variable rules Labov identifies are of a different character from the rules he talks about elsewhere (and which were referred to in the preceding chapter) that 'show how things are done with words and how one interprets these utterances as actions'. They are not therefore the kind of rules that Labov says discourse analysis needs to be concerned with: they do not deal with the pragmatic issues of how first-person intentions get textualized and how interpretations are derived from the resulting text.

With reference to the distinction made in the first chapter of this book, Labov's work on variable rules can indeed be characterized as text rather than discourse analysis. What he is looking at is the way the factors of speaker and setting are reflected in certain linguistic properties of the text. How such textual features realize discourse effects is a different matter. Such effects might, as Harris suggested, 'follow closely in the directions which the formal findings indicate', but this needs to be demonstrated. At the moment it is not easy to see how pragmatic rules that result in the actions of command, request and so on follow from rules for the variable use of the sociolinguistic marker (th).

As text analysis, indeed, Labov's work on variation has a closer affinity to corpus descriptions as discussed earlier in this chapter. The probabilistic lexical and grammatical co-occurrences of collocation and colligation that were referred to then can be seen as indicators and markers in that they reveal patterns of usage which, in correlation with kinds of speaker or settings of use, can serve to typify different language varieties as dialects or registers. Thus the corpus-based grammar referred to earlier in this chapter (Biber et al. 1999) provides an extensive account of the lexicogrammatical features that are markers of different registers. But registers are varieties of text, and, as Biber et al. note, 'texts occur and are understood in their discourse settings' and it is these settings, which are not accounted for in such descriptions, that are necessarily engaged in interpretation. Again, it is clear that an account of the occurrence of textual features is distinct from an understanding of how they function pragmatically as discourse.

We return to Brown and Yule and to the main point: constraints on co-occurrence itself, whether imposed by internal co-textual factors, or external contextual ones, have to do with the properties of text. Constraints on interpretation have to do with how text is processed as discourse. This involves tracing relationships not just between juxtaposed elements (as in collocations) but between elements which may be at a considerable textual distance from each other. And even then, as we have seen, interpretation does not follow from this tracing of semantic links. You can demonstrate the co-textual patterns that tie parts of a text together, thereby showing it to be *cohesive*, but this will not of itself indicate how the text can be made *coherent* as discourse.[3]

Such a distinction is not, however, recognized in what is widely cited as the standard work on cohesion (Halliday and Hasan 1976). For them cohesion is a feature of discourse structure which, equivalently, gives a text its texture (the terms are used in free variation). The concept is explained thus: 'We can interpret cohesion, in practice, as the set of semantic resources for linking a sentence with what has gone before' (Halliday and Hasan 1976:10). And again: 'the concept of cohesion accounts for the essential semantic relations whereby any passage of speech or writing is enabled to function as a text' (Halliday and Hasan 1976:13). Halliday and Hasan talk about the semantic linking of sentences but insist that 'a text does not CONSIST OF sentences; it is REALIZED BY, or encoded, in sentences' (Halliday and Hasan 1976:2; emphasis in the original). How a text can be encoded in sentences without then consisting of them is not made clear, but what is clear is that text is defined in terms of the semantic ties that relate different parts of it. It is co-textual cohesion that *constitutes* the text as a linguistic object. Halliday and Hasan then propose a number of distinct categories for the classification of cohesive devices: 'categories which have a theoretical basis as distinct TYPES of cohesive relation, but which also provide a practical means for describing and analysing texts' (Halliday and Hasan 1976:13). These categories represent general ways in which cohesion functions, and within each category there is a detailed list of the particular ways in which the cohesive relation is given formal instantiation. Thus reference can be instantiated by personal pronouns, by demonstrative adjectives, demonstrative adverbs, the definite article and so on. This listing of devices does indeed provide a practical means for identifying their co-textual occurrence in any particular text. What does not emerge through the detail with any clarity is how far the formal differences of these devices correspond to any difference in their cohesive function. Are personal pronouns and demonstratives, for example, simply formally different alternative instantiations of reference, or does the use of the personal pronoun constitute a different *kind* of reference from the use of a demonstrative? If so, then how are these different subdivisions of cohesive function to be defined? And are they invariably instantiated by the same formal means – do demonstratives, for example, always have to function as reference, or can they function in substitution as well?

Halliday and Hasan concede that their classification of cohesive relations is only approximate. In respect to reference and substitution as two distinctive types of cohesive relation, they comment: 'There are many instances of cohesive forms which lie on the borderline between two types and could be interpreted as one or the other. The situation is a familiar one in many fields, and when one is attempting to explain phenomena as complex as those of human language it would be surprising to find things otherwise' (Halliday and Hasan 1976:88). It would indeed be surprising to find an exact correlation between cohesive forms and functions, and one might expect some degree of indeterminacy in the model of description. Nevertheless, one might expect some attempt at explanation as to why so many forms find themselves on the borderline of two types of cohesive relation which are represented as, in principle, quite distinct: 'The distinction between substitution and reference is that substitution is a relation in the wording rather than in the meaning' (Halliday and Hasan 1976:88).

Let us consider an example. *Same* is a form that can function in either category. Halliday and Hasan provide the following to illustrate how it works as substitution:

A: I'll have two poached eggs on toast, please.
B: I'll have the same.

They comment: 'Not, of course, *the same eggs*, which would be reference, not substitution.' So in the case of substitution, the form is taken to be simply a reduced copy of some previous wording. But since the previous wording has a referential function, it is hard to see how its copying can fail to be referential as well. Although B's expression *the same* does not refer to the same eggs, it surely refers to the same dish. Compare:

A: I'll have (the) bacon and eggs, please.
B: I'll have the same.

Obviously, A and B are not going to eat the same breakfast from the same plate, but they are just as obviously both referring to the same item on the menu. The same would be the case if B were to utter the following in either of these examples:

A: I'll have poached eggs on toast, please.
    I'll have (the) bacon and eggs, please.
B: I'll have that too.

The form *that*, however, is classified under demonstrative reference, and there is no allowance made for any possible substitution function. In which case, of course, B's utterance here would have to be taken as referring to the very same portion of breakfast that A has ordered, which is pragmatically unlikely, to say the least. The fact of the matter is, surely, that we do not have two distinctive cohesive functions here at all. What we have is reference at different levels of specificity: one to the dish as itemized on the menu, the other to a token of it, an actual meal.

The same point applies to the indefinite pronoun *one* as distinct from the personal pronoun *it*. The former is assigned a substitution function, as in the example:

My axe is blunt. I must get a sharper *one*.

Here, *one* is said to substitute for *axe*, and as with our examples of *same*, we can concede that it does not refer to the blunted axe mentioned earlier, as would be the case with *it*, as in:

My axe is blunt. I must sharpen *it*.

This too, however, can be seen as an example of substitution. The difference is that whereas *one* substitutes for *axe*, *it* substitutes for *my axe*. And both items refer, *one* to axes in general, and *it* to a particular one. And in both cases the recognition of the 'relation in the wording' depends on the recognition that there is a relation 'in the meaning'.

Halliday and Hasan claim that their classification of types of cohesive relation has a 'theoretical basis'. But the only basis that is offered for identifying two of the main ones rests on a very questionable distinction between wording and meaning. Furthermore, this distinction seems to be at odds with the way cohesion in general is defined. Consider the following:

> Substitution is a relation between linguistic items, such as words or phrases; whereas reference is a relation between meanings. In terms of the linguistic system, reference is a relation on the semantic level, whereas substitution is a relation on the lexicogrammatical level, the level of grammar and vocabulary, or linguistic 'form'. (Halliday and Hasan 1976:89)

But how can one type of cohesion not be semantic, when cohesion is semantic *by definition*? 'The concept of cohesion is a semantic one; it refers to relations of meaning that exist within a text, and that define it as a text' (Halliday and Hasan 1976:4). Not being a semantic relation, substitution on this account has no cohesive function whatever. Clearly, the wording of Halliday and Hasan themselves must be interpreted to mean something other than what they actually say, for it is obvious that, as has already been indicated, one cannot even recognize a lexicogrammatical relation without identifying some semantic connection. *The same* relates to *poached eggs on toast* and *one* relates to *axe* only to the extent that these substitute items copy semantic features from the preceding expressions. Such copying can be made more or less semantically explicit. Thus we can have the following alternatives:

I'll have *the poached eggs* too.
I'll have *the eggs* too.
I'll have *the same dish.*
I'll have *the same thing.*
I'll have *the same.*
I'll have *that.*

My axe is blunt. I need a sharper *axe.*
        I need a sharper *tool.*
        I need a sharper *one.*

All of these are cohesive in that semantic features are copied from one lexicogrammatical item to another.

It may be, of course, that the term 'semantic' is being used here not in its conventional sense to signify meaning as encoded in lexicogrammatical form, but in a restricted pragmatic sense to mean what such forms are used to refer to in extralinguistic reality. Indeed this is how the term 'reference' would generally be understood. In this case, the ties between different expressions in a text would be established not by identifying links between their signification as encoded items but via an interpretation of what meanings might have been intended by using them. We would then, of course, need to go beyond co-textual occurrence and into a consideration of the kind of extralinguistic contextual factors that were considered in chapter 3, and these would have a bearing on which of the alternatives given above would be deemed appropriate on a particular occasion of use. But Halliday and Hasan quite explicitly exclude such considerations from their account. In a passage of particular significance for the theme of this chapter (and indeed for this book as a whole) we find the following observations.

> The internal and the external aspects of 'texture' are not wholly separable, and the reader, or listener, does not separate them when responding unconsciously to a passage of speech or writing. But when the linguist seeks to make explicit the basis on which these judgements are formed, he is bound to make observations of two rather different kinds. The one concerns relations within the language, patterns of meaning realized by grammar and vocabulary; the other concerns the relations BETWEEN the language and the relevant features of the speaker's and hearer's (or writer's and reader's) material, social and ideological environment. Both these aspects of a text fall within the domain of linguistics.

The familiar distinction then is drawn between the internal co-textual patterns of lexicogrammatical occurrence and the external relations that texts contract with 'the relevant features' (an echo of Firth) of the extra-linguistic context. Though the linguist distinguishes these two aspects, they are closely interrelated:

> The linguistic patterns, which embody, and at the same time also impose structure on, our experience of the environment, by the same token also make it possible to identify what features of the environment are relevant to linguistic behaviour and so form part of the context of situation. But there are two sets of phenomena here, and in this book we are concerned with the LINGUISTIC factors that are characteristic of texts in English. The situational properties of texts, which are now beginning to be studied in greater detail and with greater understanding, constitute a vast field of enquiry which lies outside our scope here. (Halliday and Hasan 1976:20–1)

The way Halliday and Hasan conceive of the interdependency of the two aspects of 'texture' here corresponds quite closely to the way code–context relations have been discussed in chapter 2 of this book. Encoded semantic meaning provides the general parameters which are then given various pragmatic settings in the light of contextual factors.

Such contextual factors, however, are beyond the scope of their enquiry, so they cannot show how these pragmatic settings come about in, for example, the achievement of appropriate reference. In other words, they cannot deal with discourse, but only with its textual trace. Since they are exclusively concerned with the linguistic aspects of co-text, they can only make statements about substitution, and these are indeed a range of cohesive devices for copying semantic features across different lexicogrammatical features of a text. Reference, as a necessarily pragmatic phenomenon, cannot be accounted for in their scheme of things. Paradoxically, the type of cohesive relation which they say is not semantic actually is, and that which they call semantic is actually not.

There is a further, and for me crucial, point to be made about this passage. It takes us back to a previous discussion about the nature of text, and forward to issues to be taken up in the next chapter. Halliday and Hasan argue that although the two aspects of text (the internal co-textual and the external contextual) are separated out for linguistic analysis, they are not experienced as separate by the language user. Agreed. But in that case, what the linguist analyses as text is not the same as what the user experiences as text. For, as I argued earlier, a text only exists for the user in association with discourse. It has no reality otherwise. One can of course isolate a text and analyse it as a linguistic object, note co-occurrences, trace co-textual semantic connections, and so on, but then it ceases to be a text as such.

We return here to the points made in chapter 2 about Halliday's two levels of text analysis. What Halliday and Hasan are exclusively concerned with is the first level of so-called 'understanding': they provide an exhaustive compendium of devices which 'relate text to general features of the language'. The second level (that of 'evaluation'), which 'requires interpretation not only of the text itself but also of the context' is excluded from consideration. The idea seems to be that once the first-level analysis is done, then this somehow provides a basis for the second. The difficulty here, as was indicated in chapter 2, is that although it may be convenient for the language analyst to divide and rule in this way, it seems to make the unwarranted assumption that language users proceed in like fashion: that they first subject a text to close semantic analysis, identifying cohesive patterns of co-textual occurrence, and then, once this is done, go on to the second stage of evaluating the pragmatic significance of their analysis. In other words, the user is represented as first processing the text, in preparation for, and as a necessary precondition on, the subsequent processing of it as discourse. Against this, I have been arguing in this chapter, and elsewhere, that there are no such separate stages, that texts are only processed for their discourse significance. Their semantic features, in this view, are relevant only to the extent that they have pragmatic point, their co-textual patterns only relevant to the extent that they key into contextual factors.

To say this is not, of course, to deny the relevance of semantic features, or the cohesive relations they co-textually contract, but only to argue the need to establish *how* they become relevant in text interpretation. The discourse process is a matter of giving appropriate pragmatic realization to the semantic meaning encoded in language, and this encoded meaning does indeed, as Halliday and Hasan point out, impose its own structure on our experience. It restricts the range of pragmatic possibility. Meaning in general, we should note, is always a relational function of mutual modification: particular linguistic elements are acted upon and their meanings are narrowed down accordingly. This modification principle operates internally within sentences in isolation as much as between sentences in texts or between utterances and contexts.[4] To take a simple lexical example, the word *open* is acted upon in very different ways by the other words it keeps company with in the expressions *open a book, open a bottle of wine, open a box of chocolates*. The activities could hardly be more different. And the differences obtain in the code, whatever the context of use. Similarly lexical items and grammatical categories can interact to different semantic effect. The present continuous aspect in English, for example, is said to denote duration over a period of time. But the nature of the duration can be quite different depending on which lexical item is involved. Thus in the case of *He is writing a note*, the period is short and uninterrupted whereas in the case of *He is writing a novel*, it is long and intermittent, and this is so whatever the particular context of use. This interdependency of meaning is obvious enough. But notice that it illustrates with particular clarity the phenomenon that Sperber and Wilson identify as defining the nature of relevance: that is to say, we recognize that the conjunction of element **a** with element **b** yields a significance which neither would have on its own. So if the understanding of sentences in isolation proceeds by this modification by conjunction, then it would appear that the decoding process is not so radically different from the inferential process as Sperber and Wilson suggest.

In pragmatic uses of language, the modification principle is extended to apply to external contextual features. The internal operation of the principle on semantic relations within an isolated sentence, or across co-textual occurrences in texts, takes us so far but no further. As was argued in chapter 2, we can think of a language as the formal encoding of the most common features of context, the most frequently adduced aspects of reality within a particular community, that part of schematic knowledge which is semantically inscribed in the code. Semantic meaning, as conventionally encoded, can be seen, in this view, as constituting a range of delimiting co-ordinates, or (in the terms used earlier in this chapter) parameters which are given different pragmatic settings in association with different contextual factors. A sentence, of its nature, will give some setting to these co-ordinates, but only in a general indeterminate way which will require pragmatic fine tuning by reference to contextual assumptions.

With this in mind, we might briefly revisit the example considered earlier:

It is raining in Paris.

Some semantic specification is in evidence here, some narrowing down of meaning. Taken in isolation it can be said to express a proposition about a certain current state of affairs in a particular location. However, people do not express propositions in semantic isolation but only to achieve some kind of pragmatic force or effect, and this will depend on making a contextual connection. The number of possible contexts this expression could relate to is infinite, but we can narrow them down by co-textual extension.

It is raining in Paris. The party has been postponed.

Now we can get things a little more into focus. The fact that the lexical item **party** collocates with **postpone** eliminates the sense of the word which was operative in the passage we considered earlier about Darwin and the natives. It eliminates the sense of political party too. No matter how strongly you feel, pragmatically (and politically), you cannot, semantically, postpone the Conservatives, for example. And now too, on the assumption that this is indeed a text and not two random sentences, we are in a position to hazard a hypothesis that what is said about the rain has the illocutionary force of explanation, that the party mentioned was to have been in the open air (for why otherwise should the rain cause its postponement?). What we are doing here is deriving a discourse from this simple text by invoking certain contextual conditions. But it still remains pragmatically unfocused. The connection between the two expressions, for example, might not be cause and effect at all. There is no explicit cohesive signal to indicate it in the text itself. It does not run: **It is raining in Paris.** *Therefore* **the party has been postponed.** And anyway, which party? And what does it have to do with me, or you, or anybody else? To answer such questions we have to provide a scenario of the kind provided to give point to the McEnroe utterance we considered in the last chapter. At this point we need to go beyond text to context. The text focuses the meaning within a narrower wave band. But there is still contextual fine tuning to be done. And until such fine tuning is done, much of the pragmatic potential remains unrealized.

In this chapter, I have argued for a clear distinction to be made between the internal co-textual relations which can be semantically traced within a text, and the external contextual relations that have to be accounted for in realizing their pragmatic meaning. In tracing co-textual relations one establishes what makes a text cohesive as a linguistic unit. To do this is to work at what Halliday refers to as the level of 'understanding' (see chapter 2). But, as has been frequently noted in the literature, cohesion does not of itself lead to the realization of a text as a coherent discourse. Identifying cohesive links by noticing how semantic features are copied across different items and how items act upon each other by the modification principle will narrow down the pragmatic possibilities, but cannot determine interpretation. For this will depend on contextual 'evaluation'. It may be convenient for analysis to focus on the cohesive properties of a text, but since texts never occur in language use without the implication of discourse, text cohesion only has point when interpreted as discourse coherence: co-textual relations are only realized by users to the extent that they are contextually relevant. It may be, furthermore, that certain co-textual features which analysis reveals are not taken as contextually relevant at all. So in reference again to Halliday's two levels of interpretation, we may find that evaluation sets conditions on what is understood rather than the other way round, that the pragmatic process of discourse realization involves regulating attention to the semantic features of a text so that some are given more prominence than others, and some indeed are disregarded altogether. These are matters which will be taken up in the next chapter.

Notes

1   It should be noted that Sinclair does not, however, agree with how Biber et al. draw on the results of such co-textual inspection in their grammatical description (see Sinclair 1999). Biber et al. say quite explicitly that they have adopted the 'descriptive framework and terminology' already established in the grammar of Quirk et al. (1985). Sinclair's view has long been that co-textual inspection does not simply yield new data to exemplify existing descriptive categories but provides evidence that they need to be changed: 'The categories and methods we use to describe English are not appropriate to the new material. We shall need to overhaul our descriptive systems' (Sinclair 1985:252). Although Biber et al.'s grammar is corpus-based, it is not, as Sinclair believes a grammar should be, corpus-driven. See Sinclair (1999), Tognini Bonelli (2001).

2   The phenomenon of semantic prosody is a co-textual relation which, like so many other findings from corpus linguistics, was first described by Sinclair, although, as is noted in Stubbs 1995, the term itself originates elsewhere. Sinclair points out (in Sinclair 1991) that certain lexical items regularly attract collocates which have unpleasant associations. BREAK OUT, for example, typically collocates with such lexical subjects as *war, violence, disagreement, disease*. It can therefore be said to have a negative prosody. For a particularly clear account of how corpus analysis can reveal such prosodies, see Stubbs 1995.

3   My early formulation of the distinction (Widdowson 1978) is not entirely satisfactory, as Hoey points out. His own formulation corresponds with the way I have drawn the distinction in this book: 'We will assume that cohesion is a property of the text, and that coherence is a facet of the reader's evaluation of a text. In other words, cohesion is objective, capable in principle of automatic recognition, while coherence is subjective and judgements concerning it may vary to reader to reader.' However, he then adds parenthetically: '(though, outside the realm of literature and student composition, there is in fact little variation)' (Hoey 1991:12). Here Hoey and I part company. I do not know what the factual basis of this assertion is, but the evidence, in fact, would seem to me to point to the opposite conclusion: what he calls evaluation (echoing Halliday) involves taking into account all manner of contextual variables, as Halliday himself recognizes (see chapter 2).

4   I have argued that S/F grammar does not address this issue of how linguistic elements are co-textually and contextually modified. There is, however, a functional approach to language description that does, namely that associated with the Prague School. Its concept of Functional Sentence Perspective (FSP) is concerned with 'how the grammatical and semantic structures function in the very act of communication' (Daneš 1964:227). In this view, linguistic elements are subject to modification in the process Firbas calls 'communicative dynamism' (CD). This, he says, 'is based on the fact that linguistic communication is not a static, but a dynamic phenomenon': 'By CD I understand a property of communication, displayed in the course of the development of the information to be conveyed and consisting in advancing this development. By the degree of CD carried by a linguistic element, I understand the extent to which the element contributes to the development of the communication, to which, as it were, it "pushes the communication forward" (Firbas 1972:78). The idea of communicative dynamism obviously precludes any direct mapping of grammar on to text, even though it is not entirely clear how far degrees of CD are dependent on contextual as distinct from co-textual factors (Firbas does not draw this distinction). One point that Firbas makes is that the degree of CD is not related to the co-textual feature of linear arrangement, which indicates that it is a function not of sequential but of structural relations among linguistic elements. This contrasts with another functional approach to grammatical description which identifies linearity as a crucial factor, namely that of Bolinger in his article 'Linear modification' published, interestingly enough, in the same year as Harris's 'Discourse analysis' (1952). Bolinger's general thesis is that 'Elements as they are added one by one to form a sentence progressively limit the semantic range of all that has preceded. This causes beginning elements to have a wider semantic range than elements towards the end' (Bolinger 1952/65:279). Thus, for instance, a participial adjective in preposed position in a noun phrase (as in **a limping man**, or **a forgotten promise**) will have a characterizing function which thereby delimits the signifying range of the noun, whereas in postposed position (as in **a man limping** or **a promise forgotten**) it will signal a 'temporary state' or 'momentary condition'. Bolinger comments that in the former case, 'the qualifying word is transferred from its literal meaning and specialized in some figurative or restricted sense . . . the participle partially loses its identity' (Bolinger 1952/65:301). The notion of on-line linguistic modification or accommodation has since been extensively explored in psycholinguistics, and seems to be consistent with recent connectionist and cognitive linguistic theories about language processing. For a detailed review, see O'Halloran (2003).

5

Pretext

At Halliday's level of 'understanding', as we have seen, it is assumed that text is processed by the close analysis of its co-textual features whereby cohesive relations are established and semantic modification recognized. This can be understood as a process of inferring how co-occurring expressions in a text are relevant to each other. We return to Sperber and Wilson. They too are concerned with the relationship between textual features, although in their case the focus is on the inferential processes that realize this relationship and which bring about contextual effects as hypothetical pragmatic possibilities. In both cases, however, making sense of language in use is represented as a serial step-by-step process of interpretation by analysis.

But although linguists and logicians might construct sense by serial analysis in this way, it does not follow, of course, that this is how ordinary people make sense of the language they use. Sperber and Wilson provide many a persuasive illustration of how the RT model works, but they are all, we should note, invented for that purpose. Actually occurring instances of language use do not figure in their discussion, and naturally one is led to wonder how far the rules of inference they propose, rather like the cohesive relations discussed in the previous chapter, are a function of their mode of analysis rather than a representation of how discourse is actually enacted in reality. One might suspect that these rules of inference are abstract constructs of ideal performance, just as rules of syntax are abstract constructs of ideal competence. Certainly when one looks at the complex untidiness of spoken interaction, the lines of logical inference are difficult to discern, and you have to disregard a great deal of data to discover their trace.

From the philosophical perspective of Sperber and Wilson the rules that Labov refers to whereby what is meant and done is related to what is said are fairly straightforward: they are essentially rules of logical inference. This is in stark contrast to how it looks from the sociological perspective of Garfinkel that was mentioned in chapter 1. As he conceives it, the task of the discourse analyst is to confront the textual data directly, warts and all, and try to work out how people actually make sense of it. To this end (to repeat the quotation given in the earlier chapter): 'What the parties said would be treated as a sketchy, partial, incomplete, masked, elliptical, concealed, ambiguous, or misleading version of what the parties talked about' (Garfinkel 1972:317). This is a far cry from the image of orderly inference that Sperber and Wilson present us with. The features of spoken interaction listed here, and indeed the very random manner of their listing, represent the very opposite of orderliness, and this is borne out by any transcript of actually occurring conversation. But if the parties concerned do not just apply inferencing rules to make sense of their interaction, how do they do it? According to Garfinkel: 'it is not satisfactory to say that members invoke some rule with which to define the coherent or consistent or planful, i.e. rational character of actual activities' (Garfinkel 1972:322). So what would be satisfactory? The parties to a conversation, the members (in ethnomethodogical parlance) of a particular community of speakers somehow impose a coherent pattern on their interaction, even though what they actually say is, to all appearances, scattered and confused. For Garfinkel too this is a rational process, but the reasoning involved is what he calls practical reasoning, and this is not a matter of simply applying rules of logical inference.

What parties say is actual linguistic behaviour, open to third-person observation, available for direct recording and subsequent analysis. What parties talk about is what they themselves make of the language they use. Though what parties say is typically incomplete, elliptical, ambiguous and so on, they nevertheless interpret it as consistent and planful. In other words, disorderly though the text may be that people produce, they nevertheless derive a coherent discourse from it in the process. Sperber and Wilson, of course, do not deal with what parties actually say but in invented utterances, devised expressly to illustrate inferential processes, so the problem of inchoate data simply does not arise. It does not arise either, or so it would seem, with written language, where the text has the appearance of ordered completion. But, as was noted in the first chapter, here appearances are deceptive.

The meanings that are constructed by linguistic analysis, then, cannot be equated with those that are constructed by language users in the discourse process. So it is, as I have already suggested, that although text can be separated out and dealt with as a linguistic object, it is never experienced by users in such contextual isolation. But context is not experienced in isolation either. It too is an analytic construct. So the linguist, as third-person observer, may examine the co-textual features of a text and adduce various contextual correlates as relevant to the projection of pragmatic meaning. But what is relevant to such analysis is not necessarily relevant to the user. I have said that people make meaning out of language by relating textual features to extralinguistic contextual factors but they do not do this by the systematic processing of data in the manner of the analyst. They do it as relevant to their purpose, and their purpose may well lead them to disregard a whole host of co-textual and contextual features that linguists and logicians have painstakingly identified. I have already suggested (in chapter 3) that the kind of inferential procedures that Sperber and Wilson propose are regulated by schematic factors, so that an awareness of different discourse conventions may, on the least-effort principle, enable the user to dispense with them. But the same principle applies more widely not only to such genre conventions of use, but to the position that users take up within such conventions. What is relevant in text is what the users choose to make relevant in relation to what they are processing the language for.

In both the SF and RT scheme of things, communication is represented as a relatively straightforward and orderly matter of linguistic processing by analysis whereby meaning is directly recovered from the textual wording. For Garfinkel, the relationship between meaning and wording is much more indirect and elusive. What parties say is an extremely distorted representation of what they mean, so communication is necessarily imprecise: their language being 'sketchy, partial, incomplete, masked' and so on. In other words (the words of T. S. Eliot) they are engaged in 'an intolerable wrestle with words and meanings' – except that they do not seem to find this wrestling intolerable. Eliot does because he is striving for a precision of meaning which it is essentially beyond the capacity of language to provide. Repeatedly in *Four Quartets* (the poem from which this quotation is taken), Eliot speaks of the frustration of his attempts to capture what he means in words which 'slip, slide, perish,/Decay with imprecision':

> Trying to learn to use words, and every attempt
> Is a wholly new start and a different kind of failure
> Because one has only learnt to get the better of words
> For the thing one no longer has to say, or the way in which
> One is no longer disposed to say it.
>
> (T. S. Eliot, *Four Quartets*)

For Eliot, then, attempts to get the better of words result in different kinds of failure. For Garfinkel, on the other hand, they result in different kinds of success. If 'one' is writing a poem one might well find that the kind of meanings one is mentally groping for are of such elusive subtlety that they are indeed hard to pin down. Certainly the reader is frequently obliged to wrestle with words and meanings in trying to understand what Eliot is getting at in his poetry. But with respect to other uses of language, even where a degree of wrestling is called for, language users do not seem to find it intolerable. They seem to think that they do get the better of words for the expression and interpretation of meaning, and the general effectiveness of daily communication, in speech, in print, on screen, would seem to bear them out. They get their message across. They make their point.

T. S. Eliot finds language intractable because he is looking for a correlation of words and meanings and so making demands on language that it cannot possibly meet. For communication, of course, cannot be a matter of such correlation. Words slip and slide because they could not otherwise function in use. They will not stay still because when they are in place in texts, they cannot. They may decay with imprecision in the sense that their semantic integrity cannot be protected, but if it were so protected, they would be pragmatically ineffective. The instability of words makes it impossible to be communicatively precise, but at the same time provides for the only communication that it possible, which is bound to be imprecise. This is because the relationship which is activated in using language to communicate is not between elemental words and meanings but between words and other words in texts which are in turn related to the contextual conditions of their production and reception. Meaning is not manifested in words, but is realized as a function of their internal and external relations. The reason why Eliot finds it so problematic to take a fix on meaning is that the text he is composing is a poem, and as such dissociated from the contextual conditions which would normally be presupposed in text production, and which would provide the necessary bearings for its interpretation. His text is in contextual limbo. In that sense the difficulties he is wrestling with are, quite literally, of his own making. What he is talking about, essentially, is a poetic dilemma, not a pragmatic one.[1]

Pragmatic meaning, in normal communicative circumstances, is bound to be imprecise and approximate to purpose. Indeed, to press for precision beyond an accepted social purpose will cut the language off from its contextual connection and undermine pragmatic effectiveness. What Eliot seeks to do in *Four Quartets* is to express meaning in the absence of the contextual limits which would normally define its pragmatic point. This naturally gives rise to interpretative uncertainty which we take as appropriate for poetry. But not for other uses of language. Here it is appropriate to be approximate. The question is, how approximate? What is it that determines the degree of precision of meaning we should press for whether at the producing or receiving end? We come to the notion of pretext.

Normal communication, that is to say, that which is part of the conduct of everyday social life, is, to use Garfinkel's terms, achieved as 'ongoing accomplishment' by the application of 'practical reasoning'. Such reasoning works out what is relevant to the communicative occasion. We should note that what makes it practical is that it is not logical, that is to say, it does not follow the procedures of rational inference, and in this respect it is a very different process from the kind of logically exact computation that is proposed in RT. This model, with its close focus on implicational connections within verbal texture, actually seems to be more suited to the interpretation of poetry than to normal contextually located uses of language, which call for a more practical, rough and ready processing whereby meanings are accomplished by selective attention. Garfinkel gives an amusing but telling example of what happens when this normal process is denied in favour of greater analytic precision. He asked his students to carry out this little experiment: 'engage an acquaintance or friend in an ordinary conversation and, without indicating that what the experimenter was asking was in any way unusual, to insist that the person clarify the sense of his commonplace remarks.' One of his students reported as follows:

> On Friday night my husband and I were watching television. My husband remarked that he was tired. I asked 'How are you tired? Physically, mentally, or just bored?'
>
> *Subject.* I don't know, I guess physically, mainly.
> *Experimenter.* You mean your muscles ache or your bones?
> *S:* I guess so. Don't be so technical.
>   (After more watching)
> *S:* All these old movies have the same kind of old iron bedstead in them.
> *E:* What do you mean? Do you mean all old movies, or some of them, or just the ones you have seen?
> *S:* What's the matter with you? You know what I mean.
> *E:* I wish you would be more specific.
> *S:* You know what I mean! Drop dead!
>
> (Garfinkel 1972:7)

Specificity is particularly out of place in casual conversation, of course, since its purpose has less to do with communication as such than with comity (see Aston 1988). So in pressing for precision, the experimenter here is denying the conditions of contextual relevance that her hapless husband takes as self-evident. Each is working to a different agenda, they bring different assumptions to their conversation, and it breaks down not because they do not understand what is being said but because these different assumptions put them at cross purposes. The husband's remarks can be taken as affective gestures of domestic intimacy, little bids for attention or togetherness. They are a kind of verbal stroking or grooming, expressions of what Malinowski referred to as 'phatic communion': being conceptually phatic in order to commune. The wife has something quite different in mind. For her the conversation is simply a pretext for getting data. From the husband's point of view, ignorant as he is of her experimental purpose, she is using his remarks as a pretext for picking a quarrel. 'You know what I mean': in other words, you know what these remarks count as, and what they count as depends on them not being subjected to analytic scrutiny.

The term 'pretext' generally refers to an ulterior motive: a pretending to do one thing but intending to do something else. In this sense, it would be normal to apply it to the wife's use of language, but not to that of her husband. But in a way, he too has an ulterior motive in that he is using language to establish intimacy. It is clear from his reaction that in mentioning his tiredness, it is not the propositional reference that matters, nor the illocutionary force, but the perlocutionary effect. He is appealing for sympathy, and his utterance fails when his wife is not affected as intended, but focuses instead on its propositional meaning. So I want to suggest that he too has a pretext and to propose that we extend the definition of the term to cover perlocutionary purpose in general. What I want to consider is how texts are designed and understood pretextually in this sense and how their effect depends on regulating our focus of attention on meaning.

The example we have just been considering is of casual conversation, and here, of course, perlocutionary effect is generally at a premium. It is a defining feature of such conversation, we might suggest, that the participants (however close their relationship) do not pay too much attention to what exactly their words mean so long as they have the desired effect of mediating comity. This, of course, is why the husband finds his wife's reaction to his remarks so irritatingly perverse. But surely in other kinds of discourse we cannot be so casual but need to take a more precise fix on what words mean. I would argue that, although there are occasions when we may indeed feel it necessary to focus attention on textual detail, it is only in order to establish to our own satisfaction what the users of the words might mean by using them, and that this inevitably brings contextual and pretextual factors into play. Consider the following comments by Johnson-Laird:

Discourse rarely depends upon speakers having complete and identical repre-sentations of the meanings of the words they use. It is perfectly possible to communicate with little or no such similarity, or else children would never learn their native tongue. Adults, too, can communicate successfully with an incomplete knowledge of meaning. When, for example, you read the sentence

> *After a hearty dish of spaghetti, Bernini cast a bronze of a mastiff searching for truffles*

you may understand it perfectly well even though, on reflection, you may not be entirely sure exactly what alloy *bronze* is, or what sort of dog a *mastiff* is, or what *truffles* are. (Johnson-Laird 1983:225)

To be sure, there are texts, particularly those concerned with such things as contractual terms and conditions, which are carefully drafted so as to formulate 'complete and identical representations' of meanings, but even here there is frequently enough lack of correspondence to keep lawyers busy with profitable litigation. Otherwise, representations of meaning do not converge into exact correspondence, and indeed it is hard to see how we would know if they did. Johnson-Laird says that we may understand the sentence he provides 'perfectly well' without being able to assign an exact meaning to the words. But we are, of course, never called upon to under-stand sentences but only texts, and texts are only produced under contex-tual and pretextual conditions. Our understanding, accordingly, is always conditional, and therefore always partial. We can never understand this sentence 'perfectly well': we can only understand its instantiation as a text, and only as well as these conditions determine. It may be true that if I were to come across this text in my reading, it might be enough for me to get the general drift but this would depend on why I am reading it in the first place. If I wished to be informed about the detail of Bernini's work as making a unique contribution to Renaissance art, then if I do not know what the words bronze or truffles or mastiff mean, I shall have understood the text very imperfectly indeed.

As was discussed in previous chapters, our understanding of a text, its realization as discourse, depends on the degree to which we can ratify the linguistic and contextual knowledge that its author presumes we share. This has to do with how far we can engage with the text at all. But there is a second condition that also comes into play: this has to do with what we are processing the text for, what we want to get out of it, the pretextual purpose which controls the nature of the engagement, and which regulates our focus of attention. These conditions naturally apply not only in the second-person interpretation of a text, but in their first person design as well. Thus a writer will make assumptions about shared knowledge of language and the world but also, crucially, will count on readers recognizing the pretext for writing, and adjusting their focus of attention accordingly. As with Garfinkel's research student and her husband, problems arise when the pretext which informs the design of a text does not correspond with that which readers bring to their interpretation of it. The writer may have pretextual pre-suppositions which, for one reason or another, may not be ratified in the reading. Consider, for example, the following text:

Hornblower, jumping for the weather mizzen shrouds, saw the eager grins on half a dozen faces – battle and the imminent possibility of death were a welcome change from the eternal monotony of the blockade. Up in the mizzen-top, he looked over his men. They were uncovering the locks of the muskets and looking to the priming; satisfied with their readiness for action, Hornblower turned his attention to the swivel gun. He took the tarpaulin from the breech and the tompion from the muzzle, cast off the lashings which secured it, and saw that the swivel moved freely in the socket and the trunnions freely in the crotch.

This passage appears in a popular novel, *Mr Midshipman Hornblower*, by C. S. Forester. What exactly, one might ask, are weather mizzen shrouds? Just what are these trunnions that run so freely in the crotch? In common with, I imagine, most readers, I have no idea. But does it matter? Can I, as Johnson-Laird suggests, understand this text 'perfectly well' in spite of such ignorance? It all depends on what I am reading for, and this in turn is influenced by what I take to be the purpose of the text. If I identify this as popular fiction and read it as such, I may be content with the general impression these words suggest: guns are being prepared for battle. This would clearly not do, however, if I have a different pretext for reading, namely to inform myself of the details of eighteenth-century naval warfare. In this case, I reach for the dictionary. But then the question arises as to how the text is designed to be read. On the reasonable assumption that Forester was aware that his readers would, for the most part, not know what these words actually mean, and would be unlikely to interrupt their reading (particularly at such a moment of dramatic action) to delve in a dictionary to find out, on what pretext, one must wonder, does he use them at all? It might plausibly be suggested that they are used to create the semblance of historical setting, to provide local colour and the illusion of authenticity. If this is so, then their very abstruseness contributes to this exotic effect: they can be taken as the verbal equivalent of period costume. In this case, we can be said to understand the text perfectly well precisely because we do *not* understand the exact meaning of these abstruse words, when we take the technical terminology as the pretext for creating an impressionistic effect.

Anthony Burgess makes a similar point in reference to the translation of the Bible: 'What has been happening to the Bible recently? There is a conviction on the part of the translators that it must be intelligible, yet some of the strength and music of the Bible as it was translated in the 1611 version precisely lies in its strangeness.'

In this view, an essential aspect of the meaningfulness of the biblical text is the effect of the seventeenth-century language, its evocative 'strength and music', its affective purport, and this is necessarily undermined by rendering it into more precise and intelligible terms. Holy script, one might say, is kept holy by its very strangeness. There is of course an alternative view, indeed a diametrically opposed one, that would argue that this strangeness is what makes the Bible remote from the reality of everyday life and that it needs to be brought down to earth and made referentially accessible for its relevance to be recognized. This after all was the motivation for the 1611 translation in the first place. Clearly, again, everything depends on pretextual assumptions and expectations, on what you read the Bible for, on what kind of text you take it to be.

For Burgess it is the evocative effect of the biblical text that is primary, not its referential intelligibility, and he takes the same view, it would seem, of church ritual:

> even when we come to the marriage ceremony we no longer have, 'thereto I plight thee my troth', and 'with all my worldly goods I thee endow'. We have, 'this is my solemn vow' and 'all that I have I share with you'. These sound as if they're not going to last, but when you say 'I plight thee my troth' it sounds like the stamping of a seal.[2]

What is important for Burgess is what the words sound like, not what they actually mean, their resonance rather than their reference. When you say 'this is my solemn vow' you know just what you are saying. In pronouncing 'I plight thee my troth', speakers will, of course, know its illocutionary force, and be aware of (and perhaps wary of) its perlocutionary effect, but may well be in as much ignorance of what the words *plight* and *troth* actually mean as, for example, the words *mastiff* and *truffle*. But the point is that it does not matter. And they cannot subsequently claim that the effect is null and void on the grounds that they did not understand what they were saying. They knew what the pretext was, and that is enough.

The main point at issue in all this is the extent to which pretext regulates the focus on meaning. In the cases we have just been considering, I have suggested that what makes these texts meaningful in one kind of reading is that they give rise to particular effects which are undermined by attempts to press for precision of meaning. But equally, of course, your reading might be regulated by a quite different pretext. Thus, you might not be content to take the Hornblower text simply as the impressionistic representation of local colour but might wish to examine the extent to which it is an accurate reconstruction of historical fact. Similarly, you may read the Bible not as a text which evokes literary effects, but as one which records literal truth. Such purposes will, of course, require greater precision in the scrutiny of the verbal texture but the precision is still a matter of selective attention determined by the pretext, and can still, therefore, only yield a partial meaning.

Hornblower and the Bible might both be regarded, in their different ways, as somewhat remote from the immediate concerns of contemporary life. But all texts, and not only those of fiction and scripture, present us with the problem of appropriate adjustment, and of how far our pretext as second-person parties can, or should, match up with the pretext that informed the first-person design of the text in the first place. Let us now consider another text, also belonging to the past, but one which is routinely invoked as of direct contemporary relevance. This is the American Declaration of Independence, in the second paragraph of which we find the following much-cited words:

> We hold these truths to be self-evident, that all men are created equal, that they are endowed by their Creator with certain unalienable Rights, that among these are Life, Liberty and the pursuit of Happiness.

The pretext here, we may say, is to evoke solidarity in a cause and to provoke political action. Its perlocutionary purpose is to create ideological unity and bring about independence, and what matters is not what the words actually mean but what effect they will have. Indeed the text is effective only to the extent that readers do not focus too precisely on the details of its formulation. If we do not acknowledge this pretext but instead take the text not as a declaration to be inspired by, but as documentary evidence to be analysed, the focus of attention changes and we read other meanings into the text accordingly. It becomes clear, for example, that the truths the authors refer to are only self-evident to themselves and have only restricted application. 'All men are created equal.' This expresses an admirable and high-sounding sentiment, but is 'all men' meant to refer to all human beings, including women? In 1776 this is unlikely. But apart from that, does it really mean all male human beings? Again, it is unlikely that signatories to this declaration would include the slaves working on their plantations as coming within the referential scope of the word 'men'. The truth that the authors of this text would hold as self-evident in this case is that such men are not created equal and have no rights, certainly not the right to liberty. The declaration of independence does not apply to them. Similarly, the reference does not include the indigenous population either. Later in the document, they are referred to as 'merciless Indian Savages, whose known rule of warfare, is an undistinguishable destruction of all ages, sexes and conditions'. What is self-evident to the authors of this text is that such men have no rights at all, not even the right to life. So what is proclaimed in this document is that all men are equal, but in denial of the semantics of the phrase, the reference is not universal, but highly restricted to certain kinds of men. One might say that what it effectively means, in Orwellian terms, is that all men are equal but some are more equal than others.

But the point is that it is a proclamation, and as such deals in grand verbal gesture which is not meant to be subjected to interpretative scrutiny. The truth is conditional on the pretext. This does not, of course, only apply to this particular declaration.[3] The use of language to make such grand gestures has been much in evidence in political rhetoric in recent times. Thus the violent destruction of the World Trade Centre on 11 September 2001 has been described as an attack on the free world, on democracy, nay, on civilization itself, as if all of these were exclusively and uniquely represented by the United States. This in turn provides the pretext for retaliation with counter-violence, but redefined in terms of a just cause and universal moral values. Thus language is pressed into the service of a political pretext and is made to mean what suits the users' purpose. In commenting on the events of 9/11 Chomsky makes the point:

> When Western states and intellectuals use the term 'international community', they are referring to themselves. For example, NATO bombing of Serbia was undertaken by the 'international community' according to consistent Western rhetoric, although those who did not have their heads buried in the sand knew that it was opposed by most of the world, often quite vocally. Those who do not support the actions of wealth and power are not part of the 'global community', just as 'terrorism' conventionally means 'terrorism directed against us and our friends'. (Chomsky 2001:75)

The expressions 'global community' and 'terrorism', then, like that of 'all men' in the Declaration of Independence, make a claim for universality of reference which on closer scrutiny cannot be sustained. But, of course, we are not encouraged to scrutinize the text, for to do so might well reveal the pretext and undermine the effect. To deconstruct the texts in which such words are used would be deemed inappropriate, perverse, and indeed a kind of treachery. The likely reactions would be similar to those of the husband in the conversation discussed earlier: 'What's the matter with you? You know what I mean.' Never mind about the meaning of the words as such, it is the effect that counts.

So much of communication seems to depend on a co-operative disregard of the meaning of words as such. As has often been pointed out, what words signify semantically plays second fiddle to the pragmatic significance we assign to them in particular contexts of use. What we do with words (to echo Austin 1962) is to subvert them to our purposes: we make them do our bidding to achieve propositional reference and illocutionary force by making appeal to mutually recognized contextual conditions. What I have argued here is that reference and force are themselves conditioned by what I have called pretextual assumptions about the perlocutionary effect that the use of language is designed to have.

These contextual and pretextual assumptions are held by particular groups of users, prime those users to understand texts in particular ways, and set the conditions for relevance. Once in place, they can indeed lend significance to language in despite of what it might otherwise signify. A somewhat extreme example of this is provided in Jerzy Kosinski's novel *Being There*. The main character, Chance, is a simple-minded gardener whose entire life has been bounded by the garden walls of his master's house. When his master dies, he is abruptly thrust into a world he cannot understand. By a series of unlikely events, he finds himself the guest of a business tycoon, Rand, and his wife, who, influenced by his appearance (he is dressed with great formality in his master's clothes), take him to be a person of wealth and distinction (Mr Chauncy Gardiner) and interpret his simple utterances accordingly. One day, Rand has a visit from the President of the United States. They talk about economic policy and the worrying trends of the financial markets on Wall Street. Chance is sitting with them, blissfully ignorant of what they are talking about and closed off in his usual innocent silence. Suddenly, the President turns to him:

'And you, Mr Gardiner? What do you think about the bad season on the street?'
    Chance shrank. He felt that the roots of his thoughts had suddenly been yanked out of their wet earth and thrust, tangled, into the unfriendly air. He stared at the carpet.

> Finally he spoke: 'In a garden,' he said, 'growth has its season. There are spring and summer, but there are also fall and winter. And then spring and summer again. As long as the roots are not severed, all is well and all will be well.' He raised his eyes. Rand was looking at him, nodding. The President seemed quite pleased.
>
> 'I must admit, Mr Gardiner,' the President said, 'that what you've just said is one of the most refreshing and optimistic statements I've heard in a very, very long time.' (Kosinski 1972:45)

What Chance does here is to pick up on the word 'season' and use it as a schematic trigger, so to speak, for talking about gardens (the only thing he knows about). This is his sole pretext, and in this respect there is a cohesive connection but without any coherent intention. Presupposing as they naturally do that Chance will have been engaged in their discussion (even if not overtly participating therein) and that what he says will (in accordance with Grice's maxim of relation) necessarily have some bearing on it, Rand and the President understand his remarks metaphorically so as to incorporate them into the context of their previous discussion. Thus they make them relevant by reading into them the reference that suits them, thereby assigning them a pretext he does not intend. And it is the effect of Chance's remarks that Rand nods at and the President comments on. They do not (fortunately for Chance) press for clarification or enquire into the validity of the supposed analogy (how are economic fluctuations comparable with naturally occurring seasons? What on Wall Street would correspond to the roots of plants?). All is well and will be well. It does not matter what Chance actually means. The point is that it sounds good. So, the contextual conditions lead Rand and the President to assign a referential relevance to the words, and at the same time what they suppose to be Chance's pretextual purpose leads them to pass over just what the words might actually mean.

This, it might be objected, is an extreme example, and a fictional one at that. But the process that it illustrates is, I would argue, a very general pragmatic one. The meaning of words in texts is always subordinated to a discourse purpose: we read into them what we want to get out of them. But to the extent that writers and readers belong to the same discourse community, and so share the same socio-cultural values and conventions of use, the writer's purpose will be recognized and ratified in the interpretation of the readers for whom the text was intended. The very social nature of communication is bound to be based on an assumption of co-operation whereby the focus of attention on meaning will be regulated. In effect, what this amounts to is a connivance at imprecision, even a conspiracy to subvert meaning so as to keep it under appropriate social control.

Of course we are not obliged to co-operate. We can engage in what has been called resistant or critical reading, whereby even if we recognize the writer's purpose, we refuse to ratify it. We can deplore the conspiracy and seek to expose it by subjecting texts to close scrutiny, probing for hidden meanings. From this perspective, every textual feature is seen to be potentially significant, its choice dictated by a socio-political motive of some kind, whether the text in question is to be found in a newspaper or a novel, in a holiday brochure or on the back of a train ticket. One fairly obvious point about such critical analysis is that since significance can only be recognized in relation to some kind of social purpose, what in effect it does is to replace one kind of pretext with another. So one might fixate on certain features of a text, take them apart, deconstruct their meaning and show that they express a particular ideological position: that is to say, what the author appears to be saying is just a pretext for saying something else. But you cannot deal with all of the textual features, let alone the complex relationships they contract with each other, so the decision of which textual features to fix on must be an informed one. What then is it informed by? Another set of socio-political assumptions that defines a discourse community other than that for which the text was designed. In other words, you too have pretextual assumptions, and they too quite naturally regulate your focus of attention on the text. Critical analysis of this kind will therefore not discover covert meanings but simply assign different ones as appropriate to a different pretextual purpose. Further elaboration and illustration of this point will be the central concern of the next chapter.

Earlier in this chapter I referred to T. S. Eliot and his intolerable wrestle with words and meanings. Let me end it with another literary quotation:

> 'When I use a word,' Humpty Dumpty said, in rather a scornful tone, 'it means just what I choose it to mean – neither more nor less.'
>
> 'The question is,' said Alice, 'whether you can make words mean so many different things.'
>
> 'The question is,' said Humpty Dumpty, 'which is to be master – that's all.' (Lewis Carroll, *Through the Looking Glass*)

There is no wrestling with words and meanings for Humpty Dumpty. He gets the better of words simply by assigning them whatever arbitrary meaning he chooses. Well, it is not as simple as that: there has to be some convention in invention, and if he is to communicate at all, he has to get some measure of consensus or collusion with a second party. But the question is not, as Alice would have it, whether we can make words mean so many different things. Clearly we can. The question is under what pretext we manage to do so.

Notes

1   As we have seen, the normal pragmatic process of interpretation involves realizing the indexical function of textual features whereby the text is used to make appropriate contextual connections: attention in this case is directed away from the text. The textual patterning in poems is designed to draw attention to itself and so to prevent a direct contextual connection. Whereas texts are normally used to make reference to a reality that is familiar, the purpose of poetic texts is to represent a reality that is not. Poets wrestle with words and meanings because they explore the possible significance of linguistic features which are not conventionally used to signify. They exploit what I have called elsewhere the 'poetentiality' in the language. For more discussion see Widdowson 1992. I take up the issue of the interpretation of literary texts again in chapter 8.

2   These extracts are taken from an article that appeared in the *Independent*, 27 November 1993. The article is an abridged version of the inaugural 'European Lecture' delivered by Anthony Burgess at the Cheltenham Festival of Literature in 1993: the year of his death.

3   How pretext regulates truth conditions is, of course, well illustrated by obituaries and other ritual and ceremonial uses of language, where is it accepted as a matter of social convention that it is proper to be 'economical with the truth'. Here the pretext is obvious. Less obvious are cases where multiple pretexts come into play, as when texts are designed to be both heard and overheard by different groups of people. Thus a presidential speech given to a particular audience may well contain so-called 'coded messages' for others on the assumption that they will recognize the different pretextual purposes and edit the text accordingly.

   Pretext clearly relates to the different participant roles in interaction that Goffman originally identified (Goffman 1981) and Levinson elaborates on (Levinson 1988).

6

Critical discourse analysis

My purpose in the first five chapters of this book has been to examine issues which it seems to me are critical for the enterprise of discourse analysis in general. I turn now to a consideration of a particular approach to discourse analysis that has become prominent and influential over recent years and which has appropriated the term critical as a designation of its distinctive character. The approach is critical in the sense that it is quite explicitly directed at revealing how language is used for the exercise of socio-political control. As van Dijk puts it:

> Critical Discourse Analysis (CDA) is a type of discourse analytical research that primarily studies the way social power abuse, dominance, and inequality are enacted, reproduced, and resisted by text and talk in the social and political context. With such dissident research, critical discourse analysts take explicit position, and thus want to understand, expose, and ultimately resist social inequality. (van Dijk 2001:352)

This critical perspective is of crucial importance in that it engages scholarly enquiry with matters of immediate and pressing concern in the non-scholarly world. What CDA has done, greatly to its credit, is to make discourse analysis relevant by relating it to a moral cause and an ideological purpose. In this respect, as I make clear in the preface to this book, I regard its work as highly significant. It happens, furthermore, that the socio-political position its proponents take up is one which I share. So I should stress that in what follows I take no issue with the critical perspective of CDA as such. My concern is with its effects on the kind of discourse analysis that is carried out, and how such analysis relates to the issues I have discussed in the previous five chapters of this book.

How then is discourse analysis done in CDA? Although, as Luke points out, 'the stances, positions, and techniques of CDA vary' (Luke 2002:98), one can identify certain features of common principle and practice which characterize the approach that has been most prominent to date. This approach has its origins in the work of Roger Fowler and his colleagues (for a succinct review, see Fowler 1996a) and was subsequently developed by others, notably Norman Fairclough, its most impressive and influential practitioner.[1] In this approach to CDA, the linguistic model that is generally invoked as particularly appropriate to the purpose is that of Halliday's S/F grammar. As an account of language as social semiotic which, as we have seen in chapter 2, claims to deal with text, it would appear on the face of it to be well suited to an analysis of discourse as social action. It turns out, however, that the application of an S/F model in CDA work is far from straightforward.

Thus, in expounding his own 'social theory of discourse', Fairclough (1992) finds it necessary to modify the model. Discourse, he explains, is itself 'constitutive' or 'constructive' of social structure (and not simply constrained by it), and one needs to distinguish between three kinds of 'constructive effect': one concerns the construction of social self or identity, another the construction of social relationships between people, and a third the construction of 'systems of knowledge and belief'. These effects, he says, 'correspond respectively to three functions of language and dimensions of meaning which coexist and interact in all discourses' (Fairclough 1992:64). They do not, however, correspond with the three functions of language that are proposed in S/F grammar. The third, the ideational, is common to both. The first two, however, the identity and relational functions, are incorporated by Halliday into a single interpersonal function. What Fairclough is proposing, then, is that we can distinguish between how discourse serves reflexively to create a first-person position or self, and how it serves as the means for establishing relations with the second-person other. We might illustrate this by reference to the figures in chapter 2:

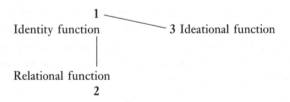

Figure 6.1

There is a good deal of theoretical appeal in this specification of discourse functions by reference to the trinity of first-, second- and third-person positions: the representation of first-person self, the relation with second-person other, the representation of third-person reality. The question arises, however, as to how this threefold distinction can be made operational in actual analysis. And this brings us to the third function in the S/F scheme of things, namely the textual. Where does this figure in Fairclough's social theory of discourse?

'Halliday also distinguishes a "textual" function', says Fairclough, 'which can be usefully added to my list' (ibid.:65). The somewhat offhand nature of this comment would seem to suggest that the textual function does not have the same status in the discourse theory being propounded as the central constitutive functions mentioned earlier. It is a useful addition. Just where its usefulness resides, however, or how it relates to these other functions, is left unclear.

Fairclough's discourse theory, then, would seem to depart from an S/F model by proposing three main functions, two of which are subdivisions of the interpersonal, and by demoting the textual function to the level of useful appendage. His apparent uncertainty as to what to do with this function is consistent with the view I expressed in chapter 2 that it does indeed have a different status from the ideational and interpersonal in that, unlike these, it is not expressive of any external social function but is an enabling device for their realization in text. The ideational and interpersonal (including the identity and relational) are, as Fairclough suggests, *discourse* functions. The textual is (true to its name) not a discourse function at all but a textual one. As such, it is not just a useful addition to discourse theory but the indispensable means whereby the theory can be exemplified by analysis. We return to the key issue of how the analysis of textual features leads to discourse interpretations.[2]

Fairclough himself outlines what he calls 'a framework for analysing texts', but without any explicit reference to the textual function as defined in S/F linguistics:

> Text analysis can be organized under four main headings: 'vocabulary', 'grammar', 'cohesion', and 'text structure'. These can be thought of as ascending in scale: vocabulary deals mainly with individual words, grammar deals with words combined into clauses and sentences, cohesion deals with how clauses and sentences are linked together, and text structure deals with large-scale organizational properties of texts. In addition, I distinguish a further three main headings which will be used in analysis of discursive practices rather than text analysis, though they certainly involve formal features of texts: the 'force' of utterances, i.e. what sorts of speech acts (promises, requests, threats, etc.) they constitute; the 'coherence' of texts; and the 'intertextuality' of texts. (Fairclough 1992:75)

This view of text analysis would appear to correspond quite closely to that proposed by Halliday, as discussed in chapter 2. The first four headings here have to do with text-internal properties, the analysis of which, according to Halliday, yields 'understanding'. The additional three headings have to do with text-external factors and constitute a second and higher level of what Halliday calls 'evaluation'. It is at this latter level that the text is interpreted as a discourse realization, or, as Fairclough puts it, as a discursive practice. But as was pointed out in chapter 2, the difficulty here is that if texts are to be taken as texts, and therefore as necessarily carrying discourse implications, they cannot be analysed as linguistic objects in isolation. It is not that the first-level analysis is carried out as an input to the second level for subsequent evaluation: this second level of interpretation regulates what textual features are attended to. Fairclough's three discursive factors are not additional to his four levels of text analysis, but are bound to be implicated in them. They do indeed 'involve formal features of texts'. The crucial issue is the nature of this involvement. Given a text, you can, of course, analyse it exhaustively into its constituent parts, and note how its morphemes, words, clauses and sentences combine. But this, as was argued in previous chapters, will tell you nothing about its essential nature as a text.

Fairclough presents his framework of analysis as the means whereby one arrives at the the constitutive discourse functions of the identity, relational and ideational kind that he has earlier specified. What the actual procedures are for drawing on this framework to infer social significance of this kind are not made explicit. We find no demonstration of how one might work through the headings that are proposed in any systematic way, ascending (or descending) the scale from 'individual words', for example, to 'the large-scale organizational properties of texts', or at what point issues concerning 'force'or 'coherence' in the second series of headings come into play. The headings constitute not so much a framework, in fact, as a check list of different factors that one might bear in mind, and put to use as and when it seems expedient to do so.

This is borne out by the example Fairclough provides of his own use of the framework in an analysis of the newspaper headline:

Gorbachev Rolls Back the Red Army

'My comments here', he says, 'will be restricted to certain aspects of the clause.' It seems reasonable to ask why, when seven headings for analysis have been outlined, only one should be singled out for special attention. It is true, of course, that this particular text cannot of itself be used to illustrate aspects such as cohesion and text structure, but then why not choose another text which would lend itself to a more comprehensive treatment? But let us consider Fairclough's comments on the clause:

> In terms of ideational meaning, the clause is transitive: it signifies a process of particular individual acting physically (note the metaphor) upon an entity. We might well see here a different ideological investment from other ways of signifying the same event, for example 'The Soviet Army Reduces its Armed Forces', or 'The Soviet Army Gives up 5 Divisions'. In terms of interpersonal meaning, the clause is declarative (as opposed to interrogative, or imperative), and contains a present tense form of the verb which is categorically authoritative. The writer–reader relationship here is that between someone telling what is the case in no uncertain terms, and someone being told; these are the two subject positions set up in the clause. (Fairclough 1992:76)

The metaphor we are asked to note is a feature of the vocabulary used in this text, but since the analysis does not concern itself with this part of the framework, there is no indication as to why it is noteworthy, or how this particular lexical choice might relate to the syntax of the clause. We are presented with 'other ways of signifying the same event' but as a matter of fact neither of them is different in clause structure from the original headline: they too are transitive, and so, on Fairclough's own account, must be assigned the same ideational meaning. The fact is that the difference in signification has to do with the vocabulary. The event is represented differently by lexical means: the choice of *The Soviet Union* rather than *Gorbachev*, of *The Soviet Army* rather than *The Red Army*, of the verbs *reduces* and *gives up* rather than *rolls back*, and so on. We should note too that sameness of the event cannot be inferred from textual evidence but only by relating the text to external contextual factors. Only then can you infer that what rolling back the Red Army actually amounts to is reducing it in size, or even, more specifically, to giving up five divisions. Whatever 'ideological investment' you might wish to see in the choice of one expression rather than another has, then, to do with the choice of vocabulary, and a knowledge of context, neither of which is taken into account in this analysis. Even if one does take these other factors into account, there still needs to be some argument as to why they might lead us to see this 'ideological investment' that Fairclough refers to.

And here we come to a further difficulty. The framework of analysis is designed as a means of revealing discourse functions. One of these is ideational: the use of language to represent knowledge and belief. But Fairclough, following Halliday, here talks of ideational meaning as already formally encoded in the transitivity of the clause. If this is so, then a particular representation of knowledge and belief is achieved automatically by grammatical choice, and is unaffected by any other factors, in which case, all the other headings in the framework that is proposed would appear, in effect, to be irrelevant. The same point applies to what Fairclough says of the interpersonal meaning of this headline:

> In terms of interpersonal meaning, the clause is declarative (as opposed to interrogative, or imperative), and contains a present tense form of the verb which is categorically authoritative. The writer–reader relationship here is that between someone telling what is the case in no uncertain terms, and someone being told; these are the two subject positions set up in the clause.

Again, the interpersonal function that is formally encoded in the grammar is equated with the interpersonal use of language: in other words, how the language is used to construct social identity and social relationships is directly inferable from linguistic forms. But declarative, interrogative and imperative are, as Labov points out (see chapter 3), linguistic categories. They are things that are said, as distinct from assertions, orders, questions, which are things that are done, and which bring all kinds of social factor into consideration. For Labov, as we have seen, the central concern of discourse analysis is to investigate the relationship between the two. But if an interpersonal function is necessarily discharged by a selection from the mood system of the grammar, then there is no distinction between saying and doing, and consequently no relationship between them to investigate. From Labov's point of view, Fairclough is not doing discourse analysis at all.

But it is not only the clause type that directly signals interpersonal significance in this analysis. Thus the occurrence of the present tense form of the verb in this text (*rolls*) is said to be 'categorically authoritative' and, as it occurs in this clause, to create relational positions of assertiveness and submission between first and second persons. Of course this tense might be used pragmatically in this way, but then one needs to explain how it does so by reference to other factors that appear under other headings in the Fairclough framework. Nobody, I imagine, would seriously argue that categorical authoritativeness is actually semantically encoded in the present tense in English. And yet this is what seems to be implied in assigning such an interpersonal meaning to it in this analysis.

Fairclough says no more about the interpersonal meaning of this headline. Rather surprisingly, he makes no explicit reference to the distinction that figures so prominently in his theory between identity and relational effects. Instead, he follows the standard S/F line and next turns his attention to the textual function:

> Thirdly, there is a textual aspect: 'Gorbachev' is topic or theme of the clause, as the first part of a clause usually is: the article is about him and his doings. On the other hand, if the clause were made into a passive, that would make 'the Red Army' the theme: 'The Red Army is Rolled Back (by Gorbachev)'. Another possibility offered by the passive is the deletion of the (bracketed) agent, because the agent is unknown, already known, judged irrelevant, or perhaps in order to leave agency and hence responsibility vague.

As we have already seen (in chapter 2) the formal property of thematic position can signal either topic or given, and so has interpersonal implications. So it does not necessarily follow that 'Gorbachev' as theme makes Gorbachev the topic of the headline, even less that it indicates that the article that follows is about him and his doings. But here Fairclough does acknowledge that you cannot read off discourse significance directly from a mode of signifying. The use of a passive construction might indeed be intended and interpreted in different ways, depending on how it figures in relation to other factors in his framework.

What, then, are we to make of this analysis, presented as an illustration of how a framework for analysing texts can be used in the service of a social theory of discourse? In the first place, very little of the framework is actually drawn upon, and there is little if any indication of how the features that are focused on ('certain aspects of the clause') relate to others under other headings in the framework. In restricting his attention to the clause, Fairclough can only make comments on what is clause-like about the headline. But this necessarily misrepresents the nature of the headline as such: the fact that it is always part of a larger text, and that its discursive function is to attract immediate attention. Hence the use of capitals, and hence, one might suggest, the use of the metaphorical *Rolls Back* and of the phrase *Red Army* which links alliteratively with it, and is more evocative than the alternative *Soviet Army*. So it is too that we cannot infer from its thematic structure as a clause what is to be topicalized in the text that follows, for the attention-seeking function of headlines makes them unreliable indicators of what the articles they are attached to are actually about.

The point is not that Fairclough's self-imposed restriction to the clause only provides a partial analysis, which could in principle be continued and complemented by taking other aspects of his framework into account. The point is that it misrepresents the very nature of the text by reducing it to a clause. What it exemplifies is what we might refer to as the *functional fallacy*. This is the assumption that semantic signification is directly projected as pragmatic significance in language use, that people make meaning by the simple expedient of activating the socially motivated linguistic encodings described in S/F linguistics.

Interestingly (and paradoxically) enough, Fairclough himself, in a passage immediately preceding the outline of his framework of analysis, points out the importance of distinguishing between meaning that is semantically encoded, and that which is pragmatically realized:

> Another important distinction in relation to meaning is between the meaning potential of a text, and its interpretation. Texts are made up of forms which past discursive practice, condensed into conventions, has endowed with a meaning potential. The meaning potential of a form is generally heterogeneous, a complex of diverse, overlapping and sometimes contradictory meanings, ... so that texts are usually highly ambivalent and open to multiple interpretations. Interpreters usually reduce this potential ambivalence by opting for a particular meaning, or a small set of alternative meanings. Providing we bear in mind this dependence of meaning on interpretation, we can use 'meaning' both for the potential of forms, and for the meanings ascribed in interpretation. (ibid.:75)

What is curious is that having made this distinction so clearly, and having stressed its importance, Fairclough should then proceed to pay no heed to it. For it is precisely because encoded meaning always gives rise to various pragmatic interpretations that one cannot talk about a particular choice from the transitivity systems of the grammar expressing a particular ideational function in use, or why one cannot talk about a mood or a tense signifying of itself a particular position or perspective. Fairclough's approach to discourse analysis, at least as exemplified here, is, I would suggest, open to criticism precisely because he fails to act on the distinction which he makes so clearly in this passage, and does not bear in mind this dependence of meaning on interpretation. And it seems perverse to court conceptual confusion by not making terminologically explicit a distinction which is so crucial to the development of a coherent theory of discourse.

As said earlier in this chapter, CDA generally takes its descriptive bearings from S/F grammar, and the functional fallacy that informs the analysis we have just been considering can be traced back to its influence. This is not to say that S/F grammar could not serve as a basis for discourse analysis.

The kinds of pragmatic meaning that are *ascribed* to particular uses of language must be related to the semantic meanings which are *inscribed* in the grammar. The externalized functions are realizations, under various contextual and other conditions, of the internalized functions that constitute meaning potential. The question is how this potential gets realized under these different conditions. One might approach this question by the thorough and systematic application of the S/F model to the analysis of texts, seeking to show how semantically inscribed meanings get realized – extended, modified, nullified even – in pragmatic ascriptions. In this way, one might hope to demonstrate the relationship between the internal semantic and the external pragmatic functioning of language, and put discourse analysis (the relationship between what is said and what is done) on a more secure and rigorous footing.

But in CDA S/F is not applied in any such systematic way. According to Fowler, it 'provides the theoretical underpinning for critical linguistics' (Fowler 1996a:5). The underpinning, however, seems somewhat insecure, for he goes on to say that actually S/F linguistics is rather too detailed and complicated for application, and that 'In practice, critical linguists get a very high mileage out of a small selection of linguistic concepts such as transitivity and nominalisation' (ibid.:8). CDA, then, does not involve the systematic application of S/F taken as a whole, but the expedient picking and choosing of whatever aspect of it seems useful for its purposes. And these purposes, as Fowler points out, might not be best served by S/F, but might call for picking and choosing from a varied assortment of other ideas, including those from speech act theory, Grice's co-operative principle, relevance theory, schema theory, prototype theory, and even the formalist theory of transformational-generative grammar. According to Fowler, ideas from all these areas, and others, can be pressed into useful service. 'It is just a matter', as he puts it, 'of bringing them within the critical linguistics model' (ibid.:11). This implies that there is already a critical linguistics model that these varied concepts can be brought within. But on Fowler's own account there is no such thing. Although, as we have seen, he does suggest at one point that S/F provides the necessary theoretical underpinning for a CDA model of description, he then finds it wanting. One can accept that all the concepts that are mentioned here might turn out to be useful in one way or another, but the crucial question is how they can be related and integrated into a theoretically coherent model of description? For, as Fowler himself acknowledges, without such a model, CDA reduces to a rather random enterprise. As he puts it:

> The original linguistic model, for all its loose ends, at least possessed a certain theoretical and methodological compactness, and I think it is important now to consolidate and develop this (essentially Hallidayan) model. If this is not done, the danger is that 'critical linguistics' in the hands of practitioners of diverse intellectual persuasions will come to mean loosely any politically well-intentioned analytic work on language and ideology, regardless of method, technical grasp of linguistic theory, or historical validity of interpretations. (Fowler 1996a:6)

Fairclough's formulation of 'a social theory of discourse', which we have been considering, can be seen as such an attempt at consolidation and development, and, as we have seen, it raises a number of difficulties. But Fairclough is not alone. Kress, for example, has also recognized the need for CDA activities to be explicitly informed by theoretical principles. As he puts it: 'It has become essential to take a decisive step towards the articulation of the theory of language, or communication, of semiosis, which is implied in these critical language activities, to develop an apt theory of language' (Kress 1996:15). What then does Kress have to propose in the way of an apt theory?

The Hallidayan concept that Kress gets high mileage from (to use Fowler's expression) is representation. This, in S/F grammar, is an alternative term for the ideational function that Fairclough comments on in his analysis of the headline we considered earlier: the clause as representation (Halliday 1994: chapter 5). But in Kress's scheme of things, this concept is linked to another which comes from an entirely different model of linguistic description, namely that of the transformation. This, as we have seen in chapter 1, is a device originally proposed by Harris, and taken up by Chomsky, for establishing formal equivalences across sentences. What Kress does is to press this formal device into functional service. Whereas for Harris, transformational operations do not tell us about 'what the author was about when he produced the text', for Kress they very definitely do. Like Fairclough, Kress would appear to subscribe to what I have called the functional fallacy in that he assumes that encoded meaning is carried intact into contextual use, that pragmatic significance is a direct function of semantic signification. What people mean by what they say is therefore signalled by their choice of wording, but since there are different options to choose from within the grammatical systems, analysis can reveal what could have been said but was not. Different wordings are different realizations of meaning potential and therefore, according to Kress, constitute different representations of reality, so that the transformation of one wording necessarily involves a transformation from one reality to another. We should note that in this scheme of things, representation is not a matter of how the transitivity sysems of S/F get realized: all three systems have a representational function. Thus a textual change of thematization, as in the use of the passive rather than the active, for example, would also have the effect of changing the representation of reality.

So, in developing his theory of language Kress gets high mileage from two concepts drawn from very different sources, transformation and representation. His model of analysis integrates the two, but only by changing them in quite fundamental ways. How, then, does the analysis work? A simple example is conveniently provided in Hodge and Kress 1993.[3] Here we find an analysis of a sentence taken from an editorial in the *Guardian* newspaper. It reads:

Picketing curtailed coal deliveries.

The authors point out that the nominalization at the beginning of the sentence encodes a process without any indication of agency, or of finite time specification. Furthermore the affected entity is also nominalized, so there is no agency or time indicated here either. Alternative options are available in the language for making these features of the process explicit (e.g. 'strikers picket a factory', 'someone delivers coal') but the author has preferred to transform these into a nominalized version, and thereby to represent the event as something abstract and agentless. 'So', we are told, 'the focus of the expression has been altered by the speaker, our vision has been channelled and narrowed' (Hodge and Kress 1993:21).

By this kind of transformational analysis, Hodge and Kress tell us, we can reveal that underlying this apparently simple sentence there is 'considerable complexity, a varied history of transformations'. One question that naturally arises at this point is the nature of this history. History is a matter of sequential events. The suggestion seems to be that in this case it is traceable to authorial motivation, that the version that appears in print here is the result of a complicated process of considered choice through a range of alternatives. No empirical substantiation is offered for such a claim, and the analysis of itself cannot of course provide it. Indeed, the point is made that the complexity of these representational effects is so considerable as to be beyond the grasp of the ordinary language user:

As readers of this editorial we should have to be alert and willing to engage in mental exercise to get beyond the seductive simplicity of the final form, with just three entities, and seemingly precise relations, where everything seems to be there on the surface. If we add to the real complexity of the sentence the fact that the verb *curtail* is a comparative, meaning roughly provide not as much X as before, we can see that few commuters on the 8.05 from Brighton would have the energy to perform the mental gymnastics required. Especially as they would have to perform them not once, but just about a dozen times on every full line of newsprint that they scan. After all the crossword is there for mental exercise. (Hodge and Kress 1993:22)

The transformational process, then, apparently only works in one direction. The mental gymnastics required by the author in order to arrive at the final form are not replicated by the reader. This seems surprising on the face of it, since one might reasonably suppose that some readers on the 8.05 from Brighton would themselves have some experience of authorship. If the textual design of meaning has a transformational history, then why, one has to wonder, can it not be traced in interpretation? The suggestion is that the recovery of the 'real complexity'of a text, and therefore of the reality that it represents, is so deeply embedded that it is beyond the capability of the ordinary reader to prise it out, and can only be revealed by expert analysis.

There is actually not much evidence here that expert analysis can reveal it either. Hodge and Kress trace the transformational history of this single sentence, but we should note that the sentence does not actually occur as such in the text at all. It has itself been extracted from a passage that reads as follows:

The Government knows that in early 1972 it was caught out by picketing in power stations which curtailed coal deliveries.

Now if structural differences always and inevitably signal different representations of reality, then we must surely take into account other structural facts in the original text: the fact, for example, that *picketing* is followed by a prepositional phrase and is itself a noun phrase constituent, that *curtailed coal deliveries* occurs as part of a relative clause, and so on. It follows, on the testimony of Hodge and Kress themselves, that the reality represented in the text is of a different kind from that which they assign to their own derived version.

It might be suggested that these structural features of the original are of no real significance and so can be disregarded, but no criteria are given for deciding which textual features are significant and which are not. On the contrary, according to the theory, all of them are significant; all are, as Kress puts it, 'ideologically saturated' (Kress 1992:174). And since 'transformations always involve suppression and/or distortion' (Hodge and Kress 1993:35), we can only conclude that by abstracting and isolating this sentence from its structural dependencies in the text, Hodge and Kress have in effect suppressed and distorted what the text itself represents.

But if transformations always result in some deformation of meaning, there must presumably be primary untransformed structures somewhere which capture this meaning in a primordial undistorted state. It is not clear, however, what such structures consist of, whether they make an actual textual appearance and, if so, how we would recognize them. What, one wonders, would an untransformed text look like? In practice it is difficult to find *any* part of a text that cannot be analysed into an alternative version and provided with a transformational history. The analysis seems endless, and it is no wonder that we are only offered a fragment or two by way of illustration. But the analysis of isolated fragments does not of its nature tell us anything about how they function in the text as a whole. As we have seen earlier (in chapter 4) textual parts contract internal co-textual relations with other parts, and with external contextual factors in all manner of ways. The only relations that Hodge and Kress are concerned with are the transformational ones that hold between constituent parts of structures abstracted from their function as textual components. In this respect, this is not an analysis of text at all.

In assigning every transformation a representative significance, Hodge and Kress take up what they call a 'strongly realist position': that is to say they 'regard all transformational analyses as hypothetical reconstructions of psychologically real processes' (Hodge and Kress 1993:35). This position is precisely that of the so-called derivational theory of complexity which flourished briefly in the 1960s (see note 5, chapter 3). This theory proposed that the complexity of a structure as indicated by its transformational history was a measure of the psychological effort needed to process it. The theory proved ephemeral. It lost its point when transformations themselves disappeared from the grammatical model on which it depended; and with them, of course, disappeared the criteria for establishing one structure as more basic or neutral than another. But empirical support for the theory had turned out to be elusive anyway. The main problem was that subjects were required to process sentences in isolation from any co-textual and contextual factors, in other words in exactly the way exemplified in the critical analysis we have just been considering. The cognitive demand made on the subjects turned out to be a function of this isolation, and changed quite markedly once the sentence was normalized by co-textual or contextual connection. In other words, the subjects were being asked to engage in a semantic analysis of linguistic constructs rather than to interpret them as pragmatic use, and not surprisingly, they found this essentially unrealistic task difficult to do.

But this is precisely the kind of mental exercise that the realist position requires and, as Hodge and Kress acknowledge, not one which readers are likely to have the inclination or capability to engage in. Yet this realist model is proposed not as just as a mode of analysis but as 'an approach to reading, a hermeneutic strategy' (Hodge and Kress 1993:160). It is, however, an approach to reading, on its proposers' own admission, that readers cannot realistically engage in. That being so, readers can never grasp the real significance of any text. This is only accessible by expert analysis, which will reveal meanings that readers ought to uncover from the text but regrettably never can.

The realist position makes the assumption that the interpretation of a text is a direct function of the analysis of its component parts, but not analysis only of what is apparent on the textual surface, but of a complex range of structural possibilities that lie beneath. It is an analysis of what is absent as well as what is present. Since there are so many parts, however, and so many transformational and other relationships beween them, the possibilities are endless. In practice, therefore, what happens is that the analyst takes a sampling from the text and scrutinizes it isolation, thereby stripping it of what makes it textual in the first place. The complex transformational history of this isolated fragment that such scrutiny expertly reveals is then said to constitute certain representations of reality. Since they are said to be revealed, and not invented, they are presumed to be there, concealed in the text all the time, though inaccessible to readers, who therefore lamentably fail to appreciate what texts really mean.

It would appear then that what CDA involves, as far as Hodge and Kress are concerned, is the assignment of pragmatic significance (the representation of a particular reality) to a fragment of language sampled from a text and cut off from its co-textual or contextual connections. The question now arises as to what motivates the sampling. What criteria are there for selecting one particular fragment rather than another? Fowler has noted, as we have seen, that CDA gets 'high mileage' from certain aspects of S/F grammar, particularly transitivity and nominalization. This raises the intriguing possibility that this high mileage is to be explained by some intrinsic property in the language itself: that there are certain encoded features (transitivity and nominalization among them) that have a greater pragmatic valency, so to speak, and are more resistant to co-textual and contextual modification. But such a possibility is ruled out by the CDA belief that no linguistic expression is ideologically neutral. All transformations suppress and distort, all language is loaded, 'ideologically saturated', as Kress puts it. So there is, apparently, no redundancy and no neutrality: every feature of a text will carry its own ideological charge. If this is so, of course, then there is no way of knowing how far the significance you assign to the fragment you have selected for treatment is or is not borne out by any other fragment you might have selected, but chose not to do so.

What is it, then, that motivates selection? As was noted at the beginning of this chapter, the work of CDA has a quite explicit socio-political pretext. As Kress himself puts it: 'The intention has been to bring a system of excessive inequalities of power into crisis by uncovering its workings and its effects through the analysis of potent cultural objects – texts – and thereby to help in achieving a more equitable social order' (Kress 1996:15).

As was argued in the preceding chapter, pretext will always come into play in interpretation, and will motivate the adjustment of focus on textual features, making some prominent, some peripheral. And so it is that pretext in CDA motivates the selection of features for special attention. The difficulty is, however, that this interpretative partiality inevitably leaves a vast amount of text unanalysed and unaccounted for. In consequence, what is uncovered are the workings and effects of texts on readers who are pretextually positioned to derive discourses from them which suit their purpose. In short, what we find in CDA are critical discourse *interpretations*. These may carry conviction with members of the same discourse community or others who share the same pretextual assumptions. But they cannot be validated by analysis.

As an example, consider the following treatment by van Dijk of an extract from the *Sun* newspaper (2 February 1989).

BRITAIN INVADED BY AN ARMY OF ILLEGALS
SUN *News Special*
By John Kay and Alison Bowyer

Britain is being swamped by a tide of illegal immigrants so desperate for a job that they will work for a pittance in our restaurants, cafes and nightclubs.

Immigration officers are being overwhelmed with work. Last year, 2,191 'illegals' were being nabbed and sent back home. But there are tens of thousands more, slaving behind bars, cleaning hotel rooms and working in kitchens. . . .

Illegals sneak in by:

- **DECEIVING** immigration officers when they are quizzed at airports.
- **DISAPPEARING** after their entry visas run out.
- **FORGING** work permits and other documents.
- **RUNNING** away from immigrant detention centres.

The first point to be noted perhaps is that anybody familiar with the *Sun* newspaper will bring clear pretextual presuppositions about it. They would know that it is designed to appeal to populist nationalistic sentiment and depends on direct impact rather than on any subtlety of argument or verbal nuance. The authors here do not disguise their negative attitude to immigrants and readers will readily recognize it (whether they actually share it or not). The article is tendentious: thus, as van Dijk himself points out, there is no mention of the employers who encourage and exploit illegal immigration. The purpose of the article is to express popular opinion (or pander to it, depending on your point of view), not to present a rational account. Readers familiar with the *Sun* would know this well enough, and would regulate their attention accordingly. They would not normally subject the text to close scrutiny to uncover its concealed significance, to find out what might be meant here other than what is explicitly said.

But van Dijk has his own pretextual agenda. This, however, is not to reveal any underlying significance that might have escaped the reader's notice. On the contrary, his purpose is to demonstrate by analysis that the racist attitude explicitly stated in the article is also, perhaps not surprisingly, implicit in the verbal texture itself. So he regulates his attention accordingly. However, there are features of this text that might be taken as counter-evidence of this attitude. Thus expressions like 'working for a pittance' and 'slaving', as van Dijk acknowledges, would seem to suggest 'commiseration with the immigrants'. One might suggest that here we have the textual indication of some underlying attitude not immediately apparent to the casual reader. But such a suggestion is not consistent with van Dijk's pretext, and so he proceeds to counter it:

> At the same time, the style of the rest of the article does not seem to confirm this journalistic mood in favour of the immigrants. Rather 'working for a pittance' also implies that 'since immigrants will do any job for any wage, they compete with white British workers'. Thus such a representation supports the familiar racist conclusion: 'They take away our jobs!' (van Dijk 1996:99)

But it is surely the purpose of critical analysis to go beyond what the style of an article *seems* to indicate by probing for evidence in the form of textual facts. The only textual fact that van Dijk examines here is the one expression *working for a pittance*. But he gives no critical attention to others which might be said to suggest sympathy with the immigrants: *slaving, desperate for a job*. One might, for example, following CDA procedure, enquire into the implications of the use of the second of these expressions. The term *slaving* (with its cognates *slave* and *slavery*) can surely be said to belong to the discredited discourse of overt racism which one imagines the newspaper would wish to avoid. We might suggest too that there is an ironic ambiguity here in the term *behind bars*, with its implication of imprisonment. It could, after all, be easily avoided (*serving/toiling in bars*). Van Dijk, however, pays no attention to these other expressions but focuses attention exclusively on *working for a pittance*.

Furthermore, this expression is taken in isolation from its co-textual connections. In the text, it is grammatically linked with the second of the phrases that van Dijk disregards: 'immigrants *so desperate for a job* that they will *work for a pittance*'. Thus one term expressive of sympathy is directly associated with another. No mention at all is made of this co-textual relation. Instead, van Dijk draws implications from the one expression that he does fix upon for which there is no textual evidence whatever, namely that immigrant workers are non-white, and that in working for a pittance they deprive white (but not non-white) British people of employment. There is nothing at all in the text that warrants these inferences: they are a function of van Dijk's reading of his own pretextual assumptions into it. And different assumptions could very easily yield quite different implications. Consider the observation made earlier that the article makes no mention of employers. We could argue that they are present nevertheless, by implication. Who, after all, owns these restaurants, cafes and nightclubs (all, we might note, symbolic of a wealthy and privileged lifestyle) and gives a mere pittance to the immigrants slaving at their menial tasks? True, there is no explicit mention of employers in the text, but then there is no explicit mention of white British workers either, and there is no reason why this should be evidence of covert significance in the one case but not in the other. Either you allow such inference of implication or you do not. You cannot have it both ways.

Van Dijk confines his comments to certain lexical features of this text, and makes no mention of its grammar. Thus, he says that the headline features 'three major negative expressions, usually associated with immigrants and refugees: "invaded", "army", and "illegals"' (van Dijk 1996:98).

Why these three expressions should be major is not explained, and no evidence (such as might be obtainable from a concordance) is given for these being 'usually associated with immigrants and refugees'. But the most obvious omission from his analysis is any comment at all on the way this headline is grammatically structured. Here we have a passive construction with the patient (Britain) thematized and the agent shifted into a prepositional phrase which is structurally dispensable. This, in Kress's terms, is a transformation, and so represents reality in a different way from the alternative non-transformed version:

BRITAIN INVADED BY AN ARMY OF ILLEGALS
AN ARMY OF ILLEGALS INVADES BRITAIN

So what, one might ask, motivates the authors' choice of the first version rather than the second?

According to Fairclough, as we have seen earlier, the passive version would have the effect of making *Britain* the topic and of making the agentivity of the *army of illegals* less prominent, almost indeed an optional extra. So the headline as actually worded would, on this account, seem to suggest a certain lack of active agentivity, and therefore responsibility, on the part of the immigrants. Van Dijk says that 'Obviously, as is the case of the use of "invaded" and "army", being "swamped" by a "tide" of "illegals" is just as threatening for the (white) British population, which is the primary audience for such style' (van Dijk 1996:98). But the use of particular grammatical forms is also part of style. And in the case of the headline here, the authors seem to have unaccountably selected a structure which gives less prominence to the threat. Furthermore, the reduced agentivity, and responsibility, of the immigrants can be seen as foregrounded by the metaphorical shift from an invading army to a swamping tide. And this second metaphor, we should note, also occurs in a passive structure in a position of secondary prominence and, what is more, is co-textually linked with just those phrases where, as van Dijk acknowledges, there 'seems to be a suggestion of commiseration with the immigrants'. If one is to use textual facts as indicators of attitude, then it seems reasonable to suggest that the immigrants are being represented here not so much as an active threat as victims acted upon by circumstances beyond their control.

So why, we must wonder, are textual features which, as we have seen, are focused on in other examples of CDA analysis, entirely disregarded here? One might argue that, in this particular case, they do not have the representational significance they have elsewhere, but then we need some explanation as to why this should be so. There is little point in proposing procedures for analysis, supposedly grounded in theory, which are then selectively applied at the whim of the analyst.

Kress, as we have seen, stresses how essential it is to articulate an apt theory of language to underpin critical analysis. Fairclough, in like manner, talks about 'the development of a new social theory which may include a new grammatical theory' (Fairclough 1995a:10). What such a theory amounts to, however, is very difficult to discern. Certainly the analyses that are offered provide no coherent exemplification of the theory at work – or of any other theory, if it comes to that. On the contrary, they exemplify no consistent analytic procedures at all. Although S/F grammar is referred to, it is not systematically applied: analysts simply take their pick of whatever grammatical and lexical features suit their pretextual purpose.[4]

Halliday has expressed the view: 'A discourse analysis that is not based on grammar is not an analysis at all, but simply a running commentary on the text' (Halliday 1994:xvi–xvii). But with the examples we have been considering, we do not even get a commentary on the text, but only on a few selected features of it. The text is taken to be a static patchwork and, as we have seen in the van Dijk example, analysis involves taking sample patches from it and assigning them special significance. Where there are features which seem on the face of it to provide possible counter-evidence against a favoured interpretation, they are downplayed, or passed over in silence.

There is nothing in the rationale of CDA that gives warrant to the kind of selective attention to textual features and selective inference of implication that characterize the analyses we have been considering. Indeed, such practices are not only inconsistent with CDA principles, but blatantly contradict them. The fact of the matter is, I would suggest, that the selective partiality of analysis in these cases is a function of pretextual purpose. What we are presented with is an interpretation regulated by pretext and the analysis is a pretence. Now of course, as with the text of the Declaration of Independence that was considered in the preceding chapter, it is perfectly natural for readers to process texts in this way. But then we need to be clear what the pretext is, and what partiality of interpretation it gives rise to. There is no reason why the partial interpretations that CDA provides should be preferred to any other: they claim a special authority only by the semblance of analysis.

And the apparent rigour with which the chosen features are analysed is, of course, very persuasive, particularly when allied to a pretext which is so obviously worthy. Another example will illustrate this. It comes from Fairclough's treatment of a television documentary about world poverty (Fairclough 1995b) which is extensively, and perceptively, discussed in O'Halloran 2003. Following the familiar CDA procedure we have already considered, Fairclough claims that the programme represents the poor as passive in that expressions that refer to them figure grammatically as Patients and not Actors. But at one point in the text, the poor apparently cease to be passive, and, inconveniently, take on the semantic role of Actor:

the poor people flock to the city

Fairclough gets round this difficulty by abandoning syntax as a criterion for passivity and turning to lexis instead: 'Interestingly, the Action here is one more usually associated with sheep – notoriously passive – than people, so the exception does not really contradict what I have said so far' (Fairclough 1995b:113). Fairclough assumes here that the usual association of the word *flock* with *sheep* will transfer intact into the text and prevail over any co-textual association it might contract there. But why then should it be the word *sheep* that accompanies *flock* into the text? For this word also denotes other groups: birds for example, and indeed people, which are not at all 'notoriously passive'. Furthermore, since the word *people* is co-textually present, this would surely be the most likely association to be activated. As O'Halloran points out: 'Intuitively, both the immediate lexical environment of "flock" and the previous co-text effect closure on the possibility that "flock" refers to a collection of sheep' (O'Halloran 2003:69).

Now of course there will be occasions when a meaning which is imported into a text will prevail over co-textual influence, as in the obvious case of metaphor. And if it really were the case that the action of flocking is 'more usually associated with sheep' then one could argue that this counteracts the effect of the immediate lexical environment. As we have seen, the claim for 'usual association' cannot be sustained by appeal to the denotation of the word since this covers groups other than sheep. But it may be, of course, that one denotation is more commonly attested in texts than another, and strength of association might then be a function of co-textual relations, and measurable by reference to actual collocational co-occurrence such as a concordance would reveal. If Fairclough's claim of 'usual association' is supported by evidence of collocational frequency, then we might concede on these grounds that he has a case: the strength of habitual lexical association can be said to override the textual effect of a particular lexical environment.

With this in mind, I consulted the British National Corpus (BNC) and was provided with a random selection of 150 occurrences of the lemma FLOCK (from a total of 759), of which 124 give clear indications of meaning. Of these, 107 are nouns, and 50 are used in reference to sheep, although in no case does the collocation give any sign of an association with passivity. Thirty-nine of the nouns refer to birds. These quantitative facts do not really provide overwhelming justification for an ovine (as distinct from avian) reading of the word in this text. The remaining 18 nouns all refer to people: but of these 12 are in the figurative sense of 'congregation' (*The vicar wants his flock . . .*), which I suppose might suggest some degree of passivity, but others (referring to pressmen, fans, female relatives) decidedly do not. So far, the actual descriptive evidence gives no very secure warrant for the idea that the word *flock* is usually associated with passive sheep.

It might be argued, however, that this is not the relevant evidence since the 107 instances of the lemma so far mentioned are all nouns, whereas in the text that Fairclough is talking about it figures as a verb. Now as has been frequently demonstrated, different morphological forms and syntactic categories of a lemma may enter into different collocational patterns, so what is really relevant as evidence for the Fairclough assertion is the occurrence of flock as a verb. The BNC sample gives 17 instances of FLOCK as a verb. And every one of them describes human actions. Sheep do not flock (nor do birds for that matter), but people do. So on the evidence of this BNC sampling of actually attested occurrence, the action of flocking is not usually associated with sheep, it is usually associated with people, and pretty active unsheepish ones at that: railway enthusiasts, journalists, golf spectators, gold-diggers all flock. There is no textual evidence whatever for the usual association that Fairclough invokes, and on which his interpretation depends. On the contrary, it is the association with people that is usual: the expression *the poor flock to the city* is in actual (textual) fact collocationally entirely normal. Therefore it does not constitute an exception and so *does* really contradict what he has to say.

What we find frequently in CDA work, then, is essentially a pretextual partiality of interpretation which is given the appearance of analytic rigour. Although S/F grammar is invoked as the informing model for analysis, it is not systematically applied, but simply drawn upon as a post hoc expedient whenever it seems convenient to the pretextual purpose. It may well be that this is the only way in which this grammar can be used, since, as I argued in chapter 2, in spite of its claims, it cannot in principle account for the co-textual relations that grammatical and lexical elements contract with each other in particular texts. But it would be of interest to put the claims to empirical test by attempting text analysis by means of a thorough and systematic application of S/F grammar. This would at least give us some inkling as to how co-textual modification works. It might even, perhaps, give some indication as to whether there are lexicogrammatical features which are more functionally salient than others. Such features – who knows? – might turn out to correlate with those (like nominalization and transitivity) that CD analysts have found, for some (as yet at least) unaccountable reason, they can get most mileage out of.

In this chapter I have raised objections to the practices of CDA on the grounds that they provide interpretations which claim, implicitly or explicitly, to be based on a close analysis of textual features but which are actually pretextually motivated. Pretext, together with context, as I have argued in chapter 5, will always condition interpretation in one way or another and there is little point in pretending otherwise. Interpretation is a matter of deriving a discourse from the text, so it can never be a direct function of text analysis itself. But this does not invalidate such analysis. On the contrary, it provides it with its purpose. For since discourses are derived from a text, so they can be referred back to it. The point about text analysis is that it can reveal what it is about the linguistic features of a text that can give rise to variable interpretation. It is a process that language users do not generally engage in, concerned as they usually are with converging on the particular discourse interpretation that is contextually and pretextually relevant to them. Analysis is what analysts do. There is no reason why they should not, from time to time, depart from their brief and hazard the occasional suggestive interpretation, their own necessarily partial discourse version. If it is clear that this is all they are doing, then no harm is done. But if the analysis is to serve its purpose, it cannot simply be done selectively to provide interpretative support. It needs to follow clear principles of procedure and be as systematic and comprehensive as possible.

The examples of analysis we have considered in this chapter, however, are, on the contrary, unsystematic, and essentially unprincipled. Certain linguistic features are picked on and others ignored. Only a part of the lexicogrammar is taken as relevant in a particular case, but no criteria for relevance are provided. Furthermore, the very fixation on such features results in the disregard of how they might be co-textually modified, and since it is by virtue of such co-textual relations that a text is a text, as distinct from an aggregate of lexicogrammatical elements, it can be reasonably argued that these are not really examples of text analysis at all. This suggests that CDA might more profitably draw on an approach to linguistic description that deals with texts in their entirety and takes explicit account of co-textual relations. Corpus analysis is just such an approach, and this we turn to in the next chapter.

Notes

1   This has been identified by Titscher et al. (2000) as one of two approaches to CDA, the second being the 'Discourse-Historical Method' developed by Ruth Wodak and her colleagues. I discuss this second approach in chapter 8.
2   It should be noted that Fairclough rejects the view of discourse as 'the analysis of text structure above the sentence' (Fairclough 1995a:7) and has made a

distinction in principle between the two concepts, not, it would seem, greatly different from that I proposed in chapter 1: 'A text is a product rather than a process – a product of the process of text production. But I shall use the term *discourse* to refer to the whole process of social interaction of which a text is just a part. This process includes in addition to the text the process of production, of which the text is a product, and the process of interpretation, for which the text is a resource (Fairclough 1989:24). In practice, however, the distinction is more honoured in the breach than the observance, as will be evident from the examples of analysis in this chapter. And it does not seem to figure as having any key theoretical status in later work: there is no explicit mention of it, for example, in Chouliaraki and Fairclough 1999.

3   Although this is published as a second edition of Kress and Hodge 1979, it is in fact not a revision but a reprint of the earlier book with an extra chapter added at the end.

4   Luke, however, sees things very differently. From his perspective, the kind of analyses I have been considering in this chapter are not unsystematic at all, but on the contrary result from 'a principled and transparent shunting back and forth between the microanalysis of texts . . . and the macroanalysis of social formations, institutions, and power relations that these texts index and construct'. These analyses, he says, 'are based upon Hallidayan analysis of formal properties of text, beginning with systematic analysis of lexical resources and categories, moving through a targeted analysis of syntactic functions (e.g. transitivity, modality), building toward the analysis of genre and text metafunction (e.g. macropropositional analysis, exchange structure)' (Luke 2002:100–1). Shunting back and forth there certainly is, but it is hard to see how it could possibly be described as principled, transparent or systematic. Luke does not himself provide examples.

7

Text and corpus analysis

In the preceding chapter, I made the point that Fairclough's claim that *flock* is usually associated with sheep, which is crucial to his interpretation of the particular text in which the word appears, can be checked out against corpus evidence. If it turns out that the word *flock*, as verb, does indeed regularly collocate with *sheep*, then, although this may not be conclusive, it will provide some substantiation to the claim. My own informal sampling of BNC findings suggested that Fairclough's intuition about 'usual association' was not, in fact, borne out by collocational evidence. Although one needs to be wary of relying too exclusively on such evidence, for associative meanings will not always and necessarily find overt textual expression, it would seem only sensible to consult it when assigning significance to co-textual occurrences in particular texts.

And elsewhere, indeed, Fairclough does consult it: in his reworking of an analysis originally proposed in Downing (1990) of the following text from *Time* magazine about a student protest in South Africa: 'Exactly how and why a student protest became a killer riot may not be known until the conclusion of an elaborate enquiry that will be carried out by Justice Cillie, Judge President of the Transvaal.' Downing makes the comment:

> The text does not pronounce on the reason for this proclaimed transition from student protest to 'killer riot', but it is implied that the most sombre aspect of the event is to be found here, not in the behaviour of the regime's police and army in rioting against unarmed schoolchildren. 'African barbarism' seems to be lurking in the wings once more. (Downing 1990, quoted in Fairclough 1995a:195)

What Downing is suggesting here is that the account here is skewed in that the expression *killer riot* already presupposes a position favourable to the authorities, which the subsequent legal enquiry is only likely to confirm. But how this relates to 'African barbarism' is not made clear. Fairclough comments:

The key expression is, of course, *killer riot*. Since what Downing calls our 'mnemonic frameworks of definition' tell us that police and army don't riot but students do, *riot* implicitly puts the responsibility onto the students. But how is it that the script of 'African barbarism' seems to be 'lurking in the wings,' as Downing puts it? If it is lurking in the wings, that is because it is evoked by some feature of the text, and textual analysis should attempt to specify what it is that evokes this script. (Fairclough 1995a:196)

This indeed is what textual analysis should attempt to do. Here Fairclough points to what is central to the whole CDA enterprise, namely the providing of textual warrant for the kind of impressionistic judgement that Downing makes. If there is meaning lurking in the wings, it should be possible for analysis to track it down and force it to make an appearance on stage. We have considered various attempts at textual analysis to that end in the preceding chapter, and found them wanting. So what kind of analysis is offered in this case? It is, in fact, very much along the same lines as before, for there is no attempt to analyse this fragment in its entirety, let alone co-textually locate it within the larger text from which it is taken. Instead, as before, a particular single feature is fixed upon as significant. What brings about the evocation of 'African barbarism'? Fairclough goes on:

It is, I think, the unusual collocation of *killer* + *riot*. *Riot*, as I have suggested, places the responsibility on the students, and killer implies not just the production of fatalities on this occasion (*fatal riot* would have done that), but the involvement in the riot (and therefore the existence among the students) of those whose nature is to kill (which is the reputation of 'killer whales', and which is implied in locutions like 'he's a killer', 'killer on the loose'). (Fairclough 1995a:196)

Unlike the analysis we considered earlier, however, reference is now made not to a usual *association* of words (as with *flock* and *sheep*) but explicitly to an unusual *collocation*. In this case, recourse is made to corpus evidence and Fairclough appends an endnote to make this clear:

The examination of collocation of *killer* + lexical item in three million words of computerized corpus data available at Lancaster University (the Lancaster–Oslo–Bergen corpus, the Brown corpus and the Associated Press corpus) seems to bear this out, though the numbers are surprisingly small with only seven collocations in all. There are two instances of *killer dust*, one each of *killer earthquake*, *killer hurricane*, *killer rabbit* and *killer sub*. All of these involve the notion of that whose nature or function is to kill. There is one instance of *killer instinct*. (Fairclough 1995a.213)

But how far do these collocations actually bear out Fairclough's claim that the expression *killer riot* implies that those involved have a natural disposition to kill? Certainly the head words themselves carry no such implication: there is nothing in the semantics of these collocates which signifies such a notion. It may be that in some cases the use of these collocations is meant to imply an intrinsic killing nature or function, as when *killer dust* refers to asbestos, for example, or, in the case of *killer rabbits*, we are in the comical fantasy world of Monty Python. We might be able to infer such implications by reference to a concordance, which provides a wider co-textual setting for these expressions. Equally, reference to a concordance might reveal that these collocations do not involve the notion that Fairclough attributes to them. Thus reference to the British National Corpus of 100 million words reveals that all of the nine occurrences of *killer instinct* relate to sporting activities and essentially involve the notion of desire to win. Similarly a *killer punch* (two occurrences) and a *killer blow* (six occurrences) have nothing to do with killing at all.

So it would appear that corpus evidence does not bear out Fairclough's interpretation of what he has identified, without explanation, as the key term in this text. In fact, the only evidence he makes use of is the actual occurrence of these collocations and not what co-textual links they may contract such as a concordance would, in part at least, reveal. He seems to make the assumption that the word *killer* itself signifies an agent whose nature and function it is to kill, and that this transfers to whatever other word it is found to collocate with. In short, although he makes reference to collocation and corpus findings, his interpretation depends on ignoring them. This seems to be borne out by his parenthetical comment on the expression *fatal riot*. This, he says, could have been used (but was significantly avoided) if the writer simply wanted to imply that the riot caused fatalities. But although it is true that the word is most frequently used in that sense, so that such collocations as *fatal disease*, *fatal accident* and so on do indeed refer to fatalities, there are many collocations which do not. A casual look at the BNC again reveals that *fatal* also collocates with such words as *blow*, *damage*, *gamble*, *error*, *mistake*, *attraction*, *fascination*, where the concordance reveals that the collocations have no reference to fatality whatever. So *fatal riot*, we might suggest, would not necessarily have served the purpose here, since it might simply have been taken to mean something like 'disastrous' or even 'fateful'.

So although the textual analysis here draws on corpus data as evidence, it does so in an entirely haphazard manner. Fairclough would seem to use descriptions of text in the same selective and expedient way as he uses descriptions of grammar. The question that was posed about S/F grammar earlier applies equally to corpus analysis: what findings would emerge if it were to be applied in a thorough and systematic way? One answer is provided by the work of Stubbs (1994, 1996),[1] which attempts to show how just such an application can substantiate the assignment of the kind of ideological stance that CDA seeks to trace.

The first thing to note is that Stubbs's data consists of a large amount of text, two books in fact. He makes the point that the texts that analysts have customarily dealt with tend to be short and fragmentary. The analyses we have been considering can be said to exemplify this tendency. I have already noted that one disadvantage of dealing with fragments is that whatever cotextual relations they contract with the larger extent of text in which they are embedded are necessarily disregarded. The interpretation, therefore, is of something taken out of co-text, and out of context, and so necessarily suspect. But such analyses not only ignore how the fragment relates to the particular text from which it was taken, but also its relationship with conventions of usage in general. Clearly to say that a particular association or combination of words is usual or unusual is to make a comparative statement: a norm is presupposed. And this, of course, is where corpus descriptions are of particular relevance, for they can provide a norm, based on an extensive empirical account of actual usage, with which the expressions of a particular text can be compared and their degree of conformity measured.

Stubbs's data for analysis, then, consists of two books: both are secondary school textbooks but one deals with the geography of Britain in an apparently factual manner, and the other is written with the express purpose of raising awareness of environmental issues. His analysis is predicated on the familiar CDA axiom, derived from Halliday, that 'all linguistic usage encodes representations of the world. It is always possible to talk about the same thing in different ways, and the systematic use of different syntactic patterns encodes different points of view' (Stubbs 1996:130). This being so, the different ideological positions of these two books should be reflected in systematic differences in their syntax, 'in their different use', as Stubbs puts it, 'of the grammatical resources of English'.

However, the analysis does not attempt to deal with all 'the grammatical resources of English' that these texts draw upon: it actually restricts itself to only two. It is easy to understand why: it is clearly not feasible to scrutinize every syntactic and lexical feature of a text for its ideological significance, even if they are taken in isolation without regard to the crucial question of co-textual modification. This is true even of small texts, let alone the extensive ones that Stubbs is dealing with. So in practice what you have to do is to select certain features and disregard the rest, and this is what Stubbs does. He does not deal with the use in these books of the grammatical resources of English as a whole, but of two particular syntactic features. This seems a reasonable thing to do on the grounds of feasibility, but it has the unfortunate consequence that it undermines the principle upon which the analysis is supposedly based. For in selecting certain particular features, you in effect rule out the possibility that any of the disregarded parts of the text might have some relevance to the identification of ideological stance. This, however, hardly squares with the idea that 'all linguistic usage encodes representations of the world', for there is no way of knowing what other ideological significance might be found (lurking in the wings) in features other than the ones selected for special attention.

One of the syntactic features that Stubbs focuses on is ergativity. This is because he has hypothesized that the main ideological difference between the two books will lie in the way agency, and hence responsibility, is expressed, and since ergative structures are devices for encoding agentless action, these are identified, in advance, as key indicators of ideological stance. So if, for example, you want to describe something as just happening of its own accord, thereby avoiding reference to any specific cause, the ergative is at hand to enable you to do so (*The vase broke* (ergative) vs *Somebody broke the vase* (transitive)). If, therefore, it turns out that a text on, say, global warming makes disproportionate use of this ergative option in describing the phenomenon, one might infer that the author's intention is to avoid specifying who is responsible (it is just happening) and from this we can further infer ideological stance. But things are not so straightforward.

To begin with, ergativity is an abstraction that is lexically and grammatically realized in different ways. When ergativity occurs as an intransitive form, it cannot encode meaning unaided but must necessarily be lexically embodied, and combined with tense and aspect. For example, many of the instances cited by Stubbs exemplify ergative verbs combining with the perfective, as in:

1. **Factories have closed.**

   (Stubbs 1996:133)

The question naturally arises as to how far the significance assigned to expressions such as (1) is a function of the perfective combined with the ergative rather than of the ergative itself. If the significant feature is indeed ergativity, then this would presumably be equally significant in association with other grammatical features of the verb phrase. Now, as grammarians tell us, the perfective signals completed action relevant to the present. In other words it allows us to focus attention not on the process but on the result. If we want to focus attention on process, we have another grammatical aspect available in English, namely the progressive. Thus we can contrast, for example:

2. Factories have closed. (ergative perfective: result)
3. Factories have been closed. (passive perfective: result)
4. Factories are/were closing. (ergative progressive: process)
5. Factories are/were being closed. (passive progressive: process)

What it would be interesting to know is whether there is a tendency for ergative verbs to occur more commonly in the perfective rather than the progressive, and this is just the kind of textual fact, of course, that corpus analysis can readily provide. But it is not provided here.

One might speculate that the ergative effect that Stubbs identifies may have something to do with the fact that the intransitive perfective (2) and its passive counterpart (3) have a formal resemblance, in that the auxiliary *have* and the past participle are common to both: *factories have (been) closed.* Indeed, one might suggest that there is some correspondence, that the intransitive perfective is a sort of shortened version of the passive, so that it is easy (deceptively easy) to slip from one to the other. The intransitive progressive bears no such formal resemblance. We might expect, therefore, that if people wanted to avoid the implication of agency associated with the passive, they would, wherever possible, use their ergative verbs actively in combination with the progressive rather than perfective aspect. So it would be of some interest to identify which combinations actually occur in these two texts. But this is ruled out if ergativity is isolated as a feature.

This matter of formal resemblances brings us to another grammatical distinction which bears on ergativity. As already indicated, the progressive is used to focus on process, the perfective to focus on a resulting state of affairs. But (again as grammarians have routinely pointed out) we have another means in English for signalling a state of affairs in dissociation from any process which might have brought it about, thereby avoiding implication of causation or agency, namely the stative:

6. Factories are closed.

Since the stative, in common with the passive and perfective, makes use of the past participle, it is not always easy to distinguish, and is prone to ambiguity. Again, it depends on how it combines with other linguistic features, including the semantics of the lexical verb, and, of course, on co-textual factors. Thus example (6) here can be understood as a passive construction, and so as implying the possibility of an absent agent (*Factories are closed* (*by unscrupulous managers*)), or as a stative construction, with no such implication (*Factories are closed* (*on Sundays*)). In the first case, *closed* can be said to contrast with the verbal *opened*, but in the second the contrast is with the adjectival *open*. Precisely the same point can be made about Stubbs's own example ((3) above):

Factories have been closed/opened (by unscrupulous managers).

as distinct from

Factories have been closed/open (for years).

But it is clear that the stative needs to be distinguished from the passive since what it encodes is a state which is not a result, and which carries, therefore, no implication of process at all.

If we are to talk of grammatical usage as encoding different 'representations of the world' these are surely crucial distinctions. But Stubbs conflates them, and indeed, he admits as much:

I studied just three patterns:

(T)   transitive verb (VERB +NP)
(P)   passive (mainly BE+VERB-ed)
(I)   intransitive (VERB)

(Stubbs 1996:134–5)

But this allows for VERB in (T) and (I) and BE in (P) to be realized in any tense or aspect form, thereby disregarding any semantic effect different co-selected features might bring about. Furthermore, in relation to the distinction just discussed (and whatever the term 'mainly' might cover) there would be no way of knowing whether the occurrence of BE+VERB -ed signalled a stative or passive function.

The difficulty is, of course, that in this kind of analysis you cannot indulge in semantic subtleties if you cannot program your computer to identify them, and so you end up with those which are manifest in forms that can be counted. So it is that even BECOME + VERB -ed, which one would suppose could always be unambiguously assigned a stative meaning, gets counted as (and so counts as) a passive. Stubbs acknowledges this in an endnote in Stubbs 1994 (omitted in the version which appears in Stubbs 1996):

> Passive included constructions with BECOME and whiz-deletions (both infrequent). Further any form with BE plus -ed (plus, of course, other endings on irregular verbs, and plus phrases intervening between BE and past participle) was coded passive, with no distinction between stative and dynamic passives. For example, the following were both coded passive:
>
> during World War 2, aircraft factories were dispersed
> the clothing industry is now dispersed.
>
> (Stubbs 1994:220)

It seems clear then that priority is given to the kind of formally marked criteria that the computer can readily recognize. So the distinction between passive and stative is ruled out as irrelevant, it seems, because it is inconvenient to manage.

But it is hard to see how it can be irrelevant if ergativity is to be associated, as it explicitly is in this analysis, with matters of blame and responsibility. One might argue that since the ergative freely combines with both progressive and perfective aspect, it always carries implications of process and result, and so to some degree raises the question of causation. But since the stative encodes a state, it is at a further remove from causation, since you have first to infer an intervening process. If that is so, the stative might be said to encode a representation in which there is an even greater avoidance of implications of blame and responsibility. It goes beyond ergativity in the avoidance of causation or agency: it is not that this is the way things happen, but this is the way things are. It focuses on the status quo. It would appear that the very principle upon which this analysis is based, namely the assignment of significance to the occurrence of specific linguistic features, logically requires that the category of stative should be recognized, even if the computer cannot easily be programmed to recognize it.

In conflating stative and passive, Stubbs disregards the syntactic environment which activates one sense of the form rather than another. But it is just such an environment, we are told (in the 1994 version) which enables us to assign ideological significance: 'the syntax co-selected with ergative verbs is likely to be ideologically significant, given its relation to the expression of topicality, agency, causality and responsibility. Such facts [*sic*] are often discussed in critical linguistics' (Stubbs 1994:207). 'Such facts.' But which facts? Even if one restricts oneself to the syntax, and leaves lexical collocation out of account, it is precisely the effect of co-selected features that the analysis does not reveal, so we cannot take as given what 'its relation to the expression of topicality, agency, causality and responsibility' might be. The only fact we have is that certain selected formal features occur with a certain frequency. But it is not a fact that they are an index of ideological significance. It is true that critical linguistics often does discuss this as if it *were* a fact. That, as I sought to demonstrate in the previous chapter, is just the problem.

Although Stubbs's analysis deals with large quantities of textual data rather than small fragments of text, it nevertheless still focuses on items in isolation from their co-textual dependencies. As he himself says, it 'starts from the Hallidayan assumption that all linguistic usage encodes representations of the world' (Stubbs 1996:130) and this he takes as implying that whenever a particular syntactic pattern is produced, a particular point of view is expressed. Thus Stubbs would appear to subscribe to what I referred to in chapter 6 as the functional fallacy, which holds that semantic encodings are carried intact into pragmatic use. What he deals with is the quantitative occurrence of a particular grammatical form across texts, but not the co-textual co-occurrence of this form with others, or the qualitative effect of such co-occurrence, such as a concordance display might reveal. It is curious that he should not do so, since he makes extensive use of concordance evidence elsewhere in his work (e.g. Stubbs 1996, chapter 4). But in this analysis it appears that, like Fairclough, he makes the assumption that significance can be read off from separate linguistic items, be they lexical or grammatical, without regard to textual modification. One can, perhaps unkindly (but taking a leaf out of the critical linguist's book), read significance into the very title of his paper (in its original version): *Grammar, Text, and Ideology*. You read attitude or point of view off from the text which itself consists of grammatical units and so the point of view is encoded in the textual features which are the same as grammatical ones. That is to say, grammar encodes text encodes discourse.

So far, discussion has focused on the need to take internal co-textual relations into consideration if we are to account for how texts mean. But as I have argued earlier, a text is only a text at all if one infers intentionality and so recognizes its discourse implications. You cannot read off significance from text as if it were a simple projection from textual features, and you could not do so, even if you managed to account for their intratextual relations. For with discourse we have to consider not just co-textual but contextual relations, and these too, of course, as was demonstrated in chapter 3, have a crucial role to play.

To take one rather simple example: one might agree that in certain circumstances one can read evasion of responsibility into the intransitive use of the ergative verb in an expression like

7. Industrial premises and shops were closing.

because in this case there is a passive alternative available which encodes causation, namely:

8. Industrial premises and shops were being closed.

But if it were the intransitive alone which encoded such significance, then it would apply equally to an expression like

9. The shops in Oxford Street close at six.

An utterance such as (9), however, is surely less likely then (7) to be pragmatically interpreted as evasive and an example of ideological stance. This, one might suggest, is because in the case of (7), prompted by the compounding of 'industrial premises' and 'shops' within the same noun phrase and perhaps by the co-selected features of continuous aspect, we are likely to take the term *shops* as being pragmatically cognate with *industrial premises*, and knowing the world as we do, we therefore infer that in this case 'close' means 'close down'. But such meanings are surely less likely to be activated in the second case (9) because the expression invokes quite different contextual associations. Here shops are places where you buy things which have normal opening and closing hours.

Or (still with shops in mind) consider the case of a text consisting of a single word, like the notice CLOSED (see chapter 1). Here there are no intratextual relations which might lead us to assign it a stative or passive sense. But its extratextual location on the shop door leads us to understand it as a stative: it is the encoded contrast with *open* that is contextually activated, not that with *opened*. The shop is in a closed state, and nobody in their right mind, surely, no matter how critically disposed, would enquire into process or causation. The shop is closed and that's that. A *closed shop* as a fixed collocate, however, is another thing altogether, referring as it does to a business all of whose employees have to belong to a trade union. This has to do not with a shop door but a shop floor. Here we might be inclined to read *closed* as a passive and to invest it with ideological significance: a closed shop has been closed by somebody as matter of deliberate action, and it might be relevant to ask who it was and why. The text CLOSED on the door of a shop activates no such enquiry. And we might then suggest (if we were of a suspicious cast of mind) that the term *closed shop* was used precisely to invoke an analogy with the stative use on the shop door so as to 'naturalize' the concept and deflect any possible implications of agency: a closed shop is just a shop which is closed. But a reading of *closed* as a passive with ideological import depends on our knowledge of the particular trade union practice the phrase denotes, and on our own political values. Of course, in saying these things I am making appeal to plausible pragmatic uptake based on the notion of 'normal' contextual connection. And one would need to see whether second-person elicitation would provide corroboration of these readings. But the point is that we need to take note of how these other perspectives come into play in interpretation. The significance is not there in the text.

And indeed this is what Stubbs himself discovers. He discusses work done by Gerbig (1993) subsequent to his own: 'an identical analysis of ergative verbs on a different corpus' (Stubbs 1996:145). Gerbig's corpus consists of texts about ozone depletion. Some of these originated from an industrial source, where one might predict that responsibility would be evaded by using the ergative to imply that ozone depletion 'just happens' and other texts orginated from environmental groups, where one might expect the use of explicit causative expressions to figure more prominently. But it turns out that 'contrary to expectation' it is actually the environmental groups that exhibit more ergativity in their texts, so its occurrence did not in this case provide corroborative evidence of ideological stance. The interesting question, of course, is: why not? Stubbs comments: 'The explanations might lie in both what is taken for granted in the texts and in the different meanings expressed by ergativity' (Stubbs 1996:145). It is greatly to Stubbs's credit that he should keep his enquiry open in this way rather than foreclose on premature conclusions. But his comments here do not just indicate minor procedural flaws or incidental shortcomings which might be remedied the next time round. They seem to me to indicate major conceptual problems in the very nature of the analysis.

Of the explanations he refers to, the second is co-textual and relates to the points I have been making about the way grammatical features act upon each other. But, again, it is not a matter of identifying different meanings that are encoded by ergativity itself, as accounted for in a grammar, and then analysing them out of the data; it is a matter of recognizing the dynamic interplay of ergativity with other grammatical and lexical features that are 'co-selected' in the textual process.

The first explanation, 'what is taken for granted', concerns contextual and pretextual factors, and takes us beyond what a computer analysis can account for. As was discussed in the earlier chapters, all texts, as the trace of a discourse process, leave things unsaid which are assumed to be taken for granted so do not need to be said, either because they are deemed to be contextually given, or irrelevant to the pretextual purpose. The difficulty is, of course, as we have seen, is that these discoursal factors cannot be directly inferred from the textual facts. One needs to relate the text externally to the conditions of its production and reception.

Stubbs would seem to concede as much in the comments he makes on Gerbig's findings. As indeed does Fairclough. In the introduction to his own collection of critical analyses, he admits that 'The principle that textual analysis should be combined with analysis of practices of production and consumption has not been adequately operationalized in the papers collected here' (Fairclough 1995a:9). But this, as I have argued in this book, is a crucial principle, for without taking account of it one is not really dealing with discourse at all but only its textual trace. Corpus analysis clearly provides a vast amount of textual fact. It can indicate what is distinctive about the occurrences of the linguistic features, lexical and syntactic, in particular texts, by referring them to a more general norm of usage. It can reveal by concordance how certain features contract co-textual relations with others in patterns of collocation and colligation, and in this respect it can be said to be the continuation, and fulfilment, of Zellig Harris's original quest for textual regularities beyond the scope of conventional grammar.

So if a particular pattern of co-occurrence, whether collocation or colligation, is regularly attested across a range of texts, then there is an argument for saying that its typicality is so systematic that it is a property of the system. Thus if, on concordance evidence, a word is typically associated with a negative or positive prosody (see chapter 4, note 2), then these features can be said to be part of its conventional semantic meaning. Furthermore, a concordance reveals that words will often combine to form commonly occurring phrases which are formulaic in different degrees of fixity and so these combinations too can be taken as having a semantic character. Corpus analysis thereby provides for an 'empirical semantics' (Stubbs 2001b:162) based not on intuited encoded abstraction but on actually attested lexicogrammatical regularity. Stubbs makes the point that 'a major finding of corpus linguistics is that pragmatic meanings, including evaluative connotations, are more frequently conventionally encoded than is often realised' (Stubbs 2001b:153). We return here to the relationship, discussed in chapter 2, between text and grammar. What corpus analysis shows is conventional regularities in patterns of usage which go beyond the customary scope of grammatical statement – hence, in Sinclair's words 'the need to overhaul our linguistic systems'. In reference to S/F grammar, therefore, we can say that now that we have observed fact rather than speculative impression to depend on, it turns out that the relationship between function and system can be extended, and that more pragmatic functioning has been systematically encoded than was previously appreciated. But we are still left with the question of how these semantic functions get pragmatically realized in relation to wider co-textual connections and to contextual factors.

Corpus analysis does not, in my view, account for context. Stubbs, it would seem, takes a different view: 'To accuse corpus linguistics of ignoring context is strange, since it is essentially a theory of context: the essential tool is the concordance, where words are always studied in their contexts' (Stubbs 2001b:156). But what Stubbs is talking about here is not context as I have defined it, but co-text (see chapter 4), and it can be readily acknowledged that the findings of corpus linguistics do have theoretical implications for grammatical description (they call for an overhaul of descriptive systems, as Sinclair puts it). We can (following Halliday) take it that the function of the lexicogrammar is to encode recurrent and conventionally sanctioned aspects of contextual reality, both ideational and interpersonal. It would follow that these encodings as they occur in texts will narrow down the pragmatic possibilities of how particular expressions are to be interpreted. So a good deal of the context is pre-coded and therefore accounted for. But by no means all of it. One might say that what the language does is to provide the general semantic variables which are assigned pragmatic value in particular instances of use. To take one of Stubbs's own examples, nominalization encodes certain features of contextual reality in compacted form, but its pragmatic significance depends on how it is related to features of context that are left unencoded: 'Nominalization allows other information to be omitted, since a noun phrase does not mark tense, but again noun phrases have many functions' (Stubbs 2001b:159).

Quite so. The semantics of nominalization allows for a range of possible pragmatic realization. The question is how far contextual (and pretextual) factors condition such realization. As Stubbs points out: 'Both convention and interpretation are involved, but it is an empirical question to decide how much meaning is expressed by conventional form–meaning relations, and how much has to be inferred' (Stubbs 2001b:153). It is indeed an empirical question. But it is not one that can be resolved by the closer scrutiny of text. What text analysis can do, as Stubbs demonstrates, is to act as a corrective to the CDA tendency, discussed in the preceding chapter, to infer significance from isolated textual features. As he says, and as was argued in that chapter: 'no conclusion whatsoever can be drawn about the ideological function of an individual grammatical form, or even of a whole sequence, independently of textual organisation' (Stubbs 2001b:160). But the conclusions to be drawn from the facts of textual organization are also limited. As Stubbs acknowledges: 'I agree with Widdowson that interpretations and patterns of language use are quite different kinds of object. They imply, respectively, agency and structure, they exist on different time scales, and they are not reducible one to the other' (Stubbs 2001b:158). Or, as I would put it, the interpretation of text as discourse is not reducible to the analysis of textual patterning. And here we return once more to Zellig Harris. As I suggested earlier, corpus linguistics can be seen as a development from his original initiative. The kind of patterning that Harris was looking for was the covert one of underlying structural equivalences discoverable by transformation. Now, of course, by means of electronic technology, corpus analysis can reveal detailed patterning on the textual surface itself. But although its findings are infinitely more informative than anything Harris could have come up with, his comments on the limitations of analysis remain relevant: 'All this, however, is still distinct from an *interpretation* of the findings, which must take the meaning of morphemes into consideration and ask what the author was about when he produced the text. Such interpretation is obviously quite separate from the formal findings, although it may follow closely in the directions which the formal findings indicate' (Harris 1952:382).

Corpus analysis takes us beyond formal findings in the Harris sense and does indeed, as we have seen, 'take the meaning of morphemes into consideration', thereby extending the scope of semantics. But we are still left with the essential pragmatic question of 'what the author was about when he produced the text'. Harris, like Stubbs, recognizes that interpretation is quite distinct from the findings of analysis, though it may 'follow closely in the direction' they indicate. How far corpus findings do indeed point in the right direction remains an open question.[2] At all events, interpretation would not seem to follow *from* analysis in any directly inferential way. They are indeed, as Stubbs says 'two quite different kinds of object', 'not reducible one to the other'. It is therefore the nature of their relationship that is the crucial issue, and this, as we have seen, is far from straightforward.

Elsewhere, however, Stubbs seems to suggest, oddly enough, that it is. He proposes an analogy with geology: geologists and corpus linguists both deal with products, rocks and texts, and both are interested in the processes that brought them about. Since, however, these are not directly observable, they can only infer them from the products that are. But the analogy is misleading. For one thing, the discourse process that leaves a textual trace is accessible to observation in a way that the process of rock formation in the Pleistocene period clearly is not. More importantly with regard to the present discussion, geologists *can* presumably infer the process of rock formation directly by a detailed analysis of the rock, particularly with the aid of computer programs. We would know nothing of such geological processes otherwise. But the essential point is that corpus linguists cannot read process from product in an analogous manner: they cannot, as we have seen, directly infer contextual factors from co-textual ones, and use textual data as conclusive evidence of discourse. In short, for geologists the rock is indeed a reducible consequence of its formation, and the process is therefore directly deducible from the product. In their case, analysis does not just indicate the structure of rocks, but how they originated, so interpretation does indeed follow closely the direction that their findings indicate, and the more precise the analysis, the greater, presumably, the precision of interpretation. But as we have seen, text analysis is not like this: it does not yield direct evidence of the discourse process that gave rise to it. And that is just the problem.

Notes

1 Stubbs 1994 appears in revised form in Stubbs 1996.
2 A recent paper, O'Halloran and Coffin (2004), opens up a particularly suggestive avenue of enquiry into the use of corpus analysis as a means of constraining the under- and overinterpretation of text. The authors make the point that collocational regularities as revealed by a concordance can be taken as evidence of how readers are positioned by the text on the grounds that such regularities are in effect profiles of their habitual expectations. Thus these co-textual patterns can be seen as analogous to schemata, which represent contextual patterns of recurrence (see chapter 3). On this account, what meaning readers assign to a particular linguistic feature will be constrained by the co-textual relations they normally associate it with, and these will be revealed, at least in part, by a concordance. The authors make the point:

> In assessing how a text positions its target audience, we as analysts have to try to check the prospect of over-interpretation and under-interpretation, and especially so if the target audience does not include us as analysts. *Totally* removing the values we bring as analysts to the text in question is difficult to achieve if indeed it is possible at all. But if we make no attempt

to keep these in check, our analysis runs the risk of being merely narcissistic and would then lack generalisability – that is, we would only be analysing from our own perspective and so could not really claim that we are interpreting text positioning from the perspective of the general target readership.

In other words, corpus findings can serve as a corrective to pretextually determined interpretation. They provide at least something in the way of secure co-textual facts to consider and, as the authors say, 'enable the generation of constrained hypotheses about reader reception'. How closely interpretation will follow the directions they indicate (to refer again to Harris) remains, however, an open question. O'Halloran and Coffin stress that their work is 'text focused rather than discourse focused' and comment: 'Using corpora and the concordancer in the ways we have shown can help to capture the reader positioning of the text. But, we make no claim whatsover that we have captured reader interpretation. Empirical analysis would be needed for the latter given its variability' (O'Halloran and Coffin 2004:24–5). I return to the question of how such empirical analysis might be carried out in the concluding chapter of this book.

8

Analysis and interpretation

This book began with the distinction between discourse and text, and subsequent chapters have tried to follow through the implications of this distinction. The main issue that recurs throughout is the relationship between them, and essentially the extent to which the analysis of a text can, as Harris originally speculated that it might, provide directions as to how it is to be interpreted. The work in CDA discussed in the last two chapters provides little in the way of substantive support for such a speculation. Its procedures are indeed not designed to do so. Instead of the thoroughgoing and systematic analytic processing of text that Harris was proposing, we find a selective focusing on specific textual features. It is not that interpretation is inferred from the analysis, but that the analysis is expediently used in support of interpretation. In short, to refer once more to Harris, CDA routinely asserts what authors were about when they produced the text without actually submitting it to detailed analysis.

This approach to the interpretation of texts is not, then, a development from the Harris initiative. It is not, in fact, an extension of the scope of linguistic description but the adoption of procedures from a quite different tradition of enquiry into textual meaning. For the interpretative procedures of this selective and expedient kind have an established precedent in the practices of literary criticism. Just as Fairclough identifies the phrase *killer riot* as the 'key expression' in his interpretation of a newspaper text (see chapter 7), so literary critics will tend to fix on particular expressions in a poetic text as having key status and bearing a particular significance. Consider, for example, the following observations.

'The room was suddenly rich' – The 'suddenly' captures that sense of unheralded insight, a sharp tang of delight, which makes a moment permanently memorable. (on Louis MacNeice: *Snow*)

Phrases such as 'blaze of darkness', 'black lamps' and 'darkness is awake upon the dark' create a sense of living darkness, a mysterious, passionate life more vital than anything in this daylight world. The various images of light, the 'blaze', 'torch' and 'lamp' heighten the sense of darkness contrast. We feel the darkness envelop us like a flood of seawater at night, yet in the deeper dark await the arms Plutonic, promising some ultimate kind of fulfilment. (on D. H. Lawrence: *Bavarian Gentians*)

The images of gulls and seeds evoke a sense of the multitude of people who respond to this challenge and who come from all parts of the world. The verbs 'clung', 'lurch', 'floated' and 'walked' are full of energy and movement. People flock to this centre of crisis, where our sickness may be healed now, or not at all. (on W. H. Auden: *Spain 1937*)

As with the examples of CDA discussed in chapter 6, the assumption here is that there is an underlying meaning inherent in the text itself which is not directly accessible to readers, but which exegetic authority can reveal by assigning special significance to certain textual features. The kind of literary interpretation these three extracts exemplify goes under the name of practical criticism, and is representative of the 'hermeneutic side of literary criticism' that, as we noted in chapter 6, Fowler mentions as influential in the early days of CDA, and it is perhaps of some interest to note, therefore, that the seventh reprint of the book they are taken from (Cox and Dyson 1963) appeared in 1979, the same year as the first published ventures into CDA (Fowler et al. 1979, Kress and Hodge 1979). 'We, like the literary critics,' Fowler says, 'were working on the interpretation of discourse.' How then, was their critical linguistic work procedurally different from practical criticism? 'They were', he tells us, 'equipped with a better toolkit' (Fowler 1996a:4). They may have had a better toolkit at their disposal, in the form of a model of linguistic description, but the problem was, as we have seen, that they put it to very limited use.

So what distinguishes CDA from practical criticism is not, as one might be led to suppose, the rigour of its linguistic analysis and the more explicit demonstration of how such analysis can point in the direction of a better-founded basis for interpretation. The distinction lies not in the procedures that CD analysts use, for these are not essentially different from those of their literary precursors, but in the kinds of texts they apply these procedures to. Essentially what CDA did was to extend the scope of hermeneutics to non-literary texts.

Such an extension was given impetus, and warrant, by the view, gaining ground at about that time, that there was no real difference between literary and non-literary texts anyway. Eagleton puts it like this:

My own view is that it is most useful to see 'literature' as a name which people give from time to time for different reasons to certain kinds of writing within a whole field of what Michel Foucault has called 'discursive practices', and that if anything is to be an object of study it is this whole field of practices rather than just those sometimes obscurely labelled 'literature'. (Eagleton 1983:205)

Fowler takes the same view, and conflates literary criticism and critical linguistics into one area of enquiry which he labels with the term 'linguistic criticism', and he writes a book about it which bears this term as its title. In his preface to the second edition of that work, ten years later, Fowler makes his position quite plain: 'Linguistic criticism is an introduction to the critical study of discourse; the chief emphasis is on those works of language hailed as "literary", but I have tried to make it clear that all texts merit this sort of analysis, and that belief in an exclusive category "literature" or "literary language" is liable to prove a hindrance rather than a help' (Fowler 1996b:v). For both of these writers, so-called 'literature' (as the scare quotes further emphasize) has nothing distinctive about it: it is indeed only something that is so called. But why, one needs to ask, is it so called? People, Eagleton tells us, have 'different reasons' for calling certain kinds of writing 'literary', but he does not specify who these people are, or what these reasons might be. But if one is to engage in the study of 'discursive practices' or, in Fowler's terms, 'the critical study of discourse', the people who read texts and the attitudes they take up in their reading are crucial factors. As has been argued throughout this book, if you do not take them into account, you are not actually dealing with discourse at all, but only with text. The essential point here is that if people identify, name, or hail a particular text as literary, they are pretextually conditioned to read it in a particular way: if they read it as literature then that is what it is. One may accept that literary texts are not distinctive in themselves in terms of their linguistic features, that there is no such thing as 'literary language', but it does not follow at all that therefore there is no such thing as literary discourse. If you are going to study discourse or discursive practices, the reasons why people call some texts literary are central to your enquiry.

But of course, just as people in general have their reasons for distinguishing literary texts from texts of other kinds, so Fowler and Eagleton have their reasons for not doing so. They too have a pretext which prompts them to read texts in a certain way, for their purpose is to enquire not into the aesthetics of verbal art, but into its socio-political significance, and prompted by such a purpose, all texts can indeed be treated alike. Whether your data are a novel or a poem, a newspaper or a political pamphlet, you can always find evidence of ideological attitude if that is what you are looking for. One can accept that literary writers, wittingly or not, do necessarily express socio-political views and values in their texts and that it is a perfectly valid exercise to track these down. In this respect, literary writers are no different from writers of any other kind. But it does not follow that they might not be different in other respects. Accepting that there is a lowest common socio-political factor in all texts does not preclude recognizing other factors that are not common, but are distinctive of certain kinds of text which, for this very reason, are called literary.

CDA began by modifying the procedures of literary hermeneutics along more explicit linguistic lines and applying them to non-literary texts. But you can, of course, do one of these things and not the other. You can make hermeneutics more linguistically explicit but still confine yourself to literary texts, and this has indeed been done quite extensively in the area of enquiry known as stylistics. As Leech puts it, 'stylistics . . . may be regarded simply as the variety of discourse analysis dealing with literary discourse' (Leech 1983). If literature is not taken as being distinctive, however, then stylistics may be even more simply regarded as synonymous with discourse analysis in general. And if this is to be critical in the CDA sense, then stylistics too is essentially an enquiry into the socio-political significance of texts.

And this is indeed one direction that stylistics has taken over recent years. It still deals with so-called 'literature' but only as a kind of documentation of social values and beliefs and as such no different from any other textual data. As Carter and Simpson put it, in a book which heralds in this new era of socialized stylistics: 'Literary discourse analysis should seek to demonstrate the determining positions available within texts, and show how "meanings" and "interpretations of meanings" are always and inevitably discursively produced' (Carter and Simpson 1989:17).[1] To analyse literature as discursive production is to examine what 'socio-historical, culturally shaped' positions are taken up in texts with regard to 'issues of class, gender, socio-political determination and ideology'. Such analysis 'takes us beyond the traditional concern of stylistics with aesthetic values towards concern with the social and political ideologies encoded in texts' (Carter and Simpson 1989:16). And so indeed it does. But a number of rather problematic questions arise.

To begin with, what seems to be suggested here is that the second concern supersedes the first and is to be preferred as necessarily more valid. There is no recognition that a concern for aesthetic values, even if traditional, might also have its own validity. Stylistics has moved on, it would seem, away from aesthetic to ideological values, from poetics to politics, and thereby can claim to have much more relevant and significant things to say about human life. But this presupposes that social and political ideologies have a unique and overriding importance in human affairs and that everything else reduces to relative triviality, including individual experience. Language, Halliday tells us, is social semiotic; but it does not follow that in using it we are restricted to social conformity. Literature, Fowler tells us, is social discourse. But it is not only that. If it were the case that every literary work, or indeed every ordinary utterance we made, was an act of social conformity, then we would have few if any of the problems of interpretation that discourse analysts, critical or otherwise, have been grappling with.

One thing that discourse analysts will agree about, whatever their theoretical or ideological bent, is that all texts admit of variable interpretation. But if this is so, it follows that to typify a text as expressing a particular set of social or ideological values, as the token of a particular discourse type, is to foreclose on this variability. Texts are not produced by ideologies but individuals, and no matter what their socio-political allegiances may be, individuals vary. George Steiner has pertinent things to say on this point:

> Any model of communication is at the same time a model of translation, of a vertical or horizontal transfer of significance. No two historical epochs, no two social classes, no two localities use words and syntax to signify exactly the same things, to send identical signals of valuation and inference. Neither do two human beings. . . . Each communicatory gesture has a private residue. The 'personal lexicon' in every one of us inevitably qualifies the definitions, connotations, semantic moves current in public discourse. The concept of a normal or standard idiom is a statistically-based fiction. . . . The language of a community, however uniform its social contour, is an inexhaustibly multiple aggregate of speech-atoms, of finally irreducible personal meanings. (Steiner 1975:47)

A stylistics concerned with the 'social and political ideologies encoded in texts' would obviously focus attention on the contours of public discourse, and consider only those textual features which are symptomatic of such communal values. The private residue of personal meanings would be irrelevant, and indeed a distraction, for the expression of these values in public discourse depends on people ignoring the private residue. And of course the kind of literary discourse analysis that Carter and Simpson favour would ignore it too in its demonstration of the socially defined public positions and values which can be traced in literary texts. This approach to literary discourse has a long tradition and there have been innumerable studies which demonstrate how literary works reflect the 'social and political ideologies' prevailing at the time. This tradition has been revitalized over recent years. Indeed, according to Weber, it is distinctive of 'most contemporary movements in literary criticism' that they aim at 'contextualizing and historicizing the literary text' and he cites as examples studies which show how Aphra Behn's play *Oroonoko* 'can be interpreted with reference to the succession problems of the Catholic King James II' and how Mary Shelley's novel *Frankenstein* 'relates to the "monsters" unleashed by the French Revolution' (Weber 2002). No doubt literary texts can be read in this way, and the tracing of their underlying socio-political significance can be very revealing. But there seems to be no reason for supposing that this is their only, or even their primary, significance. A socio-political pretext for reading is no more or less valid than an aesthetic one. Both have their own justification.

But it is the socio-political pretext that is currently privileged, to such an extent that there is a common assumption that unless it is adopted, one will not understand the 'real' meaning of a literary text at all. A striking example of this assumption is provided by a recent article by Tom Paulin about Daniel Defoe's novel *Robinson Crusoe*. This can, like any novel, be read at different levels and will be understood by readers in different ways. At one level, the level, let us say, of plot, the meaning is readily accessible: the novel is about the trials and tribulations of a shipwrecked mariner, his struggle for survival, his ingenuity in adversity and so on. At this level, there will be a general consensus as to what the novel is about. At another level, however, let us call it of theme, readers might discern a significance underlying the narrative, and might read the novel as dealing with matters concerning the human condition in general: the nature of loneliness and self-sufficiency, the need to define one's own identity and how this necessarily involves relating self to other, thereby raising issues of dependency and dominance. But according to Paulin, if we read the novel in these ways, we will have failed to grasp its essential meaning. This is what he says:

> In 1830, a few months before he died in a Soho rooming-house, Hazlitt published a lengthy essay on a new biography of Daniel Defoe in the *Edinburgh Review*, where he remarked that in *Robinson Crusoe* Defoe abandoned the political and religious subjects he addressed in his pamphlets, and confined himself to 'unsophisticated views of nature and the human heart.' Hazlitt's misreading is not uncommon. The novel is seen as the archetypal Puritan adventure story, a self-sufficient fiction which transcends the controversies Defoe addresses in his journalism. This is rather like saying that TV programmes such as *Castaway* and *Big Brother* tell us nothing about the social moments that created them. Although some recent scholars have

noticed that Crusoe's rhetoric of absolutism and submission 'places the right and might of sovereignty in the office of the monarch', as Manuel Schonhorn puts it in *Defoe's Politics* (1991), his rather lopsided, overly monarchist study, critics tend to link the novel only intermittently to the historical period it covers, and have not succeeded in offering a critical view of the text as historical allegory or parable. If Hazlitt – one of Defoe's heirs and like him nourished in Dissenting culture – missed the point, it is not surprising that later readers have also failed to grasp that *Robinson Crusoe* is an epic account of the experience of the English Dissenters under the Restoration. (Paulin 2001:15)

Generations of readers of *Robinson Crusoe*, it would appear, have failed to understand its essential meaning. They have not grasped that it is really an 'historical allegory or parable' about English Dissenters. This is hardly surprising since such an understanding depends on a detailed knowledge of the history of the Restoration which few of them are likely to have brought to their reading. Even scholars equipped with the necessary historical knowledge and with expertise in critical analysis have 'missed the point'. Now, after nearly three hundred years, however, the truth about the novel is to be revealed.

Now one can allow that Paulin is a scholar of considerable critical acuity, but even so, it is difficult to accept that he has discovered the essential meaning of the novel, that has hitherto escaped the notice of everybody else. In fact, I would argue, he has discovered nothing of the kind. What he has done is to read his own meaning into the novel in accordance with his pretextual purpose, which is to treat it as 'historical allegory or parable'. He then proceeds in the rest of his article to pay selective attention to those features of the text which suit this purpose. In other words, he uses the text as a pretext for historical commentary. There is no reason why he should not do this if he so chooses, and taking this kind of socio-political tack on a text can obviously yield readings of considerable interest. But there is no reason either why these should be privileged as more valid than others informed by different pretextual assumptions. Just as the authors of the Declaration of Independence (discussed in chapter 5) use the term 'men' to refer only to a community of which they themselves are members, so when Paulin refers to 'readers' he presumably does not mean all readers but only those within the scholarly community whose pretextual purpose, like his own, is to link the novel with its historical period. It is not that other readers outside that community have failed to grasp the meaning of the novel, but simply that they have grasped a different one by focusing attention on other aspects of the text.

The different thematic meanings I mentioned earlier that readers might assign to a literary text are a function of their recognition that the text is a literary one. To refer again to Eagleton's remarks, if readers identify *Robinson Crusoe* as a work of literature, whatever their reasons might be, then they read it as such. Paulin tells us that Hazlitt was wrong to suppose that Defoe 'abandoned the political and religious subjects he addressed in his pamphlets', because they find expression in his novel. And Paulin accordingly finds this expression. But Defoe was a novelist as well as a journalist, and *Robinson Crusoe* is a novel, not a pamphlet, and although one might call them both 'discursive practices' they are surely discursive practices of a very different kind. Even if we accept that Defoe was expressing these subjects in his fiction in some way, he was obviously not addressing them in the usual sense, for if he were, it is hardly likely that they would have remained unnoticed over three hundred years. Hazlitt, himself, we are told, was 'one of Defoe's heirs and like him nourished in the Dissenting culture', and yet he too 'missed the point'. Why, one wonders, was Hazlitt so obtuse? One must suppose that, like generations of other readers, he made the mistake of reading *Robinson Crusoe* as a work of fiction rather than as a political pamphlet.

All texts give rise to diverse interpretations, as we have seen, depending on contextual and pretextual conditions. What is distinctive about literary texts, I would argue, is that they provoke diversity by their very generic design in that they do not directly *refer* to social and institutionalized versions of reality but *represent* an alternative order that can only be individually apprehended. They focus, to use Steiner's terms, not on social contours but on personal meanings. Of course such versions are recognized as resembling those which are socially constructed, for otherwise there would be no way of engaging with them, but the relationship is one of correspondence, not direct connection. They represent a parallel and alternative world aesthetically conceived out of individual awareness. As such, they may well influence our perception of the conventional and socialized world and indeed inspire us to change it, but these I would see as incidental effects and not conditions of literary effectiveness. A novel, no matter how politically inspired, does not fail if it has no social consequence. A political pamphlet does.

If you want to address 'political and religious subjects' as matters of immediate social concern, you would be well advised to write a pamphlet or a tract which makes it plain that that is indeed what you are doing. If you write a fictionalized version of these matters in the form of a novel, then readers will read it as a novel and come up with their own diverse interpretations of what it is essentially about, which may be quite remote from your intentions. This is what Doris Lessing found readers did to her novel *The Golden Notebook*. In the preface to a new edition of her novel she has this to say:

> Ten years after I wrote it I can get, in one week, three letters about it . . . . One letter is entirely about the sex war, about man's inhumanity to woman, and woman's inhumanity to man, and the writer has produced pages and pages all about nothing else, for she – but not always a she – can't see anything else in the book.
>
> The second is about politics, probably from an old Red like myself, and he or she writes many pages about politics, and never mentions any other theme.
>
> These two letters used, when the book was, as it were, young, to be the most common.
>
> The third letter, once rare but now catching up on the others, is written by a man or woman who can see nothing in it but the theme of mental illness.
>
> But it is the same book.
>
> And naturally these incidents bring up again questions of what people see when they read a book, and why one person sees one pattern and nothing at all of another pattern, how odd it is to have, as author, such a clear picture of a book, that is seen so differently by its readers. (Lessing 1972:xix–xx)

'But it is the same book.' It is, in the sense that it is the same text, but clearly readers derive different discourse from it by reading into it their own thematic significance.

The themes they assign will no doubt be those which are socially prominent at the time of reading, but they will be those with which the readers identify as individuals. These diverse responses do indeed bring up questions of how people can discern such very different thematic patterns in a novel, but the answer has to do with the very nature of the novel as genre. Lessing seems surprised that her book should give rise to such diverse responses, and finds it odd that that these do not correspond with her own 'clear picture' of what the book is about. But there is nothing odd or surprising about this at all: on the contrary, it would be odd to find that all readers read it in the same way and were in agreement about its theme. If Lessing had written a pamphlet about politics, it would be surprising to find it interpreted as a treatise on mental illness, or vice versa, but she did not write a pamphlet or a treatise: she wrote a novel.

As did Daniel Defoe in writing *Robinson Crusoe*. So it is not surprising that, like *The Golden Notebook*, it should give rise to different responses. One may indeed, like Paulin, be able to discern in Defoe's novel the theme of religious dissent during the Restoration period, just as readers of Lessing's novel discern the themes of the sex war or mental illness. But readers who do not read such themes into the text have not therefore failed to grasp its essential significance. They are not any the less discerning: they have simple discerned something else. To suggest, as Paulin does, that readers have missed the meaning is to suppose that it is in the text itself, put there by the writer. But even if we had reason to believe that Defoe intended his novel to be 'an epic account of the English Dissenters', this does not mean that readers are bound by the intention or that any other reading of it is invalid. As the comments of Lessing make clear, readers are quite capable of inferring meanings that the writer did not intend at all. The point about novels, and about all literary texts, is that they transcend authorial intention and give rise to diverse meanings that cannot be pinned down. What a writer intended to represent is neither here nor there; it is what readers make of it that counts.[2]

All texts give rise to diverse interpretation incidentally, but literary texts of their very nature court diversity by denying direct reference to a socially constituted world and representing realities which cannot be accounted for in conventional terms. In this sense, the implication of diversity is intrinsic in their design. To suggest that a particular socio-historical reading captures some kind of primary significance lost to the unenlightened would seem to deny this intrinsic diversity and therefore the nature of literature itself. So I do not accept that the analysis of literature as social documentation is more valid than 'just' looking for aesthetic effects. I would argue, on the contrary, that such correspondences as are unearthed by the 'contemporary criticism' that Weber refers to are only significant to the extent that they do not constitute a direct reference to the actual world but contribute to the representation of an alternative one. It is when there is an assumption of direct reference, when representation is denied and the literary text becomes just like any other, that authors are held accountable and subject to persecution. Censorship, like the 'contemporary criticism' that Weber commends so highly, acts on the assumption that there is no such thing as literary representation but only social commentary that refers directly to the 'real' institutional world and so has to be held to social account.

What is of paramount importance for the kind of contemporary criticism that Weber refers to, and which Paulin's comments on Robinson Crusoe exemplify, is socio-political significance. In this respect, its treatment of literary texts is not essentially different from CDA's treatment of non-literary texts, as discussed in the preceding chapter. Indeed, as we have seen, no distinction is drawn between literary and other texts: they are all examples of 'discursive practices', and as such are all informed by socio-political purposes. But these purposes are not readily apparent and so they need to be revealed to the otherwise unsuspecting reader. The revelation is achieved by paying selective attention to those features of the text that are deemed to be symptomatic of the underlying discourse.

There is, however, an important difference between recent literary critical work and CDA, as these have been discussed so far, and this concerns the role of context. What Paulin does, and what, according to Weber, 'most contemporary movements of literary criticism' seek to do, is to 'contextualize and historicize' the text. But this, it was argued earlier, was what CD analysts signally fail to do, and one of the main criticisms levelled at their work in the last chapter was that it adduced textual evidence for interpretations without regard to the contextual conditions which gave rise to them, or those which might obtain in their interpretation. As was noted then, Fairclough himself acknowledges that insufficient attention was paid to what he refers to as the 'practices of production and consumption', and the crucial importance of context as a determining factor in discourse is emphasized elsewhere in his writing:

> Discourse is not produced without context and cannot be understood without taking context into consideration . . . utterances are only meaningful if we consider their use in a specific situation, if we understand the underlying conventions and rules, if we recognise the embedding in a certain culture and ideology, and most importantly, if we know what the discourse relates to in the past. (Fairclough and Wodak 1997:276)

Although the crucial importance of context is acknowledged in principle, there is little indication that it is taken seriously in practice in the CDA work of Fairclough and others considered in chapters 6 and 7. Here, as we have seen, the tendency is to infer discourse significance directly from the text. Indeed the assumption seems to be that it is actually *encoded* in linguistic form so that discourse interpretation is a function of textual analysis. With the CDA associated with the other author of the quotation given above, however, the case is quite different. The work of Ruth Wodak and her colleagues very definitely does take context into consideration and in this respect, as she herself points out, constitutes a quite different approach to CDA from that of Fairclough. This approach, what she calls the 'discourse-historical method', is, like the literary critical approach mentioned earlier, centrally concerned with the 'contextualizing and historicizing' of texts.

And here, of course, we make contact again with the issues discussed in chapter 3. The idea that language is essentially social action which can only be understood ethnographically in relation to a context of situation dates back to Malinowski, and it was Firth who first attempted to formulate this concept as a framework for the analysis of such action. Firth's distinction between the more immediate or local context of situation and the broader context of culture is also drawn by Wodak, although in the different terms of micro- and macro-context (Wodak 1996:20–2). In these respects, Wodak's discourse-historical method can be seen as taking up where Firth left off. But not surprisingly, informed as it is by developments in sociolinguistics and pragmatics over the intervening fifty years or so, there are considerable differences in the approach to analysis that is proposed.

It is, to begin with, much more specific. As was pointed out in chapter 3, one major difficulty with Firth's 'schematic construct' is that it is very general and vague. Thus reference is made, for example, to the 'relevant features of the participants: persons, personalities' but without any indication as to what kind of features these might be, and how one might assign relevance to them. Wodak, drawing on a wide range of sociological and sociolinguistic concepts, identifies such features more precisely in terms of the schematic constructs of culturally shared knowledge and values, which can be said to define the social person, and distinguishes these from features of personality as 'individual determinants' of context. In this way, 'persons', 'personalities', that simply occur in Firth as unexplained terms, can be assigned a conceptual significance, and one which, furthermore, can be taken as keying in with his distinction between contexts of situation and culture. For, as Wodak points out, whereas the broad macro-context of culture is relevant to an ethnographic account of generic typicality, discourse is actually realized in the local micro-context of situation with participants not simply playing out social roles, but acting as individuals. So it is not only that context is a pre-existing cultural construct to be applied, but also something that is created in the discourse process itself. As she puts it:

> The subjective experience of the individuals in an interaction has to be taken into account while analyzing discourse . . . . On the one hand, much necessary information is obtained through the ethnographic study; on the other hand, many markers and signals in the discourse itself manifest the speaker's perception and definition of context. Context is constructed and created through discourse, at the local level. (Wodak 1996:22)

Whereas Firth offers us a list of categories, Wodak develops a complex model of context designed in the form of different levels or concentric circles. This is how it is described:

> The smallest circle is the discourse unit itself and the micro-analysis of the text. The next circle consists of the speakers and audience, of the interactants with their various personality features, biographies and social roles. The next context level involves the 'objective setting', the location in time and space, the description of the situation. Then, the next circle signifies the institution in which the event takes place. And we could naturally expand to the society in which this institution is integrated, its function in society and its history. At all points, intertextuality is important; because of the specific problem under investigation, we should include other information which relates to our problem, such as other discourses of the same speakers, other events in the same institution, etc. The integration of all these context levels would then lead to an analysis of discourse as social practice. (Wodak 1996:21)

Wodak refers to this as a methodology, which would seem to imply that, unlike Firth, who just offers a schematic construct to apply, she intends this to be a procedural model which incorporates a mode of application. The proposal seems to be that analysis moves systematically through the levels or circles, presumably integrating them by adjusting findings from one level in the light of findings from the next. Or it may be that there are other methodological possibilities for integrating these context levels. Be that as it may, the question we need to consider is how this concentric model of context gets operationalized in the process of actual analysis. Fortunately, again unlike Firth's, the discourse-historical method that subscribes to this methodology has produced abundant samples of analysis for us to consider.

Unfortunately these do not provide much in the way of an explicit exemplification of the methodology proposed. There is no space to substantiate this by looking at a range of samples in detail, but it seems reasonable to take as representative an analysis that is specifically selected as illustrative of the approach by Wodak and her colleagues themselves. This is to be found in a chapter in Titscher, Meyer, Wodak and Vetter 2000 which sets out to identify what is distinctive about the discourse-historical method as compared with the approach to CDA taken by Fairclough. Among the principles adduced is that 'setting and context should be recorded as accurately as possible' and, although there is no explicit reference to the concentric model of context given above, one must assume that such accurate recording requires the systematic application of its procedures. A second principle concerns intertextuality, and here there is an explicit link with the model.

As there is with a third: 'texts must be described as precisely as possible at all linguistic levels', which, presumably, refers to the 'micro-analysis of text' that is said to take place at the 'smallest circle' of contextual analysis. We are then presented with an article from an Austrian newspaper and an English translation. We might reasonably expect that what is to follow is a demonstration of how the texts can be analysed in accordance with these principles and procedures.

But no such demonstration is provided. The setting and context, the detailed specification of which is said to be so crucial to this method of analysis, are summarized in one short paragraph. This, it is true, begins by situating the text in its historical setting: 'The text arises out of discussions concerning the housing of 800 Romanian refugees in the district of Kaisersteinbruch – the high point of an eighteen-month long discussion of Austria's responsibility to refugees and immigrants from the former Eastern Bloc.'

Here we have a degree of precision in the 'description of the situation': the number and nationality of refugees and the place where they were housed are both exactly specified. But the question arises, of course, as to why these particular details, and not others, should be identified as contextually significant. What is the relevance of the fact that these refugees are Romanian, rather than say Hungarian? And why is particular mention made of the district of Kaisersteinbruch? What Austrian readers of this text would know, but others probably would not, is that Kaisersteinbruch is situated near the borders with Slovakia and Hungary and is the site of a military barracks, which explains why the refugees are housed there. To refer to it as a district is not only imprecise, but actually quite misleading. In short, the recording of the situation to which this text relates is very sketchy indeed. We are not even told the date of publication of this article, so we cannot actually refer it to the geopolitical state of affairs obtaining at the time. For a method that insists on the primary importance of knowing 'what a discourse relates to in the past' this seems a particularly curious omission.

But this is only the first sentence of what purports to be the description of the setting and context of this article. What of the rest of it? The paragraph continues:

> There had been some discourse of sympathy and imposition of will from pro-revolutionary reports of the suffering of the Romanian people. This had already become a discourse concerning the expulsion of troublesome asylum-seekers. Because of this there arose a discourse of justification, in the sense that those whose sufferings had aroused sympathy were now to be excluded for matters of violence, crime and social parasitism. (Titscher et al. 2000:162)

What we are presented with here is not a description of contextual features at all, but an interpretation which leaves such features out of account altogether. If the authors were to be consistent with their own method, their conclusions here about different discourses would have to depend on a careful appraisal of contextual factors. But there is no indication here as to what contextual factors were considered nor how they gave warrant to their conclusions. What we have here, in short, is not the specification of setting and context as a necessary precondition on interpretation, but ready-made interpretations which, in effect, serve as a kind of pretextual priming, designed to dispose us to read this text in a particular way.

A similar disparity between principle and practice is evident too in the description of the text itself 'at all linguistic levels'. The themes of this article, for example, are said to 'reflect those of prejudiced migration debates at the international level' with its 'metaphors of threat' ('streams', 'floods', 'masses'). None of these terms, however, appears in this text, and so in this respect at least it clearly does *not* reflect these debates, and no other linguistic feature is given in evidence that it does. We are told that 'The complete text corpus, beyond this short sample text, displays a xenophobic attitude', but we are given no indication as to what linguistic features serve to display it. In fact only five linguistic features in the text are explicitly mentioned at all: the noun phrases *refugees, Eastern refugees, economic migrants*, which are said to be 'clearly marked by negative content', and *Eastern neighbours, asylum-seekers and refugees*, which are said to be 'vague formulations'. How *refugees* can be both clearly marked and vague at the same time, or why *Eastern neighbours* is vague but *Eastern refugees* is not, is left unexplained.

Such 'vague formulations', it is claimed, cast the refugees in an unfavourable light and in effect pander to prejudice against them. When one looks at the actual text, however, there is nothing vague about the description of refugees at all. On the contrary, it is markedly precise:

> Our country has had to cope with 3 great waves of refugees over the past 34 years:
>
> In 1956, after the Hungarian revolution, suppressed with considerable bloodshed, 182,432 people crossed its borders.
> In 1968 after the crushing of the Prague Spring, 162,000 Czechoslovaks fled to our territory.
> In 1981 after the imposition of martial law in Poland 33, 142 refugees sought political asylum. (quoted in Titscher et al. 2000:161)

No notice is taken in the analysis of what is surely particularly noticeable about this description, namely the exactitude with which the numbers of refugees from each country are cited, in two cases down to the last digit. But not only is there nothing vague about this description, there is nothing negative about it either. Even a perfunctory look at the grammatical level of this text reveals that each of the three sentences here is cut to the same structural pattern whereby what is thematized (in the grammatical sense) is the circumstances that caused these people to seek refuge in the first place, described in considerable detail. It seems reasonable to propose, therefore, that what is made prominent here is the oppression that the refugees suffered as victims. After all, there are alternative patterns available which could have been used to different effect. The text could have been written as follows:

> Our country has had to cope with 3 great waves of refugees over the past 34 years:
>
> 182,432 people crossed its borders after the Hungarian revolution in 1956. 162,000 Czechoslovaks fled to our territory after the Prague Spring in 1968. 33,142 refugees sought political asylum after the imposition of martial law in Poland in 1981.

If one wanted to lay emphasis on the sheer number of refugees involved ('streams', 'floods', 'masses') so as to imply a potential threat, and avoid any reference to anything that might induce sympathy with their plight, then this would surely be the preferred version. But the text under analysis takes a quite different form, and one which, on the face of it, would seem to express a very different attitude: one which presents the refugees in a much more positive and sympathetic light. So in reference to the point made earlier, the theme of the text, as indicated by its thematization, does not reflect that of 'prejudiced migration debates' in which refugees are represented as a threat, but exactly the opposite. It has to be said that it seems somewhat perverse to assign significance to a text on the basis of linguistic features that do not actually occur in it ('streams', 'floods', 'masses') and in disregard of linguistic features that do.[3]

The brief interpretative commentary that is provided on this text may have its merits, and may even carry conviction and so fulfil its pretextual purpose, but it cannot seriously claim to result from the systematic application of methodological procedures which yield an accurate record of setting and context, or a precise description of text at all linguistic levels. What in fact we are presented with here is not an analysis but an interpretation.[4] It may be, of course, that this interpretation is the result of an exhaustive analysis that we are not privy to, that the context of this newspaper article has been subjected to a rigorous analysis beforehand and that the text in the original has already been precisely described at all linguistic levels. But if we are to make any judgement on the validity of this approach, we obviously need to know just how the analytic findings give warrant to these particular discourse interpretations. There seems little point in providing such a complex theoretical and procedural apparatus for analysis without demonstrating how it actually works.

There seems to be a curious disparity between the highly elaborate theoretical 'framework' which is said to inform the discourse-historical method in principle, and the rather simple, even simplistic, results that it yields in practice. There is a parallel here with the other approach to CDA that was discussed in earlier chapters. This is said to be 'within the framework' of Halliday's S/F grammar but, as was noted, it does not apply this grammar with any degree of systematic rigour. In practice, as Fowler points out, what happens is that analysts of this persuasion get high mileage out of a few selected features of the grammar and leave the rest aside. The complexity of this model of linguistic description is not made operational. Similarly, having devised an extremely complex model of context, the discourse-historical approach then appears to avoid using it.

In consequence, what we are presented with is shown to be not the result of anything resembling a precise consideration of textual and contextual factors, but a reflex of pretextual purpose. Attention is paid to specific features of text and context, to be sure, but only selectively, as regulated by pretext. This kind of linguistic criticism actually bears a close resemblance to literary criticism as traditionally practised, as Fowler acknowledged in his account of CDA discussed earlier in this chapter (Fowler 1996a). In Fowler's view the essential difference lies in the fact that CDA, having 'a better toolkit', is able to achieve greater precision in describing the linguistic features of text. One might say that Wodak and her colleagues have developed a toolkit for the description of contextual features, which is an advance on Firth, who really provides no tools at all. But in both cases, though having an impressive toolkit at their disposal, analysts are not disposed to put it to any systematic use, so that in effect, and in practice, what is said to distinguish linguistic criticism from literary criticism disappears. In consequence, what CDA has to say about texts is not essentially different in kind from the examples of practical criticism cited at the beginning of this chapter. The pretext may be different, political on the one hand, aesthetic on the other, but what we find in both cases is impressionistic interpretation.

This may carry conviction and it may be innovative and insightful, even inspiring, but ultimately it can only be taken on trust, since it is not grounded in any principled methodology of analysis. There is of course the difference that literary criticism makes no claim that it is: no models of language or context are adduced as lending authority to interpretation. In CDA they are, but it is almost as if their purpose is to lend prestige and face validity to the critical enterprise rather than to serve as a procedural basis for analysis.

To suggest such a thing is perhaps to be needlessly provocative. Nevertheless, this marked disparity between what CDA, in both of its manifestations, claims to do in principle and what it does in practice calls for some explanation. I consider what possible explanation there might be in the next chapter.

Notes

1 The title of this publication is identical to that of Carter 1982 except that the term 'discourse' has been inserted, thereby implying that discourse is not taken into account in the earlier volume. Actually, it *is* taken into account, but not in the exclusively socio-political sense that was to become dominant by 1989. For further comment, see Widdowson 1992:192–3.

2 It is interesting to note that the intolerance of other readings which Paulin seems to express here is at odds with the attitude expressed in another of his texts: the following poem indeed would appear to ridicule the very process of assigning socio-political significance to literary texts that he himself practises.

Where Art is a Midwife

In the third decade of March,
A Tuesday in the town of Z

The censors are on day-release.
They must learn about literature.

There are things called ironies,
Also symbols, which carry meaning.

The types of ambiguity
Are as numerous as the enemies

Of the state. Formal and bourgeois,
Sonnets sing of the old order,

Its lost gardens where white ladies
Are served wine in the subtle shade.

This poem about a bear
Is not a poem about a bear.

It might be termed a satire
On a loyal friend. Do I need

To spell it out? Is it possible
That none of you can understand?
(Paulin 1993)

Censorship is, of course, testimony to the plurality of meanings that can be derived from the same text on different pretexts. A poem about a bear might well be taken as a satire, just as *Robinson Crusoe* can be read as an historical allegory about English Dissenters. But it does indeed need to be spelled out, and it is perfectly possible, and valid, to understand it differently, and a poem about a bear is still a poem about a bear, whatever further significance might be assigned to it.

3 It is perhaps also worth pointing out in passing that on the matter of precision of textual description, there is also, of course, the obvious difficulty here that a description of the translated text, precise or not, provides no secure basis anyway for assigning significance in the original.

4 One might suggest, using a distinction originally proposed in Fairclough (1989) and taken up in O'Halloran (2003), that what we are given here is not so much interpretation as explanation. Interpretation is defined as the on-line process of assigning meaning to the specific features of a text, which in the present case would presumably involve linking these features with particular contextual factors. Effectively, this stage is bypassed here and instead we are provided with an explanation, that is to say an account of the significance of this text in broader socio-cultural terms, unsupported by a description of the interpretative process on which the explanation is based.

9

Approach and method

As was noted at the end of the last chapter, although there is a good deal of discussion about models and procedures of analysis in the CDA literature, it is rare to find any explicit and systematic demonstration of their application. We find the statement 'Texts must be described as precisely as possible at all linguistic levels' (Titscher et al. 2000:160), but with no accompanying demonstration of how this has been, or even could be, actually done. We are told:

> What differentiates CDA from some Foucaultian versions of discourse analysis used by social scientists is that it is, in the terms of Fairclough (1992) a 'textually-oriented' discourse analysis, i.e. it anchors its analytical claims about discourses in close analysis of texts. Convincing social scientists of the value of CDA in social research is very much a matter of convincing them that detailed analysis of text will always enhance discourse analysis. (Chouliaraki and Fairclough 1999:152)

Since close and detailed analysis is said to be not only central to CDA, but what actually differentiates it from other kinds of discourse analysis, we would expect to find it abundantly exemplified in the literature. Given the importance of convincing social scientists of its value in social research, we would expect that Fairclough 1992, with its title *Discourse and Social Change*, would provide a particularly convincing demonstration of such analysis.

In this book Fairclough develops a theory of discourse as hegemonic struggle whereby power is exercised to construct social reality. One of the key concepts that is adduced to account for how this power is exercised is intertextuality. This is defined as 'the property texts have of being full of snatches of other texts, which may be explicitly demarcated or merged in and which the text may assimilate, contradict, ironically echo and so forth' (Chouliaraki and Fairclough 1999:199).[1]

Intertextuality, as defined here, is not easy to trace. There are times, it is true, when its occurrence is obvious, as in newspaper headlines like:

PRINCE TAKES ARMS AGAINST BAD ENGLISH

Here the word 'Prince' (which refers to the Prince of Wales) cues us to recognize the next three words as an obvious intertextual echo of Shakespeare's *Hamlet*. But there are innumerable cases where it is impossible to decide whether a sequence of three words, or even a longer stretch of text, is the 'snatch' of another, especially, of course, when it is 'merged in'. As corpus analysis reveals, all texts are composite of regularly occurring patterns (see chapter 6) and so they all have traces of other texts and in this sense they are all intertextually constructed. So when do we have a 'snatch' and when not?[2] We obviously need clear descriptive criteria to apply if the concept is to have any operational value. Establishing intertextual traces, then, is problematic enough, but Fairclough actually sets himself an even more difficult task. He is not only, or indeed primarily, interested in tracing textual features but in assigning them significance as realizing different attitudes, values, ideologies, in short as symptomatic of different discourses. It is actually not intertextuality as such he is concerned with but inter-discoursality, or inter-discursivity. The problem that intertextuality, as defined above, presents us is how we *identify* textual features. The problem of inter-discursivity is the even less tractable one of how these features, once identified, are to be *interpreted* as significant.

How then does Fairclough deal with these difficulties? Chapter 6 of Fairclough 1992 has the promising title 'Text Analysis: Constructing Social Reality'. In it (pp. 169–74) we find the following text which is to be subjected to analysis, taken from a booklet (*The Baby Book*) about pregnancy.

Antenatal care

The essential aim of antenatal care is to ensure that you go through pregnancy and labour in the peak of condition. Inevitably, therefore, it involves a series of examinations and tests throughout the course of your pregnancy. As mentioned above, antenatal care will be provided either by your local hospital or by your general practitioner, frequently working in cooperation with the hospital.

It is important to attend for your first examination as early as possible, since there may be minor disorders that the doctor can correct which will benefit the rest of your pregnancy. More particularly, having seen your doctor and booked in at a local hospital, you will usually receive the assurance that everything is proceeding normally.

The first visit

Your first visit involves a comprehensive review of your health through childhood and also right up to the time you became pregnant. Just occassionally [*sic*] women may suffer from certain medical disorders of which they are unaware – such as high blood pressure, diabetes and kidney disease. It is important for these problems to be identified at an early stage since they may seriously influence the course of the pregnancy.

The doctor and the midwife will also want to know about all your previous health problems, as well as discussing your social circumstances. We do know that social conditions can influence the outcome of the pregnancy. For this reason, they will ask you details about your housing, as well as your present job. In addition they will need to know if you smoke, drink alcohol or if you are taking any drugs which have been prescribed by your doctor or chemists. All of these substances can sometimes affect the development of a baby.

Examination

You will be weighed so that your subsequent weight gain can be assessed. Your height will be measured, since small women on the whole have a slightly smaller pelvis than tall women – which is not surprising. A complete physical examination will then be carried out which will include checking your breasts, heart, lungs, blood pressure, abdomen and pelvis. The purpose of this is to identify any abnormalities which might be present, but which so far have not caused you any problems. A vaginal examination will enable the pelvis to be assessed in order to check the condition of the uterus, cervix and the vagina. A cervical smear is also often taken at this time to exclude any early pre-cancerous change which rarely may be present.

A word or two first about the text itself. The first thing to note is that it is a fragment, so there is no way of knowing how it functions in relation to the rest of the booklet. Actually it is a series of fragments, for the three extracts that we have are discontinuous: a whole subsection between the second and third has, we are told, been omitted, though we are not told why. So the first point to make is that the data to be analysed has already, in a sense, been tampered with, and oddly enough in a way that precludes establishing intertextuality within the text itself. But not only is the sample a fragment, the analysis is fragmented too, for it starts not, as one might have expected, from the first section but from the last. Whatever reason there might be for this is not explained. There may be a procedural principle at work here, but since it is not made explicit, the analysis seems to be unsystematic. But how close and detailed is it?

The analysis of this third section reveals that there is a predominance of sentences which consist of two clauses (referred to, oddly enough, as simple sentences) expounding purpose and reason relations:

Clause 1 *so that/ since/ in order to/ to* Clause 2.

These are textual facts which nobody, I imagine, would wish to dispute. But this is what Fairclough refers to as the description dimension. The facts have now to be interpreted. There is the difficulty, though, that description itself to some degree implies interpretation. Fairclough himself points this out:

> Description is not as separate from interpretation as it is often assumed to be. As an analyst (and as an ordinary text interpreter) one is inevitably interpreting all the time, and there is no phrase of analysis which is pure description. Consequently, one's analysis of the text is 'shaped and coloured' by one's interpretation of its relationship to discourse processes and wider social processes. (Fairclough 1992:199)

But as has been pointed out in previous chapters of this book (and particularly in chapter 5) 'ordinary text interpreters' pay only very selective heed to textual features and so do not notice what underlying significance they might have. It is precisely this underlying significance that CDA claims to be able to reveal by analysis. But it now turns out that there is actually nothing separate or distinctive about analysis: the analyst too necessarily pays selective attention to textual features according to whether they are 'shaped and coloured' by interpretation. And since this is inevitable, the only close and detailed analysis there can be is of those features of it that interpretation has already singled out as significant. This would, of course, explain why these particular fragments were extracted from the whole text in the first place, and why the analysis does not proceed in the orderly, systematic fashion we might expect. The analysis is partial and selective because it is contingent on the interpretation.

But what then is the status of the interpretation? Fairclough as analyst is not in the position of the 'ordinary text interpreters' for whom the text is designed, so there is no reason to suppose that the necessary partiality of his interpretation corresponds with theirs. As O'Halloran and Coffin point out (see chapter 7, note 2), 'In assessing how a text positions its target audience, we as analysts have to try to check the prospect of over-interpretation and under-interpretation, and especially so if the target audience does not include us as analysts' (O'Halloran and Coffin 2004:24).

With this in mind, let us consider what interpretation Fairclough assigns to his description of clauses in this text: 'The message that comes across is one of re-assurance: everything that happens during antenatal care is there for a good reason.' This may be the message that comes across to Fairclough but he cannot know, of course, whether the same message comes across to the readers for whom this text was designed. For all he knows, they may not be reassured at all. One might reasonably conclude from internal textual evidence that the intended *illocutionary force* of this passage is explanation. But reassurance is a *perlocutionary effect*. The only way of finding out whether this is indeed the effect is to ask the pregnant women for whom it is written. One might even consider asking the producers whether this was intended. But you can only read such an effect off from the text like this by assuming a vicarious identity.

But the analyst here assumes not only the identity of the consumer but that of the producer as well. Fairclough sets out to demonstrate that there are two contending discourses here, given expression by two different 'voices': medico-scientific on the one hand, and what (borrowing from Habermas) he refers to as 'lifeworld' on the other. His description seeks to demonstrate that the dominant discourse is a medico-scientific one, and that the social reality of pregnancy is constructed in its terms. The pregnant women are positioned as compliant patients (grammatically and medically). The medical staff are in control. Evidence for this is said to be found in the second section of the extract where there is a shift from third to first person ('The doctor and midwife' to 'We'). This apparently makes it clear that the text is produced by medical staff: it is their voice which speaks. In the next piece of text, however, we are told there is evidence of two voices in the following sentence: 'Your height will be measured, since small women on the whole have a slightly smaller pelvis than tall women – which is not surprising.' Fairclough's interpretation runs as follows: 'the tagged-on comment "which is not surprising" comes across as the lifeworld voice of the prospective patient, or indeed of the medical staff in their non-professional capacities' (Fairclough 1992:172).

Again, we might ask 'Comes across to whom?' We just do not know whether this comes across to the prospective patients since they have not been consulted. But anyway, if this voice is indistinguishable from that of the medical staff 'in their non-professional capacities' how can we talk about two voices anyway? Are we to suppose that the medical voice is always uniform and unmodulated by lifeworld concerns, that medical staff in their professional capacities are necessarily and inevitably detached, objective, and technical in their treatment of patients? The analysis continues:

> But notice the contrast in voices between this and the second clause of the sentence ('since small women on the whole have a slightly smaller pelvis than tall women'), which is a reason clause. This is in the medical voice: 'pelvis' is a medical term, the clause consists of an authoritative assertion, which we take to be grounded in medico-scientific evidence. It is also far more typical of the extract as a whole: most reason clauses are in the medical voice.

What is it that characterizes this medical voice? What textual evidence can we adduce to identify it? Technical vocabulary perhaps? 'Pelvis' is identified as a medical term, which seems reasonable enough. But what of 'breasts', 'heart', ' lungs', ' blood pressure', 'abdomen'? Are these all medical terms as well? The point is, surely, that you cannot talk about pregnancy at all, in any voice, without using terms like this. So if the patients were to employ them would they too be using contrasting voices, enacting some hegemonic discursive struggle by using non-lifeworld capacities?

But if it is not lexis which is the defining feature, then what is? We are told that 'most reason clauses are in the medical voice'. Some are, then, and some are not. Which is which? We are not told, but unless we know what makes a reason clause medical as distinct from lifeworld, there is no way of knowing that the particular clause we are considering ('since small women on the whole have a slightly smaller pelvis than tall women') is 'far more typical of the extract as a whole' than the phrase 'which is not surprising'. What is it that makes it typical? We have no way of knowing because the type is left unspecified. We are told that 'this clause consists of an authoritative assertion, which we take to be grounded in medico-scientific evidence'. But the clause consists of nothing of the kind. It consists of linguistic constituents. Whether it is an assertion or not, and certainly whether it is an authoritative assertion or not, and how it is taken to be grounded, are interpretations based on an assumption of attitude assigned to the producer in advance. '. . . which we take as grounded . . .' Who is 'we'? Do the prospective patients take it in this way? There is no way of knowing, but Fairclough simply assumes that they do.

But we have not yet finished with this particular clause. The phrase 'on the whole' is singled out for comment: 'The hedging of the assertion ("on the whole") is interesting. On the one hand its vagueness suggests a shift into the voice of the lifeworld, while on the other it marks the cautious and circumspect ethos we associate with scientific medicine' (Fairclough 1992:173). In this case, it seems, there is no way of knowing which voice is operative. But even if we opted for the lifeworld interpretation, it could still be taken as the voice of medico-scientific authority, but subtly modulated so that it sounds as if it was not. Fairclough goes on to provide further evidence of this ruse. First he summarizes the findings of his analysis of the given extract: 'The clauses of reason or purpose, consistently cast in the voice of medicine, give the sort of rationalization and argumentation one would expect from medical staff, which contributes to the construction of medico-scientific ethos in the extract.' The clauses of reason and purpose, we should note, are now represented as *consistently* expressive of the medical voice: it is not just (as stated earlier) that *most* of them are cast in this idiom, *all* of them are. They contribute to 'the construction of a medico-scientific ethos'. What else contributes we are not told. But we are given an example of a text which contrasts with it. This reads as follows:

> Throughout your pregnancy you will have regular check-ups. . . . This is *to make sure that both you and the baby are fit and well, to check that the baby is developing properly,* and, *as far as possible to prevent anything going wrong.*

The italics are provided by Fairclough. He comments: 'The italicized expressions are evidently closer to the voice of the lifeworld than equivalent ones in *The Baby Book*' (Fairclough 1992:173). If these are evidently closer, what is the evidence? Why, one is bound to wonder, is 'check-up' not italicized as lifeworld (cf. the equivalent terms 'examination' and 'test', which figure in the medico-scientific *Baby Book*). Why, on the other hand are 'This is' and 'and' not italicized? How can the single use of 'and' mark a shift into a different voice? So in what respects exactly are these italicized expressions 'closer to the voice of the lifeworld'? To the extent that they comprise clauses of reason and purpose, one might suppose, on Fairclough's own argument, that they are just as close to the medical voice. Fairclough himself seems uncertain about their status. He continues: 'but I feel nevertheless that there is an ambivalence of voice in the *Pregnancy Book*.'

We might expect that reference might now be made to the clauses that have already been described, or to some other textual features, to lend support to this feeling. But we get nothing of the kind: 'The reason for this is that medical staff often do shift partly into a lifeworld voice when talking to patients . . . and the italicized expressions *could* be used by medical staff. It therefore remains unclear whether the producer of the *Pregnancy Book* is writing from the patient's perspective, or from that of (a 'modernizing' position among) medical staff' (Fairclough 1992:173). But this is an interpretation without description. It is simply an assertion, unfounded in this particular text. It remains unclear whether the text producer is using one voice or another because there are no clear textual criteria which would enable us to distinguish them. We would not know whether there is a shift or not, and even if we had convincing linguistic reasons to suppose there was, we would not know whether this textual shift implied a corresponding discourse shift, or was simply a rhetorical ploy.

The medical voice is elusive, and yet it is crucial to Fairclough's argument that it should be identified since not otherwise can he demonstrate intertextuality, and show how the discursive practices of authority position people by borrowing other voices, thereby exercising deception by disguise. So medical people pretend to adopt lifeworld values in much the same way as advertisers assume the guise of advisers and politicians adopt the idiom of ordinary talk. Fairclough's contention, and it is central to his theory of discourse and social change, is that people in power shift voices in subtle ways to exert their influence. In the present case, medical staff will assume a voice expressive of a patient perspective so as to keep them in their place.

The whole argument depends on the assumption that there are separate and distinguishable discourses. There is a community of social subjects, the medical staff which has its own distinct discourse expressive of its own distinct ethos. The position it adopts necessarily precludes the perspective of the patient, which is a different social subject, belonging to a different discourse – a lifeworld one. So although medical people may appear to adopt this perspective they do so only as a tactical ruse to win over the patient by a kind of covert intertextual colonization.

You can, of course, interpret these texts in this way, but the question is how far it is warranted by (or 'anchored in') textual analysis. As we have seen, Fairclough accepts that his analysis will always be 'shaped and coloured' by interpretation in some degree, and this is indeed borne out by the analyses we have been considering. But to what degree? How far does the licence run? Fairclough himself suggests an answer. There are, he says, two kinds of interpretation:

> Interpretation 1 is an inherent part of ordinary language use, which analysts, like anybody else, necessarily do: make meaning from / with spoken or written texts. People make meanings through an interplay between features of a text and the varying resources which they bring to the process of interpretation 1. Interpretation 2 is a matter of analysts seeking to show connections between

both properties of texts and practices of interpretation 1 in a particular social space, and wider social and cultural properties of that particular social space. Notice that interpretation 1 is part of the domain of interpretation 2; one concern of interpretation 2 is to investigate how different practices of interpretation 1 are socially, culturally and ideologically shaped. (Fairclough 1996:49–50)

It is clear from this that interpretation 1 is the normal pragmatic process that both analysts and ordinary interpreters engage in; and it is this that 'shapes and colours' description and results in what we might call analysis 1. But what CDA is concerned with is Interpretation 2.[3] This is apparently something that analysts alone come up with, and has to do with the social, cultural and ideological significance of texts. It is here that CDA claims to be distinctive as an approach to discourse analysis and to contribute something of value to social research. We need to note, however, that on Fairclough's own account above, interpretation 2 must, by definition, result from some mode of analysis which is free of the distorting influence of interpretation 1. In the absence of any explanation of just what this mode of analysis (analysis 2?) consists of, or how it would work, we can only suppose that it is meant to be exemplified by the practices we have been considering. But as we have seen, social significance (Interpretation 2) is assigned entirely on the basis of a single shaped and coloured analysis (Interpretation 1). It is certainly not based on an investigation of 'how different practices of interpretation 1 are socially, culturally and ideologically shaped'. The only practice on view is Fairclough's own. There is no consideration at all of how other 'ordinary text interpreters' might read this text. The assumption seems to be that they are bound to read it in the same way, or if not, perhaps, that they are reading it in the wrong way. The implication is that the distinction Fairclough himself makes between interpretation 1 and interpretation 2 does not apply in his case.

The question naturally arises as to whether the text can admit of an alternative analysis which might provide the basis for a different, if equally partial, interpretation. Let us consider the matter.

At the most general propositional level, we can say, uncontroversially, that this text is about pregnancy. Again uncontroversially, we can say that, as a matter of fact, this is both a physical process, something that involves the human body, and a personal experience, something that involves the individual human being. So there are obviously two very different ways of talking about it: objectively as fact, from the third-person perspective of the outsider observer; and subjectively as affect from the perspective of the first person, the insider participant. Medical staff naturally take up the first position, and prospective mothers the second: naturally, because these positions are determined by the nature of the process, not by any socially sanctioned assignment of role. But the purpose of the interaction between these parties is in some way to mediate between them. The prospective mothers need to know something about their bodies, the medical staff on the other hand can only talk to the human beings. Any medical text, therefore, is likely to have features which reflect this dual perspective.

So it is that in our present text we find a continual shifting from non-participant third-person to participant second-person reference which reflects a relative distancing from the concerns of the individual. The pregnant women are both addressed and talked about. Thus the participant phrases '*your* pregnancy', '*your* local hospital', '*your* general practitioner' co-occur with the non-participant equivalents '*the* doctor', '*a* local hospital', '*the* pregnancy'. But the participant expressions always come first and the non-participant ones take on a dependent anaphoric function. One way of interpreting these textual facts is to suggest that the writer's first concern is to acknowledge the insider perspective. Not all non-participant expressions are anaphoric, however. In the third extract, we find reference to both 'your pelvis' and 'the pelvis'. But the former is associated with 'your breasts, heart, lungs, blood pressure, abdomen' and the latter with 'the uterus, cervix and the vagina'. We might note that the former list becomes lexically more medical (compare the sequence: 'your abdomen, lungs, blood pressure, heart, breasts'), and this we might interpret as marking a gradual distancing into non-participant reference. This then becomes dominant in the second paragraph, where there is only one single occurrence of the second person ('which so far have not caused you any problems'). In this paragraph, we might suggest, the medical perspective takes over: appropriately enough, one might suggest, since this particular extract is, by its title, quite explicitly about examination. It is about human bodies, not human beings.

But the medical perspective, we should note, comes in the second, not the first paragraph of this third extract: again it is the participant perspective which comes first. This would account for the occurrence of the phrase 'which is not surprising'. For Fairclough, as we have seen, this is the interpolation of a contrasting lifeworld voice, a kind of 'slippage', like the occurrence of 'we' in the second extract. But they can both also be read as support for the participant orientation which is predominant in the paragraphs they occur in. Actually the paragraph in which 'we' appears is the second paragraph of this third extract, not the first, and it might seem that the principle of establishing participation before medical distancing is not evident in this case. But notice that participation is already keyed into the beginning of this first paragraph ('Your first visit', 'your health', 'you became pregnant'), and then in the remaining two sentences we find a shift entirely into the non-participant mode with no second-person presence whatever.

I am not saying that this is how the text should be interpreted. I am simply pointing out that there is a pattern discernible in this text which Fairclough makes no mention of, and which gives rise to a rather different interpretation of its purpose and possible effect: one which is more cooperative than conflictual, which invokes no hegemonic struggle, and which is rather more favourable to the medical profession. I would argue that Fairclough does not notice this pattern because he is looking for something else. And of course he might argue that I have only noticed it because I am determined to be contrary. This is probably true: I would not have subjected the text to scrutiny if he had not provoked me to do so. But this is just the point. We come to the same text with different contexts in mind and with different pretextual purposes, regulate our attention to textual features accordingly and so read our different discourses into it.

I would not make any claim that what I have offered here is a close and detailed analysis of the text, and certainly not that it has revealed anything significant about how social reality is structured. But Fairclough here does make such claims for a similarly selective and subjective exercise. The interesting thing is that elsewhere he expresses principles which actually oppose such practices, and ought to preclude them. For example: 'But texts may be open to different interpretations depending on the context and interpreter, which means that social meanings (including ideologies) of discourse cannot simply be read off from the text without considering patterns and variations in the social distribution, consumption and interpretation of the text' (Fairclough 1992:28). But later in the very same book we find the analyses that we have been considering above, where contextual factors are *not* taken into account, where different interpretations are *not* allowed for, but are subsumed within a single one, where social meanings *are* simply read off from the text.

We return to the question I posed at the end of the last chapter. Why is it that there is such an obvious disparity between the theoretical aspirations of CDA and its actual descriptive accomplishments, between what in principle it claims to do, and what it actually does in practice?

One reason for it, I think, might be attributed, in part at least, to the apparent confusion we find in the literature between the concepts of approach and method. In Wodak's writing the two terms are used interchangeably: her 'discourse-historical method', for example, is described as a different approach from that of Fairclough or his colleagues. Now although it seems reasonable to talk about an approach to analysis as being informed by certain theoretical ideas and indeed in conformity with certain ideological assumptions, to talk about a method of analysis implies a set of operational procedures, replicable in their application. One can evaluate the analytic validity of the findings as data to the extent that they are consistent with the procedures without regard to how they might be interpreted, which is a different matter altogether. A method makes an approach operational and provides data to be interpreted as evidence for its tenability.

CDA, as its proponents have always insisted, is an approach to discourse analysis that is ideological in intent. It is committed to the cause of social justice and its purpose is to expose exploitation and the abuse of power: 'CDA sees itself as politically involved research with an emancipatory requirement: it seeks to have an effect on social practice and social relationships' (Titscher et al. 2000:147). This is discourse analysis with a mission, a mode of political action. As such, it is interested in the language of texts only to the extent that it is symptomatic of something else, namely the underlying socio-political motives that inform it. In this respect, as an approach, it has, curiously enough, much in common with Chomskyan linguistics. Language is for Chomsky, as he himself acknowledges, an epiphenomenon, of interest only as a source of evidence for underlying mental processes. Linguistics, as he has famously put it, is for him a branch of cognitive psychology. But, as his detractors have pointed out, this means that all those aspects of language which have no bearing on this mentalist enquiry simply get left out of account. In like manner, CD analysts would appear to think of linguistics as a branch of political sociology and to pay similarly selective attention to those aspects of language that suit their particular line of enquiry.

Chomsky does not need a comprehensive account of what he calls Externalised or E-language to make his mentalist point. Such an account is, indeed, a distraction, as he has made abundantly clear. By the same token, one can argue that Fairclough, and others who subscribe to his approach to CDA, do not actually need a comprehensive grammatical description to make their political point. As we have seen (in chapters 6 and 7) although they routinely invoke S/F grammar as the authority for their analysis, they actually make very little use of it. But if they are 'politically involved', there is no reason why they should. The analysis of a text by way of a methodical application of S/F would simply distract them from their purpose.

Similarly, it might be suggested, the reason why the detailed model of context that Wodak provides is not actually implemented in practice is that it is simply not necessary to do so: interpretation can be assigned to a text without such close attention to contextual detail.

The discourse-historical method differs from the CDA associated with Fairclough in that its primary focus of attention is on context rather than text. But in both cases only certain features are attended to, and this, of course, is because the focus is adjusted to suit the purpose of the undertaking in the first place, which is explicitly to reveal, and remedy, prejudice and injustice. In short, the focus is regulated by pretext. In consequence, and in spite of its name, the discourse-historical method, like Fairclough's CDA, is not actually a method of analysis but an approach to interpretation. Such a characterization would seem on the face of it to be consistent with what Luke has to say of CDA in a recent, and highly favourable, review of its work: 'To treat CDA as a formalized corpus of analytic and methodological techniques might be to miss the point altogether. Critical discourse analysis is more akin to a repertoire of political, epistemic stances' (Luke 2002:97).

Nevertheless, Luke acknowledges that some link needs to be made between techniques and stances and indeed he asserts that the work of Fairclough and that of Wodak constitute 'major attempts to formalize and codify approaches'. 'These', he says, 'synthesize a corpus of text analytic techniques drawn from a number of related areas: systemic linguistics, sociolinguistics and the ethnography of communications, ethnomethodology, pragmatics and speech act analysis, and narrative text grammar analysis.'

This is an impressively comprehensive list of areas of linguistic enquiry, but although they are said to be related, there is no indication as to what the nature of this relationship might be, nor of how these different areas get synthesized into techniques of analysis. Luke provides neither explanation nor example. He continues: 'In turn, approaches to text analysis are integrated with concepts from contemporary social and cultural theory drawn, variously, from Frankfurt School critical theory, neoMarxist, poststructuralist and feminist cultural studies, Bourdieuan sociology, and, most recently postcolonial and multiculturalist theory. How we stitch these together into an intellectual, explicitly political project is the task at hand' (Luke 2002:98).

This is, to be sure, an imposing, not to say ostentatious, list of intellectual influences, but, again, we are not told how they are variously drawn on: 'variously' – that is to say, one assumes, selectively. But on what principled basis are these concepts selected? They are, we are informed, integrated with techniques for text analysis already synthesized, even though they have not yet, apparently, been 'stitched together', this being a 'political project' still to be undertaken.

So although Luke talks in laudatory terms about the formalization, codification, integration and synthesis that characterize work in CDA, he leaves us in the dark as to how these have been achieved, and provides no evidence by way of substantiation. We have to take his assertion on trust. He later tells us that 'Though they vary considerably in technical specification, there [*sic*] share a common strategy. CDA involves a principled and transparent shunting back and forth between the microanalysis of texts using varied tools of linguistic, semiotic, and literary analysis and the macroanalysis of social formations, institutions, and power relations that these texts index and construct' (Luke 2002:100).

As has been noted earlier (see chapter 6, note 3), on the evidence of analysis we have considered, the shunting back and forth are very far from principled and transparent. Indeed there is little in the way of analysis at all, either at a micro-linguistic or at a social macro level, let alone any systematic tracing of a relationship between them. Luke himself provides no illustration of this shunting strategy. Indeed, in his lengthy survey of developments in critical discourse analysis he provides not a single example of actual analysis of any kind.

One gets the distinct impression that the purpose of this survey is not, as one might expect, to explain or exemplify CDA but to promote it, and it is difficult to resist the conclusion that the theories adduced in its support are paraded to impress. Certainly it is hard to reconcile the ideal image of CDA as a coherent approach, with a method to match, with the examples of analysis we have been considering.

Luke makes the point that, as a result of advocacy, 'CDA has achieved some degree of stability, canonicity, and, indeed, conventionality', and so it has. But of course advocacy has to do with how persuasively a case is argued. The validity of the argument is a different matter. He adds that 'CDA has produced different, innovative analyses of a range of texts' and this we can readily concede. Its analyses are, to be sure, different and innovative, not to say inventive, and not infrequently suggest intriguing possibilities of interpretation. In this respect, indeed, they are very like their precursors in literary criticism. The central question, however, in respect to both literary and linguistic critical analysis, is how far their findings follow from replicable procedures, in short how methodically the approach can be applied. Later in the same paragraph from which the above quotations are taken, after listing (but not illustrating) a number of such innovative analyses, Luke comments: 'Graduate student theses openly declare CDA as a method and supervisors needn't look far for paradigmatically sympathetic examiners' (Luke 2002:99). But declaring CDA as a method does not make it one, any more than advocating it makes it valid.

As we have seen, just as there is no shortage in the CDA literature of references to theories that are, variously, drawn on to inform the approach, so there is no shortage of references either to models of analysis, of both text and context, that are drawn on, equally variously, to inform the method that makes it operational. The difficulty is in the shortage of explicit demonstration as to just *how* they are drawn on in any principled way. The evidence of the analyses considered earlier suggests that S/F grammar is simply put to expedient use to suit a pretextual purpose. Now, of course, all analysis is partial up to a point: one cannot exhaustively describe every textual feature, let alone the complex co-textual relations that such features contract with each other. There has to be selective attention. But it is precisely for this reason that we need a set of explicit methodological procedures. Similarly with context. As we saw earlier, Wodak distinguishes between the macro and micro levels of context. The former corresponds closely to a Malinowski perspective, the latter to that of Sperber and Wilson (see chapter 3). 'The goal of sociological investigations is to bring together these two dimensions in all their complexity' (Titscher et al. 2000:27). But it is then conceded that this is actually impossible. The passage continues:

> In specific analyses one can pursue the so-called 'discourse-sociolinguistic approach'. One [*sic*] the one hand a considerable amount of information is acquired through an ethnographic perspective, and on the other hand the discourse marks particular cases where the context is relevant. There remains a final problem, however: how can one decide how much contextual knowledge is necessary? Where does a context begin and end?

Where indeed? Some features of context, micro or macro, are relevant, necessary for analysis, and some are not. We are back to Firth, and to Sperber and Wilson and the familiar difficulty of defining the concept of relevance. For Titscher et al. this is a residual problem, mentioned almost as a footnote. But as we have seen from previous chapters (and particularly chapters 3 and 4) this problem is central to the whole enterprise of discourse analysis, and how it is resolved operationally will crucially determine what methodological procedures are to be applied and what kind of analysis will result as a consequence. Titscher et al. make no attempt to engage with this problem but content themselves with the comment: 'the aspects of context that are to be included and excluded must be precisely argued and justified within the concrete analysis of a particular case. And these decisions should take into consideration the theoretical questions posed by the analysis' (Titscher et al. 2000:28). It may be, of course, that the relevance problem does not admit of any methodological solution, and that all we can do is to follow the expedient procedure proposed by Titscher et al. but be quite explicit about our reasons for including certain aspects of context, and excluding others, in particular cases. To do so would at least allow for the possibility of other people proposing alternative analyses, and interpretations based on them, by including and excluding different aspects of context. But I submit there is little evidence in CDA analyses of this procedure at work. It is hard to find examples where such reasons are 'precisely argued and justified'. Typically there is no explanation provided at all as to why certain contextual, or textual, aspects are deemed to be relevant, nor why others have been excluded from consideration altogether. We are expected to take the analysis on trust.

Again, what critical discourse analysts say they do, or should do in principle, seems to be at variance with their practice. And again, one is led to surmise that the ideological commitment to a socio-political cause, which is so intrinsic to this critical approach, does not actually need explicit methodological procedures of this kind. If it can achieve its persuasive purpose otherwise, there is no point in precise argumentation or justification. Indeed, it can be plausibly argued, the development of a method of analysis which is explicit and replicable might well undermine the pretextual purpose of the approach in that it would allow for the possibility of alternative findings which did not support that purpose. After all, if your mission is to reveal the underlying truth of things, it will not be in your interests to provide people with the means for questioning the revelation.

It can be argued, then, that there is a fundamental, and necessary, contradiction between the approach of CDA and the methods it claims to apply, in that applying the methods would undermine the cause embodied in the approach. But at the same time, there has to be the appearance of methodological rigour to match the theoretical sophistication of the approach, for not otherwise would the analysis carry conviction.

And of course it is crucial to the approach that it should. When discussing the beginnings of CDA, Fowler expresses the concern that it might be 'a damaging admission' to acknowledge its development from literary criticism (Fowler 1996a:4). One can appreciate his concern: CDA would not want to be associated with mere 'aesthetic values' (to use Carter and Simpson's words quoted earlier), concerned as it is with the more significant quest for 'the social and political ideologies encoded in texts' (Carter and Simpson

1989:16). But, as I have argued earlier, although the pretext is different, the mode of interpretation is the same. In both cases what we get is, as Halliday puts it 'not an analysis at all, but simply a running commentary on the text' (Halliday 1994:xvi–xvii), and in both cases too the commentary is effective to the extent that it has *affective* appeal, that it carries conviction, resonates persuasively with the attitudes, emotions, values of the reader. And since it is the avowed pretextual mission of CDA, as an approach, to induce socio-political awareness and inspire social action, this kind of commentary is very well suited to its purpose. Promoting the cause of social justice does not depend on being methodical in analysis, nor even on being coherent in argument. The case for CDA is subservient to its cause, and if the case carries conviction that is all that counts.

So one way of countering the criticism I have been levelling at CDA in these chapters is simply to say that it is beside the point. The cause CDA espouses is so crucial to human well-being, one might suggest, that it transcends the rather tiresome conventions that constrain the conduct of academic enquiry. There is no reason why such conventions should be deferred to anyway: they are surely only those partial and privileged ways of representing reality which happen to be currently sanctioned by scholarly authority. In the present post-modern period, such authority, indeed any authority, is suspect. But it is not only that my criticism of CDA can be dismissed as based on a mistaken adherence to outmoded convention, it can also be understood as opposition to the cause itself. If furthering the cause depends on a denial of conventional standards of scholarship, this is a difficult if not impossible charge to counter.

But I do not think that it does depend on such a denial. I believe that one should question the value of scholarship that is closed off from real world concerns, and I entirely agree that it should engage with such pressing issues as social injustice and the abuse of power. But the only reason why anybody should pay any attention to what scholars have to say about such issues is that they are assumed to have the intellectual authority to do so, and this authority depends on an adherence to the principles of scholarly enquiry. The only way in which scholars as scholars can promote a cause is by presenting a case, and one which does not compromise these principles but conforms to them. The principles are not absolute and fixed, of course, and they necessarily can yield only partial truths about the world, but they do provide an agreed and relatively objective framework of reference within which ideas and procedures, claims and findings, can be evaluated. One might take the view that, in this day and age, they should be made subservient to socio-political values, and that the exposure of the evils of social injustice is too important to be hampered by academic convention: if this mission can be accomplished by persuasive rhetoric and expedient analysis, then so be it. But what if these devices fall into the wrong hands? For they can, of course, be used to further any cause, right-wing as well as left, democratic as well as dictatorial, evil as well as good. They are indeed the stock in trade of all polemic and propaganda, and have a long and by no means honourable history in human affairs. If people have the necessary conviction and commitment to a belief, they will always find their witch.

But let me make it clear once more that to say this is not to question the cause that CDA is committed to, or the integrity of its motives in exposing deception and the abuse of power. Now more than at any other time in history perhaps is it crucial to be critical about the way language is used, with sickening hypocrisy, for the distortion of truth and the suppression of human rights, and it is to the great credit of CDA that it has made us aware of this. But if the exposure is to be effective, underwritten by scholarly authority, it needs to be based on consistent principles and replicable procedures of analysis and interpretation. Otherwise, there is the obvious risk that the critical cause itself is discredited because of the shortcomings of the case presented in its support.

Notes

1 This is quoted in Chouliaraki and Fairclough 1999 but it is not entirely clear whether the formulation comes from Kristeva 1986 or Fairclough 1992. No page reference is given for either.

2 Here we have another case of CDA following the lead of literary criticism (see the discussion in chapter 8), which has long recognized the phenomenon of intertextuality. As Culler puts it: 'A major point on which there would be agreement . . . is that literary works are to be considered not as autonomous entities, "organic wholes", but as intertextual constructs: sequences which have meaning in relation to other texts which they take up, cite, parody, refute, or generally transform. A text can be read only in relation to other texts' (Culler 1981:38). What CDA does is to apply this literary critical principle to all texts. (For a discussion of the difficulty of establishing criteria for intertextuality, and generally making the concept operational in actual analysis, see Widdowson 1992:201–4.)

3 Interpretation 2 is what Fairclough elsewhere calls 'explanation'. See chapter 8, note 4.

10

Conclusion

This book has been an inquiry into issues which were first raised fifty years ago, and which have remained stubbornly problematic ever since. It all begins with Zellig Harris and his attempts to find patterns in text beyond those accounted for in sentence grammar. Since then developments in text analysis, particularly in the work of corpus linguistics, have revealed that there are indeed such patterns, but not of the kind that Harris envisaged. Harris sought to bring underlying patterns of morphological equivalence to light by transforming the structures that actually occurred in texts. The patterns revealed by corpus analysis are essentially lexical and not morphological, and they are present on the textual surface. The reason why they are not immediately apparent, and so need to be revealed, is not that they are invisible in the text but that they are unnoticed by text users. No transformational operations are required to change the textual data: all you need is a concordance which will display their regularities.

Harris can be credited with initiating the quest for texual patterning, but he was really looking for the wrong kind in the wrong place. The issue he originally raised about language beyond the sentence has now, we might say, been resolved, even if the nature of the resolution is not at all what he had in mind. There is, however, a second issue that Harris raises, and this seems to be as far from resolution as it was fifty years ago. This has to do with what bearing the findings of textual analysis have on interpretation. As we have seen, Harris suggested, optimistically, that interpretation might 'follow closely in the direction such findings indicate'. Subsequent work in discourse analysis does not provide much support for such optimism.

As we have seen, there has been no shortage of cases where discourse interpretation has followed closely on text analysis, but without the texts themselves being closely analysed. In the preceding chapters we have considered several examples which amply illustrate Toolan's criticism: 'Too often, an elaborate theoretical and interpretive superstructure is build upon the frailest of text-linguistic foundations' (Toolan 1997:93).

But the question arises as to what kind of text-linguistic analysis would provide a more substantial foundation for interpretation. Interpretation is the process of deriving a discourse from a text and will always be a function of the relationship between text, context and pretext. Any text has the semantic potential to mean many things, and which meaning gets pragmatically realized depends on how these other factors come into play. No matter how detailed the analysis of a particular text might be, the textual features that are activated in interpretation are only those which are perceived, consciously or not, to be contextually and pretextually relevant. If that is so, then what we need to enquire into is how different contexts and pretexts can act upon the same text to give rise to diverse interpretations.

The interpretations that CDA proposes, based on selective attention to certain textual features, are often very appealing. But the appeal, I have suggested, lies in the justness of the cause they espouse rather than in the analytic precision of the case made in support of it. And the appeal is all the harder to resist when the interpretations are presented as underwritten by impressive theoretical authority. CDA work is indeed imposing. But that, I would argue, is just the problem with it. One can admire the ingenuity of its practitioners, and acknowledge the inspirational insights they provide about possible meanings, even agree that they have identified in a text something significant that we were hitherto unaware of. In this respect what critical discourse analysts have to say about texts has very much the same effect, and the same value, as the similarly imposing interpretations of literary critics. In both cases, we may be inspired to follow their example, and their lead, by replicating their procedures to confirm their findings, or to conduct work of a comparable kind on other texts.

The difficulty is that there is so little in the way of explicit procedures for us to follow. Given a text, how do we set about analysing it? How do we know which features to focus on and which not? Context is crucial, we are told, but how is it crucial? Which aspects of context are relevant to which features of text? If it is the case that textual, contextual and pretextual factors are interdependently activated in interpretation, then a change in one of these factors will necessarily affect the significance of the others. So we surely need some procedures for identifying these factors and demonstrating their interdependency by proposing alternative interpretations, and alternative texts.

The need for explicit and workable procedures for analysis has not gone unnoticed. Here, for example, is what Fowler has to say on the matter:

> A comprehensive methodological guide, tailored to the needs of the discipline, on the lines of the last chapter of *Language and Control* [i.e. Fowler et al. 1979], is needed, but of course more formal and more extensive than that

early 'check list': a textbook specifically designed for the teaching of critical linguistics. Meanwhile, there is a need for published analyses to be more explicit, less allusive, about the tools they are employing. What I am saying is that we need to be more formal about method, both in order to improve the analytic technique, and to increase the population of competent practitioners. At the moment, students do not find it easy. (Fowler 1996a:8–9)[1]

As the title of their book indicates, Titscher et al. (2000) think of CDA as a method, but, as we have seen, their account of it comes nowhere near to being 'a comprehensive methodological guide'. Wodak describes her approach to CDA as a method and talks about methodology, but offers little more than a 'check list' by way of guidance as to how to make the method operational. Luke appears to believe that the need that Fowler identifies has already been met, referring as he does to 'a formalized corpus of analytic and methodological techniques' (Luke 2002:97),[2] though he gives no indication of what they are, let alone how they actually work. 'Graduate student theses openly declare CDA as a method', he tells us (Luke 2002:99). But if they lack the 'comprehensive methodological guide' that would make them 'competent practitioners', then one has to wonder what kind of theses these graduate students are producing, and what criteria the 'paradigmatically sympathetic examiners' are using to evaluate them.

One is led to expect that the approach, or theory, or stance, of CDA is to be supported by an explicit set of methodical procedures, and the question must arise as to why they are not forthcoming in its literature. I suggested in the last chapter that there may indeed be some significance in their absence in that if such procedures of analysis were provided they could be used to come up with findings in support of unwelcome alternative interpretations. But another, if related, reason for avoiding too much systematicity of method has been suggested. One of the subheadings in the first chapter of Chouliaraki and Fairclough (1999) is 'CDA – Theory or Method'. The authors assert that it is both. The theory, they say, 'is a shifting synthesis of other theories', and this being so, they argue, the method that relates to the theory must be similarly unfixed and unstable:

> Given our emphasis on the mutually informing development of theory and method, we do not support calls for stabilising a method for CDA (Fowler 1996; Toolan 1997). While such a stabilisation would have institutional and especially pedagogic advantages, it would compromise the developing capacity of CDA to shed light on the dialectic of the semiotic and the social in a wide variety of social practices by bringing to bear shifting sets of theoretical resources and shifting operationalisations of them. (Chouliaraki and Fairclough 1999:17)

Anything in the way of an agreed methodology is not only unnecessary for CDA, it appears, but inimical to its essential purpose. Its capacity for shedding light must be left to range like a free spirit unconstrained by methodological routine. Or even, it would seem, by theoretical consistency, for with such continual shifting there can clearly be no settling into a stable theory either. We are left with nothing that is secure enough to take our bearings from. It is difficult to see how CDA in this view can be based on any secure guiding principles at all. Stabilization of method, Chouliaraki and Fairclough concede, would have institutional and pedagogic advantages (not the least of which, as has already been noted, is that it would enable people to do their own analyses and come to their own conclusions). But such stabilization of method, and theory, is not just an advantage, which one might dispense with, but the essential condition of any kind of rational and empirical enquiry. It sets the terms for accountability and without it any light that CDA sheds can really only be the reflection of subjective attitude.

Of course, to return to a point touched on in the last chapter, what I have said about the shortcomings of CDA here (and elsewhere) assumes the validity of established conventions of academic enquiry. But this validity can be questioned. The approach that CDA takes may claim to be informed by a quite different set of assumptions and premisses, a radically new epistemic order, and one based more on moral than on rational principle. It may be that it is indeed time to question our cherished beliefs, and to look for alternative modes of enquiry more directly relevant to the pressing socio-political issues of the world we live in. CDA is quite explicit about its socio-political stance and its interventionalist mission, but there is no comparably explicit recognition of any change of epistemological principle that this might involve. If CDA is initiating a new order, there is little discussion or demonstration of what this might be. On the contrary, it is extremely conventional in its mode of argumentation, and there is no indication that the theories it invokes or the analyses it presents constitute a shift into a radically different mode of enquiry. There is no grappling here with intellectual uncertainties, no confrontation of opposing paradigms. Nothing comes across as posing any real problem. We are told that CDA is carried out within the framework of Halliday's grammar, that all aspects of context are to be taken into account, that the approach is consistent with the theories of Foucault, Bourdieu, Habermas, Marx and so on. Everything is presented as straightforward. There is no suggestion that there might be some difficulty about synthesizing these different theories, or about deciding on which categories of S/F should be applied, or about deciding on how the relevance of particular features of text and context are determined. In short, the problematic issues that I have been exploring in this book are apparently not seen as problematic at all.

Critical discourse analysis is not critical about its own principles and practices. Perhaps it is too much to expect it to be. People who are committed to a particular approach, or paradigm of enquiry, or school of thought are, naturally enough, not disposed to question it. This point is indeed stressed in CDA itself and provides the essential motivation for its analysis, the purpose of which is to expose the fallibility and bias of what has become naturalized and taken for granted. But what applies to the discourse of others must apply equally to that of CDA itself. In taking up a position which allows us to identify as problematic what it takes to be self-evident, we are, paradoxically, questioning the validity of CDA by following its lead.

The central problem that CDA exemplifies and does not address takes us back to the first chapter of this book and the distinction between text and discourse that I proposed there. Text, I argued, is the overt linguistic trace of a discourse process. As such it is available for analysis. But interpretation is a matter of deriving a discourse from the text, and this inevitably brings context and pretext into play, which is why the relationship between text analysis and discourse interpretation is such a problematic one, and the reason why CDA figures so prominently in the second half of this book is that it exemplifies so clearly what is problematic about it. I made the point there that 'critical discourse analysis' was actually a misnomer since what its findings typically consisted of were interpretations, necessarily conditioned by particular contextual and pretextual factors. The objection I raised was to the claim that CDA interpretations have a privileged status, a unique validity even, because they are based on the analysis of textual facts.

But if one accepts my argument, it is true of all interpretations, and not just of critical ones, that they cannot be directly derived from analysis. It would seem to follow that not only is 'critical discourse analysis' a misnomer, but so is 'discourse analysis' *tout court*. So long as it is confused with text analysis, I think this is indeed the case. There is, however, another way in which this term can be taken. We can use it to refer to the process of enquiring into how textual facts and contextual and pretextual factors act upon each other in the interpretative process. As corpus analysis has revealed so clearly, there are regularities of co-textual patterns in text, and this in itself would lead one to conclude that there are corresponding regularities in the way texts are processed as well, and such a correspondence is proposed and exemplified in O'Halloran and Coffin 2004 (see chapter 7, note 2). So one way of proceeding in our enquiry might be to establish default interpretations of texts based on psycholinguistic research on co-textual processing and by postulating an 'idealized lay reader' along the lines proposed in O'Halloran (2003). These model interpretations could then be systematically related to different contextual and pretextual conditions in elicitation experiments to find out whether one can establish how textual features are variously activated. Such procedures, of course, put discourse interpretation at a considerable remove from the circumstances of actual use, but they would at least provide something definite in the way of a stable frame of reference for further investigation.

One kind of further investigation might be to explore the circumstances of actual use directly by taking into account what Fairclough calls 'the practices of production and consumption', which he acknowledges have not been 'adequately operationalised' in his own work (Fairclough 1995a:9). Ethnographic enquiries might be carried out, for example, into how groups of readers of different socio-cultural background and political persuasion actually respond to texts of various kinds. A possible technique for collecting data here might be modelled on that which Bartlett used in his original enquiry into the nature of the schema (Bartlett 1932). Since, as was argued in chapter 3, the concept of the schema is central to an understanding of context, Bartlett's technique would, on the face of it, seem to be particularly appropriate to our purpose. It involved asking subjects to read a North American folktale, 'The War of the Ghosts', and then to rewrite it from memory (see chapter 3, note 3). The rewritten versions reduced and reformulated the original in various ways, and these were taken as evidence of how interpretation is mediated through socio-culturally informed schematic preconceptions. Following the same procedure, different groups of readers could be asked to read and recall a newspaper article, or provide summaries of varying length, to see how far their responses provided evidence of the relative significance they assigned to different textual features.

Another possible empirical procedure is suggested by the modest exercise in alternative interpretation that I presented in the last chapter. Here I demonstrated how a shift of focus on textual features gives warrant to a different reading of the text in question from the one proposed by Fairclough. To what extent either reading would correspond with how the text is understood by the readers it was designed for is an open question. But it is also a question that is open to empirical enquiry. One way of proceeding would be to elicit the reactions of these readers to the original text and a version of it in which the linguistic features I have focused on have been systematically changed. For example:

Original	*Reworded version*
The essential aim of antenatal care is to ensure that **you** go through pregnancy and labour in the peak of condition. Inevitably, therefore, it involves a series of examinations and tests throughout the course of **your** pregnancy. As mentioned above, antenatal care will be provided either by **your** local hospital or by **your** general practitioner . . .	The essential aim of antenatal care is to ensure that **women** go through pregnancy and labour in the peak of condition. Inevitably, therefore, it involves a series of examinations and tests throughout the course of **the** pregnancy. As mentioned above, antenatal care will be provided either by **the** local hospital or by **the** general practitioner . . .

Slight though this example is, the procedure of retextualization that it exemplifies obviously has considerable potential. Whatever textual feature is identified as significant, be it lexical or grammatical, or even typographical, can be systematically altered and the effects of the alteration empirically investigated. All of the interpretative findings based on selective analysis that were discussed in previous chapters can, indeed, be reformulated as instructions for retextualization. If a particular word, or sequence of words, or syntactic structure is identified as having key significance for interpretation, then the obvious thing to do is change it and see what effects the change gives rise to. This procedure might even serve as a reflexive check on the analyst's own impressionistic claims, whether the rewordings are then put to empirical test or not.

I make no grand claims for these proposals. They are little more than tentative suggestions, but they indicate ways in which what Fairclough calls 'a "textually oriented" discourse analysis' might be more rigorously carried out. They constitute, in some measure at least, a method for establishing some empirical evidence for how texts are 'open to different interpretations depending on the context and interpreter' (Fairclough 1992:28). In this respect they would seem to be entirely consistent with CDA concerns.[3] How far this method, or indeed any methodically applied set of replicable procedures, is consistent with the persuasive purpose of CDA and the furtherance of its ideological mission is a different question. And here we return to the matter I raised at the end of the last chapter, and bring this book to a conclusion.

The issues in discourse analysis that this book has been concerned with are critical in two senses. They are issues in the first place (and in the first half of the book) which, as I see it, are critical to any academic enquiry into the nature of language use, into the relationship, in Labov's phrase (cited in chapter 3), of 'what is done to what is said and what is said to what is done'. These issues are critical because they have to do with principles of intellectual rigour, rational argument and empirical validation according to which academic enquiry is conventionally conducted. But this book has also been concerned with issues that arise in critical discourse analysis, an approach to the study of language use explicitly informed by ideological commitment and directed at advancing a socio-political cause. The question arises as to how far such an approach can, or should, be constrained by normal conventions of enquiry. How far, in other words, is there any point in being critical in the first sense about an approach that is critical in the second?

CDA, as it currently most widely perceived and practised, presents us with a serious dilemma. Because of its moral stance and its avowed mission to expose the abuse of power through language, it has an appeal which is well-nigh irresistible. But the very strength of its appeal as an activist cause works to its disadvantage as an approach to discourse analysis. For the appeal is essentially ideological, a function of shared conviction, and it is sustained by the sense of commonality, and solidarity, in belief and purpose which has little if anything to do with the rationality. If people can be persuaded into conviction by moral appeal, they do not need to be convinced by intellectual argument or rigorous analysis. If the cause is just, one might suggest, the only case that we need to present is one that will lend it expedient support, and whether the case is conceptually coherent or empirically well founded is, as the idiom has it, only of academic interest.

Only of academic interest. This implies that what is academic is irrelevant, and an endorsement of just that view is not hard to find in the present climate of opinion. The very term *academic* seems suggestive of something arcane, an aloof and elite indulgence in abstract scholarship, and academics are often at pains to dissociate themselves from 'the academy' and insist that what they do must be accountable to the non-scholarly world. But the crucial point is that what they do is only of any value to the non-scholarly world to the extent that it is scholarly. Whatever contribution academics, as academics, can make to an understanding and amelioration of the human condition is by virtue of what they know that other people do not, and the distinctive ways in which they put their intellect to work. These ways conform to certain agreed conventions of enquiry which yield particular versions of reality, alternatives to those of everyday experience, but in reference to which everyday experience can be differently understood.

Now the proponents of CDA can be regarded as activists in that they are critical, but as discourse analysts they are academics. They work in university departments, write papers in learned journals in the accepted scholarly idiom, and in general lay claim to the authority of academic scholarship. That being so, it seems reasonable to be critical of their work, *as discourse analysis*, where it appears not to conform to the conventions of rationality, logical consistency, empirical substantiation and so on that define that authority. It seems to me that the promotion of the critical cause by persuasive appeal at the expense of analytic rigour deflects critical attention from the academic shortcomings of CDA and so does the cause a serious disservice.

One further, and related, point. Academics engage in intellectual enquiry and do research, and it is this part of their work which is currently given priority and prestige, and for which they, and their institutions, are most rewarded. But they also teach, and the prime purpose of their institutions is to educate students. It seems to me that teaching students discourse analysis, and educating them into a recognition of its significance, must involve initiating them into the principles of scholarly enquiry, and thereby developing in them an awareness of what is problematic about discourse analysis. The purpose of education, I would have thought, is not to persuade students into an unquestioning allegiance, but, on the contrary, to get them to resist persuasion by inducing in them an informed scepticism of received opinion. The conventions of academic enquiry provide the general means for the independent appraisal of ideas. And students also need to know how these can be made operational in practice. They need to be provided with a methodology: a set of explicit and replicable analytic procedures for them to apply not only in producing their own analyses but in evaluating the analyses of others that are presented to them as exemplars. If students are not taught principles and procedures that they can apply for themselves, they have no means of questioning the ideas and interpretations they are presented with, and these then, carrying the imprimatur of higher authority, simply become 'naturalized', confirmed as unquestionably valid. But then in effect students are subjected to precisely the kind of hegemonic process that CDA sets out to expose. To the extent that CDA does not provide for independent initiative, its practices as discourse analysis not only are incompatible with its ideological purpose, but flatly contradict it.

The kind of CDA work that I have considered in this book has become extremely widespread and influential over recent years and has, as Luke puts it 'achieved some degree of stability, canonicity, and indeed, conventionality' (Luke 2002:99). But, as I have sought to show, it has, by academic standards, serious shortcomings as an approach to discourse analysis – shortcomings, furthermore, which actually compromise the very cause which motivates it. But the cause is not in itself incompatible with the requirements of academic enquiry: on the contrary, I have argued that it can only be effectively furthered by meeting them. And there are other ways of following a critical agenda, ways briefly outlined earlier in this chapter, in which doing critical discourse analysis is not inconsistent with being critical about discourse analysis – ways whereby, while keeping faith in the cause, we give support to the case with more consistent and cogent argument.

Notes

1 Toolan makes much the same point. He refers to the lack of 'congruence of methodology' and the need for CDA to be more consistent and systematic in method: 'Standardization of methods, questions, assumptions and parameters assayed is likely to strengthen the method, clarify it, and make it both more teachable and learnable' (Toolan 1997:99).

2 One of the subheadings of Luke's account of developments in CDA reads: 'Techniques in search of a theory' (Luke 2002:103). The implication here is that the techniques are in place and what is now needed is a theory for them to work on. This is in itself a curious reversal of the normal process: it rather calls to mind the Queen's pronouncement in *Alice in Wonderland*: 'Sentence first – verdict afterwards'. But, anyway, one would not have thought there was much evidence in the literature that people working in CDA have a problem in finding theories. On the contrary, what is most striking about the literature is the abundance of theory on display. As pointed out in the preceding chapter, and as Fowler and Toolan indicate, it is a systematic methodology of analysis that is missing. I would submit that what we find most obviously in CDA is the very opposite of what Luke suggests, namely theories in search of a technique, an approach that lacks a method.

3 An empirical project roughly along these lines is, in fact, reported in Wodak 1996. Informant responses were elicited to three different versions of a news bulletin: 'the original form and two "simplified", reformulated versions'. However, just how the original text was 'simplified' is described in very brief and general terms: 'Special emphasis was laid on shortening long and complex sentences, as well as on the expansion of nominal phrases and the explicit highlighting of contextual relationships or contradictions within a given news item – in short, on the general increase in the semantic coherence of individual stories' (Wodak 1996:103). The retextualizations were not, it would seem, done in any explicit and systematic way, so there was not, nor could there have been, any consideration of what effect specific textual changes have on how the texts were understood.

References

Aitchison, J. 1998. *The Articulate Mammal*. London: Routledge.

Aston, G. 1988. *Learning Comity: An Approach to the Description and Pedagogy of Interactional Speech*. Bologna: Cooperativa Libraria Universitaria Editrice.

Austin, J. L. 1962. *How to Do Things with Words*. Oxford: Clarendon Press.

Bartlett, F. C. 1932. *Remembering*. Cambridge: Cambridge University Press.

Biber, D., S. Johansson, G. Leech, S. Conrad and E. Finegan (eds). 1999. *Longman Grammar of Spoken and Written English*. London: Longman.

Bloor, M. and T. Bloor. 1995. *The Functional Analysis of English: A Hallidayan Approach*. London: Edward Arnold.

Bolinger, D. L. 1952/65. Linear modification. *Publications of the Modern Language Association of America* 67. Reprinted in D. L. Bolinger, *Forms of English* (1965). Tokyo: Hokuon. Page reference to the reprint.

Brown, G. and G. Yule. 1983. *Discourse Analysis*. Cambridge: Cambridge University Press.

Carter, R. (ed.). 1982. *Language and Literature: An Introductory Reader in Stylistics*. London: Allen & Unwin.

Carter, R. and P. Simpson (eds). 1989. *Language, Discourse and Literature: An Introductory Reader in Discourse Stylistics*. London: Allen & Unwin.

Chafe, W. 1992/2003. Discourse: Overview. In W. Bright (ed.) (1992)/W. Frawley (ed.) (2003), *International Encyclopedia of Linguistics*. New York: Oxford University Press.

Chomsky, N. 2001. *9–11*. New York: Seven Stories Press.

Chouliaraki, L. and N. Fairclough. 1999. *Discourse in Late Modernity: Rethinking Critical Discourse Analysis*. Edinburgh: Edinburgh University Press.

Cook, G. 1995. Theoretical issues: Transcribing the untranscribable. In G. Leech, G. Myers and J. Thomas (eds), *Spoken English on Computer*. London: Longman.

Coulthard, R. M. 1977/1985. *An Introduction to Discourse Analysis*. London: Longman.

Cox, C. B. and A. E. Dyson. 1963. *Modern Poetry: Studies in Practical Criticism*. London: Edward Arnold.

Culler, J. 1981. *The Pursuit of Signs: Semiotics, Literature, Deconstruction*. London: Routledge & Kegan Paul.

Daneš, F. 1964. A three level approach to syntax. *Travaux Linguistiques de Prague* 1.

de Beaugrande, R. 1980. *Text, Discourse and Process*. London: Longman.

Downing, J. 1990. US media discourse in South Africa: The development of a situation model. *Language and Society* 1.1, 39–60.

Eagleton, T. 1983. *Literary Theory: An Introduction*. Oxford: Blackwell.

Fairclough, N. 1992. *Discourse and Social Change*. Cambridge: Polity Press.

Fairclough, N. 1995a. *Critical Discourse Analysis: The Critical Study of Language*. London: Longman.

Fairclough, N. 1995b. *Media Discourse*. London: Edward Arnold.

Fairclough, N. 1996. A reply to Henry Widdowson's 'Discourse Analysis. A Critical View'. *Language and Literature* 5.1, 49–56.

Fairclough, N. 1989. *Language and Power*. London: Longman.

Fairclough, N. and R. Wodak. 1997. Critical discourse analysis. In T. van Dijk (ed.), *Discourse Studies: A Multidisciplinary Introduction. Volume 2: Discourse as Social Interaction*. London: Sage.

Firbas, J. 1972. On the interplay of prosodic and non-prosodic means of Functional Sentence Perspective. In V. Fried (ed.), *The Prague School of Linguistics and Language Teaching*. London: Oxford University Press.

Firth, J. R. 1957. *Papers in Linguistics (1934–51)*. London: Oxford University Press.

Foucault, M. 1972. *The Archaeology of Knowledge*. London: Tavistock.

Fowler, R. 1996a. On critical linguistics. In C. R. Caldas-Coulthard and R. Coulthard (eds), *Texts and Practices: Readings in Critical Discourse Analysis*. London: Routledge.

Fowler, R. 1996b. *Linguistic Criticism*. Oxford: Oxford University Press.

Fowler, R., B. Hodge, G. Kress and T. Trew. 1979. *Language and Control*. London: Routledge & Kegan Paul.

Freedle, R. O. (ed.). 1977. *Discourse Production and Interpretation*. Norwood, N.J.: Ablex.

Garfinkel, H. 1972. Remarks on ethnomethodology. In J. Gumperz and D. Hymes (eds), *Directions in Sociolinguistics: The Ethnography of Communication*. New York: Holt, Rinehart and Winston.

Garnham, A. 1985. *Psycholinguistics: Central Topics*. New York: Methuen.

Gerbig, A. 1993. The representation of agency and control in texts on the environment. Paper presented at the AILA Conference, Amsterdam.

Goffman, E. 1981. *Forms of Talk*. Philadephia: University of Pennsylvania Press.

Grice, H. P. 1975. Logic and conversation. In P. Cole and J. Morgan (eds), *Syntax and Semantics. Volume 3: Speech Acts*. New York: Academic Press.

Halliday, M. A. K. 1989. *Spoken and Written Language*. Oxford: Oxford University Press.

Halliday, M. A. K. 1994. *An Introduction to Functional Grammar*. 2nd edn. London: Edward Arnold.

Halliday, M. A. K. and R. Hasan. 1976. *Cohesion in English*. London: Longman.

Harris, Z. 1952. Discourse analysis. *Language* 28, 1–30.

Hodge, R. and G. Kress. 1993. *Language as Ideology*. 2nd edn. London: Routledge.

Hoey, M. 1991. *Patterns of Lexis in Text*. Oxford: Oxford University Press.

Hymes, D. H. 1968. The ethnography of speaking. In J. J. Fishman (ed.), *Readings in the Sociology of Language*. The Hague: Mouton.

Hymes, D. H. 1974. *Foundations of Sociolinguistics*. Pittsburgh: University of Pennsylvania Press.

Johnson-Laird, P. N. 1983. *Mental Models*. Cambridge: Cambridge University Press.

Kosinski, Jerzy. 1972. *Being There*. New York: Bantam Books.

Kress, G. 1992. Against arbitrariness: The social production of the sign as a foundational issue in Critical Discourse Analysis. *Discourse and Society* 4.2, 169–91.

Kress, G. 1996. Representational resources and the production of subjectivity: questions for the theoretical development of Critical Discourse Analysis in a multicultural society. In C. R. Caldas-Coulthard and R. Coulthard (eds), *Texts and Practices: Readings in Critical Discourse Analysis*. London: Routledge.

Kress, G. and R. Hodge. 1979. *Language as Ideology*. London: Routledge & Kegan Paul.

Labov, W. 1969. *The Study of Non-standard English*. Champaign, Ill.: National Council of Teachers of English.

Labov, W. 1972. *Sociolinguistic Patterns*. Philadelphia: University of Pennsylvania Press.

Lee, D. 1992. *Competing Discourses*. London: Longman.

Leech, G. N. 1983. *Principles of Pragmatics*. London: Longman.

Lessing, D. 1972. *The Golden Notebook*. London: Michael Joseph.

Levinson, S. C. 1983. *Pragmatics*. Cambridge: Cambridge University Press.

Levinson, S. C. 1988. Putting linguistics on a proper footing: Explorations in Goffman's concepts of participations. In P. Drew and A. Wootton (eds), *Erving Goffman: Exploring the Interaction Order*. Oxford: Oxford University Press.

Lock, G. 1996. *Functional English Grammar*. Cambridge: Cambridge University Press.

Luke, A. 2002. Beyond science and ideology critique: Developments in critical discourse analysis. *Annual Review of Applied Linguistics* 22, 96–110.

Lyons, J. 1966. Firth's theory of 'meaning'. In C. E. Bazell, J. C. Catford, M. A. K. Halliday and R. H. Robins (eds), *In Memory of J. R. Firth*. London: Longman.

Malinowski, B. 1923. The problem of meaning in primitive languages. Appendix to C. K. Ogden and I. A. Richards, *The Meaning of Meaning*. London: Routledge & Kegan Paul.

Mey, J. 1993. *Pragmatics: An Introduction*. Oxford: Blackwell.

O'Halloran, K. A. 2003. *Critical Discourse Analysis and Language Cognition*. Edinburgh: Edinburgh University Press.

O'Halloran, K. A. and C. Coffin. 2004. Checking overinterpretation and underinterpretation: Help from corpora in Critical Linguistics. In C. Coffin,

A. Hewings and K. A. O'Halloran, *Applying English Grammar: Functional and Corpus Approaches*. London: Hodder Arnold.

Paulin, T. 1993. *Selected Poems 1979–90*. London: Faber.

Paulin, T. 2001. Fugitive Crusoe. *London Review of Books*, 23.14, 19 July.

Quirk, R., S. Greenbaum, G. Leech and J. Svartvik. 1985. *A Comprehensive Grammar of the English Language*. London: Longman.

Schiffrin, D. 1994. *Approaches to Discourse*. Oxford: Blackwell.

Searle, J. R. 1969. *Speech Acts*. Cambridge: Cambridge University Press.

Sinclair, J. M. 1985. Selected issues. In R. Quirk and H. G. Widdowson (eds), *English in the World*. Cambridge: Cambridge University Press.

Sinclair, J. M. 1991. *Corpus, Concordance, Collocation*. Oxford: Oxford University Press.

Sinclair, J. M. 1997. Corpus evidence in language description. In A. Wichmann, S. Fligelstone, T. McEnery and G. Knowles (eds), *Teaching and Language Corpora*. London: Longman.

Sinclair, J. M. 2001. Review of Biber et al. (1999). *International Journal of Corpus Linguistics*, 6.2, 339–59.

Sperber, D. and D. Wilson. 1995. *Relevance: Communication and Cognition*. 2nd edn. Oxford: Blackwell.

Steiner, G. 1975. *After Babel: Aspects of Language and Translation*. Oxford: Oxford University Press.

Stubbs, M. W. 1983. *Discourse Analysis*. Oxford: Blackwell.

Stubbs, M. W. 1994. Grammar, text, and ideology: Computer-assisted methods in the linguistics of representation. *Applied Linguistics* 15.2, 201–23.

Stubbs, M. W. 1995. Corpus evidence for norms of lexical collocation. In G. Cook and B. Seidlhofer (eds), *Principle and Practice in Applied Linguistics*. Oxford: Oxford University Press.

Stubbs, M. W. 1996. *Text and Corpus Analysis*. Oxford: Blackwell.

Stubbs, M. W. 2001a. *Words and Meanings*. Oxford: Blackwell.

Stubbs, M. W. 2001b. Texts, corpora, and problems of interpretation: A response to Widdowson. *Applied Linguistics* 22.2, 149–72.

Titscher, S., M. Meyer, R. Wodak and E. Vetter. 2000. *Methods of Text and Discourse Analysis*. London: Sage.

Tognini Bonelli, E. 2001. *Corpus Linguistics at Work*. Amsterdam: John Benjamins.

Toolan, M. 1997. What is critical discourse analysis and why are people saying such terrible things about it? *Language and Literature* 6.2: 83–103.

Trudgill, P. 2003. *A Glossary of Sociolinguistics*. Edinburgh: Edinburgh University Press.

van Dijk, T. A. 1996. Discourse, power and access. In C. R. Caldas-Coulthard and R. Coulthard (eds), *Texts and Practices: Readings in Critical Discourse Analysis*. London: Routledge.

van Dijk, T. A. 2001. Critical discourse analysis. In D. Tannen, D. Schiffrin and H. Hamilton (eds), *The Handbook of Discourse Analysis*. Oxford: Blackwell.

Weber, J. J. 2002. The critical practices of Henry Widdowson. In *Language and Literature* 11.2, 153–60.

Widdowson, H. G. 1978. *Teaching Language as Communication*. Oxford: Oxford University Press.

Widdowson, H. G. 1979. *Explorations in Applied Linguistics*. Oxford: Oxford University Press.

Widdowson, H. G. 1983. *Learning Purpose and Language Use*. Oxford: Oxford University Press.

Widdowson, H. G. 1990. *Aspects of Language Teaching*. Oxford: Oxford University Press.

Widdowson, H. G. 1992. *Practical Stylistics*. Oxford: Oxford University Press.

Widdowson, H. G. 2000. Critical practices: On representation and the interpretation of text. In S. Sarangi and M. Coulthard (eds), *Discourse and Social Life*. London: Pearson Educational.

Widdowson, H. G. 2002. Verbal art and social practice: a reply to Weber. *Language and Literature*, 11.2, 161–7.

Widdowson, H. G. 2003. *Defining Issues in English Language Teaching*. Oxford: Oxford University Press.

Wilson, D. 1994. Relevance and understanding. In G. Brown, K. Malmkyaer, A. Pollitt and J. Williams (eds), *Language and Understanding*. Oxford: Oxford University Press.

Wodak, R. 1996. *Disorders of Discourse*. London: Longman.

Index of names

Index of subjects